S0-BFB-779

"The Whole Wide World, Without Limits"

AMERICAN JEWISH CIVILIZATION SERIES

Editors

MOSES RISCHIN
San Francisco State University

JONATHAN D. SARNA
Brandeis University

*A complete listing of the books in this series
can be found online at http://wsupress.wayne.edu*

"THE WHOLE WIDE WORLD, WITHOUT LIMITS"

International Relief, Gender Politics,
and American Jewish Women,
1893–1930

MARY McCUNE

WAYNE STATE UNIVERSITY PRESS   DETROIT

Copyright © 2005 by Wayne State University Press,
Detroit, Michigan 48201. All rights are reserved.
No part of this book may be reproduced without formal permission.
Manufactured in the United States of America.
09 08 07 06 05   5 4 3 2 1

Library of Congress Cataloging-in-Publication Data

McCune, Mary.
The whole wide world, without limits : international relief, gender politics, and American
Jewish women, 1893–1930 / Mary McCune.
p. cm. — (American Jewish civilization series)
Includes bibliographical references and index.
ISBN 0-8143-3229-3 (hardcover : alk. paper)
1. Jewish women—United States—Political activity—History—19th century. 2. Jewish
women—United States—Political activity—History—20th century. 3. Jewish women—
United States—Social conditions—19th century. 4. Jewish women—United States—Social
conditions—20th century. 5. Jewish women—United States—Societies and clubs—History—19th century. 6. Jewish women—United States—Societies and clubs—History—
20th century. 7. National Council of Jewish women—History. 8. Hadassah (Organization)—History. I. Title: International relief, gender politics, and American Jewish women,
1893–1930. II. Title. III. Series.
E184.36.W64M36 2005
305.48'8924073'09041—dc22
2004017351

∞ The paper used in this publication meets the minimum requirements
of the American National Standard for Information Sciences—
Permanence of Paper for Printed Library Materials, ANSI Z39.48–1984.

Grateful acknowledgment is made to the Mary Dickey Masterton Fund
for financial assistance in the publication of this volume.

Dedicated to
FRANK J. BYRNE
and my family

In memory of
FRANK L. BYRNE
(1928–2002)
and HARRY E. MCCUNE
(1927–2004)

CONTENTS

ACKNOWLEDGMENTS

This book started as a dissertation at Ohio State University, where I had the great fortune to work with a number of remarkable people who helped me combine my interests in women's, Jewish, American, and European history. Susan Hartmann was a model adviser, keeping me focused while at the same time allowing for, and fostering, my disparate interests. Leila Rupp always urged me to look at the wider context. Her comparative perspective helped me draw connections between American Jewish women and the broader international communities with which they interacted. Both these women have continued to be wonderful role models for me as scholars, teachers, and writers. David Hoffmann kindly agreed to join my committee at a late date, offering useful insights from the Russian and Eastern European contexts. Without Michael Berkowitz I would never have embarked on a study of Jewish women nor would I have learned Yiddish, which he continually urged me to employ in my research. For years he has been a consistently strong advocate, even from the other side of the Atlantic Ocean. Neil Jacobs taught me my "alef-beys," at first in his free time and then later in more formal settings. His tutoring opened the doors for me to the world of the Workmen's Circle women.

Other scholars have also generously contributed to the development of this project. Pamela S. Nadell provided insightful criticism and substantial encouragement while also introducing me to the wider world of Jewish women's studies. Daniel Soyer and Carolyn Shapiro-Shapin assisted with the complexities of the Yiddish language, mutual aid provision, and American Jewish and medical history. Shulamit Reinharz, Mark Raider, and readers at *American Jewish History* and *Feminist Studies* helped me improve the portions of the manuscript that appeared in their publications as articles. I thank the two journals and the University Press of New England for their kind permission to reprint in this book portions of articles which first appeared as "Social Workers in the *Muskeljudentum:* 'Hadassah Ladies,' 'Manly Men,' and the Significance of Gender in the American Zionist Movement, 1912–28," *American Jewish History* 86 (June 1998): 135–65; "Creating a Place for Women in a Socialist Brotherhood: Class and Gender Politics in the Workmen's Circle, 1892–1930," *Feminist Studies* 28, no. 3 (2002): 585–610; and "Formulating the 'Women's Interpretation of Zionism': Hadassah Recruitment of Non-Zionist Women, 1914–1930" in the anthology *American Jewish Women and the Zionist Enterprise* (2004).

This work would not have been possible without the assistance of archivists and librarians in Washington, D.C., New York City, Cleveland, and Pittsburgh. I would especially like to thank Susan Woodland at the Hadassah Archives and Leo Greenbaum at the YIVO Institute for Jewish Research. Research for this project was supported by grants from the Elizabeth D. Gee Fund, Department of Women's Studies, and a Graduate Student Alumni Research Award, both of Ohio State University; a Foreign Language and Area Studies fellowship from the U.S. Department of Education; the Myer and Rosaline Feinstein Center for American Jewish History at Temple University; and the Memorial Foundation for Jewish Culture. Finally, I would like to thank Moses Rischin, Jonathan Sarna, Arthur Evans, Kathryn Wildfong, and Annie Martin of Wayne State University Press for helping me transform a dissertation into a manuscript and for patiently answering my numerous questions throughout the entire process.

On a personal level, I owe Sean Martin and Lisa Jenschke a debt of gratitude for their friendship and support over the years, first as we all struggled to learn Yiddish and later as we endeavored to find a place for ourselves in the world beyond graduate school. Together with Patricia Levi, they have sustained me through many difficult periods. Kathleen Van De Loo gave me the courage to return to academic life and taught me the discipline necessary to succeed. Kelly Meyer listened to my rambling thoughts, usually over pitchers of beer, and in the process helped me develop my arguments. The generous hospitality and friendship of Patricia Levi, Carol Gibson, and their families, and of Jennifer Schwartz not only allowed me to extend my research trips but also made them infinitely more enjoyable. The History Department and Women's Studies Program at the State University of New York at

Oswego have provided a warm and supportive environment in which to make the final changes to the manuscript. I would especially like to thank Geraldine Forbes, J. Douglas Deal, Gwen Kay, Robert Cole, and Jean Dittmar for all their help and encouragement.

This book is dedicated to my husband, Frank J. Byrne, and to my family, especially my mother and two sisters. As the youngest child in a large family of Catholics, Protestants, Jews, a Buddhist, and several atheists (some of whom are still in the closet), from my earliest days I could not help but be aware of the complex relationship between personal identity, family or communal allegiance, and public activism. This is due in no small part to the efforts of my mother, who worked to promote her children's personal growth while also stressing the importance of respecting the beliefs of others. Her lifelong fascination and engagement with the world have furnished me with a powerful, courageous, and tolerant model for living that I have always sought to emulate in my own teaching and research.

Abbreviations

AJC   American Jewish Committee

AJCong   American Jewish Congress (also Congress)

AJRC   American Jewish Relief Committee

ARA   American Relief Administration

AUAM   American Union Against Militarism

AZMU   American Zionist Medical Unit

CRC   Central Relief Committee

DIA   Department of Immigrant Aid (a section of the NCJW)

ERA   Equal Rights Amendment

FAZ   Federation of American Zionists (prewar Zionist movement)

ICW   International Council of Women

IWSA   International Woman Suffrage Alliance

JDC   American Jewish Joint Distribution Committee (comprising AJRC, CRC, and PRC)

JWB   Jewish Welfare Board

JWO   Jewish Women's Organization

NCJW   National Council of Jewish Women (also Council)

NCW   National Council of Women

NEC   National Executive Committee of the Workmen's Circle (Arbeter Ring)

NFTS   National Federation of Temple Sisterhoods

Abbreviations

NWC	National Workmen's Committee on Jewish Rights
PEC	Provisional Executive Committee for General Zionist Affairs
PJWERA	Palestine Jewish Women's Equal Rights Association
PRC	People's Relief Committee
UPA	United Palestine Appeal
WCJW	World Congress of Jewish Women
WZO	World Zionist Organization
ZOA	Zionist Organization of America

NOTE ON
YIDDISH TRANSLITERATION

Yiddish names, words, and phrases have been transliterated according to the guidelines of the YIVO Institute for Jewish Research. Words are transliterated exactly as they appear in the original text, except in those instances where a common spelling appears in English ("Asch," for example, rather than the "Ash" of the original). Hebrew words appearing in Yiddish are transliterated according to their Yiddish pronunciation. Foreign words are italicized the first time they appear in the main text. Foreign words in titles are not italicized in the notes except where they are italicized in the original.

Introduction

Woman's sphere is in the home, they told us. The last thirty years have been devoted to proof of our boast that women's sphere is the whole wide world, without limits.

Hannah G. Solomon, "American Jewish Women in 1890 and 1920: An Interview with Mrs. Hannah G. Solomon," *American Hebrew* 106 (April 23, 1920)

Hannah G. Solomon, founder of the National Council of Jewish Women (NCJW; also Council), could well have been describing the achievements of many women's organizations besides her own in the era preceding World War I. From the end of the Civil War through the 1890s, the decade of the NCJW's birth, American women from across the ideological spectrum slowly embraced causes outside their homes, entering into the wider arena of public life. By 1920 substantial numbers of women not only participated in civic affairs but also turned their attention overseas.[1] Solomon acknowledged how critical the war was in altering forever the contours of women's sphere. No longer bound to the confines of domestic, local, or even national issues, American women now considered their realm "without limits," as evidenced by the postwar international activities of such groups as the Women's International League for Peace and Freedom and the League of Women Voters.[2]

The war years affected American Jewish women even more profoundly than it did non-Jews. The unique plight of Jews in Europe and Palestine awakened in American Jews a keen sense of responsibility for their coreligionists overseas. Women quickly joined men in organizing relief for Jews trapped in war zones. Once the armistice was signed, Jewish women, like many others, did not return home to focus solely on domestic affairs. Rather, they opted to expand their wartime programs both nationally and internation-

I

ally. Like other American women, Jews used their experiences in the war years to claim a permanent place for themselves in the worlds of international politics and global relief and to redefine their relationship to men in the public sphere.

Speaking at the 1923 World Congress of Jewish Women (WCJW), NCJW leader Rebekah Kohut asserted that World War I proved conclusively that the most pressing issues were global rather than local. Women could no longer remain at home caring only for those in their own communities; the world demanded more active female intervention. "Who better than women know the needs of women and children," she asked, "and knowing them who can and should help in the solution of these problems?"[3] For women like Kohut, relief work—social welfare activism brought to the international level—required feminine input. Prior to the war Progressive women like Jane Addams and Lillian Wald had opened settlement houses to aid the immigrant populations, while others worked to clean up the cities, curb the use of alcoholism, reform "wayward" girls and much more. Just as Kohut did, these activists argued that women had unique attributes to contribute to the public sphere, and that female activism amounted to a form of "social housekeeping."[4] During the war women of all backgrounds and faiths turned their attention to the war effort whether working on behalf of peace, like Jane Addams, or in support of military preparedness.[5] Jewish women behaved similarly. They energetically raised funds for Jewish refugees and drew attention to neglected groups in this population, primarily women and children. While all American women involved in public activism achieved a sense of empowerment through their wartime endeavors, the experience of Jewish women differed in a special way. Relief work enlivened in these women a deeper sense not just of gender identity but of communal identity as well. "If women are not for women," Kohut declared at the World Congress, "how can we hope to advance the cause of Jewish womanhood?"[6] Jewish women, less active than their gentile sisters prior to the war, mobilized through relief work to engage with the public sphere on a level unprecedented before the conflict.

Because the American Jewish community disagreed on matters of religious observance, class politics, and the proposed establishment of a Jewish nation-state in Palestine as advocated by the

Zionists, women created a variety of means by which to express their personal identity collectively. The American Jewish community consisted of several sub-groups, including the Sephardic Jews who had emigrated in the colonial era, Jews from German lands who arrived in the United States in the mid-nineteenth century, and the most recent wave of immigrants hailing from Eastern Europe—most notably the Russian Pale of Settlement. Divided by language and national origin, American Jews also split over religious observance—while most religious East European Jews were Orthodox, many German Jews followed the Reform branch of Judaism. Many other Easterners were nonreligious socialists.[7] Jewish organizations reflected this diversity of experience. Some women, seeking to avoid controversial political or religious discussions, joined the moderate NCJW. Others embraced groups committed to Zionism, socialism, or secular Jewish identity. Still others dedicated their efforts to the maintenance of their synagogues through work in the local synagogues' sisterhoods and in the National Federation of Temple Sisterhoods founded in 1913.[8] Women established and joined a wide array of organizations, often more than one at a time. Personal identification—as a Zionist, a socialist, religious or secular—was closely entwined with public activism.

This book explores women's involvement in three of these organizations—the NCJW, Hadassah (the Women's Zionist Organization of America), and the socialist Workmen's Circle (*Arbeter Ring* in Yiddish)—during the first three decades of the twentieth century. Investigation of these groups presents the opportunity to explore a wide range of Jewish women, from upper-class to working-class, assimilationist to Zionist. The NCJW and Hadassah were the largest and most prominent Jewish women's groups of the period between World Wars I and II. The Workmen's Circle, while not solely a women's association, was a major forum for working-class, secular Jewish activism.[9] The women in the NCJW tended to be upper class and of Central European-Jewish descent. Their organization pursued a broad reformist agenda yet often refrained from taking official positions on controversial issues, like Zionism, that might divide the membership. Hadassah usually appointed women of middle- or upper-class Central European origin to leadership positions, although rank-and-file members frequently came from Eastern European backgrounds. The overwhelmingly working-class membership of the Workmen's Circle generally traced its origins to Eastern Europe and communicated primarily in Yiddish. In this early period, the great majority of Circle members were non- (if not anti-) Zionist, embracing instead a form of cultural nationalism most closely associated with the General Union of Jewish Workers in Lithuania, Poland, and Russia (known as the Bund).[10]

All three groups responded quickly and extensively to the refugees' cries for help during World War I, and because the situation in Eastern Europe did not significantly improve after November 1918, they continued to involve themselves in international relief well into the postwar period. Women contributed to regional, state, and national relief drives administered by men while simultaneously launching a host of national and local programs of their own. Despite stereotypes depicting them as chatty, charitable, sewing-circle ladies, these women did not limit themselves to sewing and fund-raising alone, as important (and undervalued) as such work was. Their myriad involvement in relief projects aimed at helping Europe's and Palestine's unfortunate led women to consider the future prospects of those populations. In the war years and during the 1920s, American women began to debate ever more intently what type of programs and what overall solutions would most effectively ameliorate the plight of their coreligionists overseas. Often perceived as being removed from the rough-and-tumble world of male politics, women participating in relief work found themselves grappling daily with questions of ideology, nationalism, and political statehood. In turn, these women redefined the "political" itself by introducing new topics and concerns into the agendas of their movements and also through the very real political consequences of their seemingly apolitical acts, particularly in the realm of Zionism.[11]

Women's traditional role of caring for their people provided important rhetorical and practical models for the varying manifestations of Jewish nationalism that arose during this crisis period, even as it was overlooked by contemporaries and later historians of the era. The American Jewish female tradition of "charity work" served as a critical foundation upon which other U.S. Jewish groups could construct an ethos of caring for world Jewry.[12] Within such a framework, American Jews came to understand their location in the "family" of world Jewry as comparable to that of fortunate siblings whose responsibility was to help those living in less agreeable circumstances.

Participation in international relief endeavors brought women into indirect contact with great numbers of Jews in Europe and Palestine and introduced many of them to the world of international politics. Jewish women, like men, sought solutions to the "Jewish problem," solutions that were necessarily influenced by such broader forces as antisemitism and anti-Bolshevism. Relief work, initially aimed at helping Jews weather the storms of war, induced Americans, even the non-Zionists and anti-Bundists, to construct varying notions of Jewish identity, all of which transcended regional boundaries. Whether they adhered to Zionism, Bundism, or the idea of a "civil religion," World War I and the exigencies of the postwar period provided women with an entrance into international politics and simultaneously facilitated the construction of a modern American Jewish identity intimately connected to philanthropic activities for Jews in other lands.[13] Gender was central to this construction: far from being apolitical, the philanthropic-based identification, so effectively promoted by Hadassah in particular, enabled non-Zionist American Jews, most notably women, to begin to accept the idea of Jewish settlement in Palestine as one refuge among many, although not as a Jewish homeland or nation-state, a decade before the Nazis rose to power in Germany. While global political considerations plainly guided U.S. Jewish activism, women's ethic of caring for fellow Jews simultaneously offered a model of "nationalism" that proved more appealing to many middle-class Jews than did, for instance, political Zionism or Bundism. By downplaying traditional notions of the political and highlighting more "apolitical" feminine pursuits, work that they held in common with non-Zionist organizations, Hadassah successfully promoted the Zionist ideal and, ultimately, that movement's geopolitical goals as well.

In addition to examining the role played by international events and women's activism in the development of Jewish nationalism and collective American Jewish identity, this book also explores how women's organizations influenced their members' more personal definitions regarding what it meant to be a Jew. Women's entrance into the public sphere revealed to them the great complexity of modern Jewish identity. Large-scale relief work introduced Jewish women to international politics and to Jews from foreign lands, but more immediately women found themselves encountering, perhaps for the first time, the diversity of their own national community. Associating with those who shared many concerns yet who differed from them in fundamental ways revealed subtle, and not always openly acknowledged, divisions among American Jews. The war and the events of the inter-war period demanded that a woman consciously evaluate her stance regarding Zionism, Bundism, Bolshevism, and what all of these could possibly "mean for the Jews." Discussing such issues also forced her to recognize the rifts that existed in her own community. All Jewish relief groups, including the women's groups, envisioned ties binding together the world's Jews, and all of them advanced solutions to that community's plight. But just as they could not unite behind one political program for solving Europe's and Palestine's Jewish "problem," Americans Jews came to realize that ideological barriers existed even among their own relatively united national community—barriers informed by class and other personal differences. In the end, involvement in relief work made American women more cognizant of their political beliefs but also of their class status, regional origin, religious affiliation, primary language, and more.

In similar fashion, interactions with Jewish men during this period compelled women in all three groups to articulate a more distinctly female, if not feminist, consciousness.[14] Men's all too frequent disregard for their capabilities led women in each group to conceptualize more explicitly a positive female identity, to work vigorously to promote that identity, and to claim for themselves a more activist role. Regardless of their differences, women in all three organizations entered the 1920s with a firm sense of themselves as women, laying claim to a strongly gendered identity, both personally and organizationally. Although women in the NCJW, Hadassah, and the Arbeter Ring followed widely divergent political programs, each of them affirmed women's right to public work and to equality with men, however differently they defined "public," "work," and "equality." All three groups also pursued to varying degrees a policy of gender separatism, arguing that organizing on their own provided women with greater opportunity for leadership than they received in mixed-sex organizations.

Despite the unique path Jewish women took during the war years, they were clearly not divorced from trends affecting gentiles in this period. During and after the war women of all religions and ethnicities participated in relief work and concerned themselves with questions of public policy affecting women. Many women also continued to organize independently of men, even as women of a younger generation disavowed such strategies as outmoded and old-fashioned.[15] Notwithstanding their constituting a minority population, Jewish women behaved in the same fashion as other women of their class, although the issues that often motivated them to action, such as Jewish nationalism or antisemitism, differed substantially from those of their gentile counterparts. All three organizations borrowed ideas from and collaborated on similar agenda items with other women's groups. Socialist Jewish women maintained closer contact with other socialists than they did with women in either Hadassah or the NCJW. Like gentile socialists, Circle women struggled to define "equality" in a movement that all too often ignored gender difference or, at best, put questions regarding gender equity on the back burner, to be solved by the revolution.[16] Similarly, although committed to helping the poor and to interacting with lower-class Jews through their work, women in the NCJW established much closer, more productive bonds with non-Jewish women of their own socioeconomic status, embracing pressure group politics after 1920 just as countless other middle-class women's groups of that era did. This book seeks to integrate a fuller picture of the Jewish American female experience into the general U.S. women's history narrative. By examining the interactions of a diverse collection of Jewish women with gentile women's organizations, we can gain a better understanding of the points of resemblance between all American women while remaining sensitive to the many unique aspects of Jewish women's history.[17]

Although they shared much in common with gentiles like themselves, women in the three groups studied here never ignored or downplayed their Jewish identity. Jewish women's groups were not "single-issue" groups, nor did they wish to be. Women in these three organizations negotiated their needs and demands as women with those as Jews. In each case, these negotiations produced different outcomes, different models of how best to advocate for Jewish and gender interests. The NCJW and Hadassah came much closer to one another than either did to the socialists in terms of creating organizations that held similar beliefs regarding gender identity, modes of activism for women, and appropriate projects for those overseas. Yet the leadership of these two groups fundamentally disagreed over the question of Zionism. In other words, as this book will show, there was no one way to be an American Jewish woman and no single method by which to advocate for all Jewish women's interests. Like other minority women, Jews had long recognized that they could never simply join gentiles in organizing together as "women." Their Jewishness proved to be too central a component of their identity to sublimate in a bid for suffrage or for other issues advanced by the major women's groups of the era; coalition work better suited their needs. Yet while coalition work gave them the space they needed to organize around Jewish identity, women in these three groups soon found that "Jewishness" proved to be every bit as complex. Just as no single women's group could ever truly speak for all American women, so Jews found it impossible to create one organization that could incorporate the position of each and every American Jewish woman, despite the stated intent of both the NCJW and Hadassah to do just that.

American Jewish women often found themselves between worlds while they struggled to integrate their gender, religious, class, and ethnic identities. Historical scholarship has tended to replicate the dilemmas these women faced during their lifetimes. As Jews they are marginalized in standard narratives of U.S. women's history, even though Hadassah and the NCJW surely rivaled other organizations in size and importance.[18] In histories of Jewish relief agencies, socialism, and Zionism during the war years, they are again relegated to positions behind the scenes as men take center stage.[19] Although Jewish women, most notably the Yiddish-speakers, have tended to fall between the cracks in historical scholarship and subdisciplines, it is not for lack of documentation. Women in the NCJW and Hadassah were especially prolific writers, seeming to relish the opportunity to express their organizational point of view publicly. I have been very fortunate to deal with groups of women exhibiting tremendous public candor. This study rests primarily on the documents originating with the three organizations, including convention materials, newsletters, and periodicals, along with material in the broader Jewish press. Each group produced a regular organizational publication—the NCJW's *Jewish Woman*, Hadassah's *Bulletin* and later *Newsletter*, and the women's column in the Workmen's Circle paper *Der fraynd* (The Friend). Each group also published selections from the proceedings of their yearly or, in NCJW's case triennial, national conventions. These proved quite valuable in the case of the Workmen's Circle, where national office documents remain unprocessed and difficult to access fully. The early Arbeter Ring conventions debated a variety of issues relative to women's participation in the organization. Even more critical were the anniversary publications of Arbeter Ring branches. Here one finds a host of "greetings" from *froyen klubn* (women's clubs), which, while quite formulaic, also frequently offer surprising insight into women's perceptions of their organization, especially of its earliest years. National board meeting minutes for the NCJW and Hadassah also proved invaluable in offering a glimpse behind the often sanitized discussions in the published convention proceedings.

This book is organized in a broadly chronological fashion. The first chapter details the founding and early years of the NCJW, Hadassah, and the Workmen's Circle, with particular attention to the role played by gender and class in these groups' formation. Women's adherence to a particular political ideology alone was not sufficient to determine the shape of their organizational lives, since class status also played a critical role. Yet in all three groups the women's interactions with men of the same class eventually produced a distinctly female consciousness. In each organization, uneasy collaboration with male counterparts led women to articulate more forthrightly their belief in their own abilities even as the groups held widely divergent ideas about liberalism, Zionism, and socialism.

The war years are the subject of chapter 2, which examines women's participation in the major relief efforts and in their own projects during World War I. While women cooperated closely with Jewish men, they did not abandon interactions with other women, including gentiles. These ties with other women sustained female consciousness during a period when women felt a great urgency to subordinate their own needs to the dictates of the larger relief mission. Chapter 3 looks at how the two all-female groups, the NCJW and Hadassah, fought after the armistice to resurface from their wartime submergence in male-led endeavors. Both the NCJW and Hadassah struggled after the war to break free of male leadership directives, even though, given their different organizational ties to male-led groups, each forged a unique path to independence. At the same time, both Hadassah and the NCJW increasingly used a rhetoric of female difference and maternalism to justify their move into the public sphere and toward autonomy.

Chapter 4 continues the focus on the NCJW and Hadassah by exploring the organizations' recruitment strategies and the alliances each made with other women's groups during the 1920s. While divided over the issue of Zionism, women in both groups found themselves drawn closer together as members began to acknowledge similarities in organizational projects and language. The final chapter returns to women in the Workmen's Circle, detailing their postwar activism and use of separatist strategies. Although they never participated in battles for independence like those of the NCJW and Hadassah, during the inter-war period many Circle women began to promote the formation of separate women's groups within the larger organization. Ultimately these groups affected a change in the tenor and focus of the postwar Workmen's Circle.

Circle women joined other Jewish and gentile American women in making the "whole wide world, without limits" their sphere in the post-suffrage, inter-war period. The war years proved to women that they could participate in public activism on behalf of Jews and women in general. Over the years, as they helped first immigrants and then war victims and refugees, Jewish women developed an ethic of caring for others, one that shared important features with the voluntary efforts of contemporary, gentile women's organizations. In the process of aiding other Jews, women moved decisively into the public sphere, promoting gender interests and participating in debates about the nature of Jewish identity and nationalism. Their dedication to finding a way to be both Jewish and female in the public sphere significantly influenced the construction of modern American Jewish identity.

CHAPTER I

Creating Organizations
for Women, 1892–1912

At the Columbian Exposition in 1893, participant Helen L. Bullock exclaimed, "We are all doubtless aware here that Columbus discovered America. America's uncrowned queen, Miss Frances E. Willard [founder of the Women's Christian Temperance Movement], once said the greatest discovery of the nineteenth century is the discovery of woman by herself."[1] Although speaking of all women, Bullock might have been talking specifically of Jews.

Part of a small community, though recently growing as a result of massive immigration from Eastern Europe, American Jewish women created few organizations of any size before the late nineteenth century. But because of heightened Jewish immigration and middle-class Americanized Jewish women's beliefs about their proper function in and duty toward society, during the 1890s and early 1900s Jewish women once again began to organize. Unlike earlier synagogue-based benevolent societies, which were often under the tutelage of local rabbis or other prominent men, these new organizations remained in the hands of their female founders. The groups were national in scope and achieved more than could have ever been imagined by women in the earlier charitable groups.

But Jewish women in the United States never constituted a monolithic group, and this was particularly the case at the turn of the century. Differences in class combined with language and cultural diversity resulted in a rich and far from unified community.

Some Jewish women spoke only English, others Yiddish, and still others were bi- or multilingual. Like men, they had diverse ways of understanding their Jewish identity and contemplated a variety of means by which to improve conditions for Jews in the United States. Some women fervently believed in free-market liberalism, while others vowed to work against capitalism in the pursuit of socialism. After the turn of the century, growing numbers of women became intrigued by the Zionist mission to create a Jewish homeland overseas. In essence, women from across the ideological, political, and class spectrums began to, as Willard had, discover themselves. Part of that discovery resulted in joining others in organizations that best expressed these varied understandings of Jewish and female identity.

The foundational histories of the Workmen's Circle, the NCJW, and Hadassah, the Women's Zionist Organization of America, illustrate the diverse ways that women organized to realize their goals. The women's life experiences influenced how they conceptualized the Jewish community—its problems as well as the solutions that they, collectively, would devise. Women's backgrounds and ideological outlooks also shaped the way they thought about gender relations within that community, specifically about women's rights and duties. Some women, seasoned by participation in radical movements, maintained strong beliefs in gender equality and joined organizations, such as the Workmen's Circle, that theoretically supported such equality. These women, often from the working class, generally avoided female-only organizations, viewing them as bourgeois, middle-class, and separatist. Others grew up in social settings where it was suitable for men and women to inhabit separate, though complementary, spheres. These women often found separatist organizing more in line with their convictions about the gendered nature of society. Indeed, some came to believe that breaking entirely from men's groups gave them leadership opportunities they could never have in mixed-sex organizations.

The founding and prewar agendas of the Workmen's Circle, the NCJW, and Hadassah reveal what the members of these three organizations thought about women's capabilities and their place in the Jewish community and society at large. Women in these groups all faced similar obstacles in organizing (or in the Workmen's Circle case simply joining) their associations. Men's resistance, sometimes expressed as a trivialization of women's desire for public work, played an important role in spurring Jewish women to action. Male attitudes galvanized women in each group to articulate more clearly their ideas about women's roles in the movements for societal reform and to pursue their own self-defined goals. The types of projects women initiated in the years before World War I show the importance of gender politics in the Jewish community and how women used various separatist strategies to achieve their aims.

Women in a Socialist Brotherhood

In 1892 a small group of radical workers, including Tillie Falter and Jennie Gordon, met in New York City to start a mutual aid group for secular Jews who rejected the traditional benevolent organizations' ritualism and lack of interest in political matters. This was the nucleus of what would become the Workmen's Circle, or Arbeter Ring. The group considered itself the "Red Cross of the labor movement," providing strike funds, sickness benefits, and burial costs to its members. By 1900 it established three branches in New York and Brooklyn, and late in that year these branches resolved to establish a national order. In 1905 the Circle claimed nearly 5,000 members in ninety chapters, predominantly located in and around New York City. Twenty years later the group's membership reached a peak of 85,000 and included people living in "country-cities" far outside New York.[2]

The Arbeter Ring's first members were overwhelmingly Yiddish-speaking immigrants from Eastern Europe. In the early twentieth century working-class members dominated the order; semiskilled and skilled workers comprised eighty percent of its ranks.[3] The Circle required that members join a union if possible and that they pledge to vote for working-class parties, which in practice meant the socialists.[4]

Initially socialist internationalists, over time Circle members became ever more concerned with Jewish identity while agitating for working-class unity. This form of cultural nationalism did not equate to establishment of a Jewish nation-state, as did the political nationalism of the Zionists. Rather it promoted the idea that secular Jewish culture, traditions, and most importantly the Yiddish language be allowed to survive in multiethnic (preferably socialist) states. All ethnic minorities in these states would educate children in their own "national" language—Yiddish, not Hebrew, for Jews. The organization most closely associated with this sort of national sentiment was the General Union of Jewish Workers in Lithuania, Poland, and Russia (the Bund), founded in Vilna (Vilnius), Lithuania, in 1897. The Bund and the Workmen's Circle strengthened their close ties following the failed 1905 Russian Revolution, when many Russian Jewish radicals fled to the United States—more than a few of them Bundists who later joined the Workmen's Circle. The Circle held a prominent position in the New York Jewish left, alongside labor unions with high Jewish membership such as the International Ladies Garment Workers Union and the Amalgamated Clothing Workers of America, the Yiddish daily *Forverts* (*Forward*), and the Socialist Party. It maintained close relations with all these groups working together in pursuit of common interests.[5]

Although women numbered among the earliest members of the order, they remained a minority; for most of its history the group was considered "in essence, a *men's* organization"[6] [emphasis in original]. Some people in the Circle attributed the discrepancy in membership rates to the greater numbers of men immigrating to the United States and to the poverty of working families. Women's domestic responsibilities also severely limited their membership in the years prior to World War I. Many postwar reminiscences describe the trouble that women, especially those who were married, had in leaving their homes at night. One male member, writing in 1939, recalled that once women who had been active in the Bund married, they became so consumed with household duties that they failed to continue their youthful activism. Women, he remembered, tried to attend Circle meetings but most only managed to do so occasionally. Becky Cohen remembered that even as late as 1927 it was difficult to get women to the meetings more than once every two weeks or so since they were "sitting at home, cooking, washing, and raising the children."[7]

More subtle, but potentially more significant, factors than immigrant poverty and domestic burdens also curbed female participation. Gender dynamics often left women feeling alienated from this socialist workers' brotherhood. Circle women confessed to feeling out of place when they first began to attend meetings. Yeta Golding, for instance, joined the Circle due to her interest in the diverse programs it offered, but she did not feel entirely relaxed at first. "Only one thing irked me," she remembered, "I was the only woman at the meeting! Something made me feel so *unheym-lekh* [uncomfortable] . . . like a miserable, poor person . . . a woman!"[8] Others also noted the singularity or absence of female members. One man stated bluntly that women were so rare a presence in Circle life that he sometimes did not know whether a particular member even had a wife. Not only were women physically absent, they seem to have been missing from men's conversations as well.[9]

Some contemporaries insisted that more than poverty and domestic responsibilities stifled women's desire to attend meetings. To Golde Shibka, it was "incomprehensible" that more women were not involved in the Workmen's Circle given their prominence in Bundism. Intimating that the cause of low female enrollment resulted from men's reaction to female participation, she asserted that even when a woman paid dues, "psychologically" the branch remained "a men's branch."[10] The Circle's own historian, Maximilian Hurwitz, conceded that men adhered to gender norms brought with them from their native *shtetlekh* (small towns). "Despite their radical professions of faith in women's equality to men," he acknowledged, "[radical Jewish men] regard this as a man's world and think in masculine terms."[11]

While many women lamented that they had neither the time nor the psychological fortitude to join the Circle, they found ways to build community—especially with women in similar predicaments. Pregnant women and those with young children, for instance, received help from other wives. Yent Smit remembered many nights when she had to stay home alone with her children "until the gray of day" while her husband went out to various gatherings, a sentiment echoed by the main character of Tillie Olsen's well-known short story "Tell Me a Riddle."[12] Unlike that character, who grew lonely and estranged from her husband, Smit relied on neighbors to alleviate the isolation brought on by her husband's absences. Like other women of her generation, she insisted that the sacrifice was worthwhile even if "the price [we] paid . . . was high." Similarly, members of women's Branch 244-B, looking back from 1938, declared that while at first they could rarely attend meetings, "we put up with it because we felt that [the Circle] did good

work."[13] These women continued to maintain faith in the importance of the organization and the work it did regardless of their
personal alienation. Such commitment eventually led some women
to demand an equal voice in the movement. Yet prevailing ideas
about men's and women's proper roles would color the Circle's
reception of those women who tested their organization's profession of gender equality. The response they received would spur
them to press aggressively for equal rights while insisting the Circle become more responsive to women's unique needs.

Jewish Women's Congress to National Organization

Virtually at the same time that working-class women were struggling against the isolation they felt in their homes and the alienation they experienced at Arbeter Ring functions, middle- and
upper-class Jewish women in the United States were establishing a
national Jewish women's organization, the National Council of
Jewish Women. The NCJW, created not long after the Arbeter
Ring founders first met in a small, crowded, New York apartment,
grew quickly to become a prominent national organization devoted
to Judaism and social welfare. The women who developed this
organization inhabited an entirely different world than that of
Arbeter Ring women. While members of both groups expressed
frustration with their domestic duties and often felt estranged from
their male peers, wealthier Jewish woman had an important advantage over working-class immigrants—the ability to hire domestic
servants, which gave them the opportunity to engage more freely
in voluntary activities.[14] An example of this greater freedom was the
preparation for the 1893 Jewish Women's Congress, held during
the Chicago World's Fair. Prominent Jewish women from across
the nation gathered at this congress, at which time they laid the
foundations for the NCJW.

The Jewish Women's Congress was just one small part of the
broader effort to valorize women's achievements at the World's
Fair. Susan B. Anthony and other activists initially sought to play
an equal role in the development of the fair's program and exhibi-
tions. Their request denied, the women were shunted aside into a
separate Board of Lady Managers. However, this did not stop them
from displaying women's talents in the general program by convening a Women's Congress. Bertha Honoré Palmer chaired the board

and took her duties seriously. According to historian Anne Scott, Palmer "had no intention of being a token."[15] Hannah G. Solomon, like Palmer a Chicago Woman's Club member, brought the same determination to her organizing efforts on behalf of Jewish women.

Raised in a well-to-do family of Reform Jews, by 1893 Solomon had been active in the women's club movement for years. She and her sister bore the distinction of being the first Jews admitted to the prestigious Chicago Woman's Club and, as Solomon later commented, were "probably the only Jewesses many of the members ever had met."[16] Like other activists, Solomon remained involved in public work, in both the Jewish and gentile worlds, during the years she raised her three children. Her commitment to women's and Jewish issues eventually led her to try to revive the Chicago Conference of Jewish Women's Organizations, a group which, she later asserted, was a "living refutation of the hackneyed argument that women cannot work constructively and in harmony together."[17]

Recruited to preparations for the World's Fair by Palmer and Ellen Henrotin, Solomon formulated a plan for Jewish women to participate in this event. Viewing Jewish identity as primarily a religious matter, she opted to affiliate with the Parliament of Religions rather than with the Women's Congress planned by her friends.[18] Given the paucity of Jewish women's national organizations at the time, it proved difficult even to identify women of national prominence. Indeed, Solomon herself knew of only a few who might have fit the bill. An even greater obstacle than the lack of nationally recognized figures proved to be a number of men who expressed doubts about the viability of the enterprise. These men not only joined Solomon in questioning whether enough women could be rounded up for such a gathering, but they went further by challenging the very idea of Jewish women organizing separately from women of other religions. Not unlike latter-day separatist feminists, such men believed that Jewish women should join together with other women. Unlike these feminists, however, the men believed women should leave religious matters alone.[19]

Despite this attitude, Solomon and her colleagues were determined to affiliate with the Jewish Congress of the Parliament of Religions rather than with the Women's Congress. Some historians have seen this action as evidence of the NCJW's resistance to fem-

inism, since at this crucial moment its founders identified themselves as Jews first and women second.[20] This view, in essence, forces
a stark division in identity that these Jewish delegates did not necessarily make themselves. Moreover, Jewish women were not alone
in seeking a female voice in religious proceedings. Prominent
Christian activists like Elizabeth Cady Stanton and Frances Willard
also participated in the Parliament of Religions. Finally, given that
no representatives from African American women's organizations
were included on the Board of Lady Managers and few black
women were invited to make presentations to the Women's Congress, it is perhaps not surprising that Solomon sought a venue
where Jewish women could openly express both their Jewish and
female identities without risking marginalization.[21]

If Solomon feared the disappearance of Jewish women in the
final Women's Congress program, she quickly learned they were
not going to receive much floor time in the Jewish men's Congress
either. Like the men Bertha Honoré Palmer encountered, Jewish
men were far from enthusiastic about the prospect of active female
involvement. In an anecdote retold many times in various NCJW
histories, Solomon described one particular meeting to which she
was invited by male organizers. They quashed all her suggestions
for ways that women might participate, making their lack of interest abundantly clear. For instance, when Solomon proposed that
two women be allowed to make presentations to the Parliament of
Religions as representatives of the Jewish Congress, the men
ignored her. Finally, Solomon could hold her tongue no longer and
put the question to them point-blank:

> "Mr. Chairman," I inquired, "just where on your program are the
> women to be placed?"
> "Well," hemmed and hawed the chairman, "the program seems
> complete just as it stands."
> "Very well," I replied, "under these circumstances we do not care
> to cooperate with you, and I request that the fact of our presence at
> this meeting be expunged from the records."[22]

In retelling the incident, Solomon's granddaughter dispensed with
her grandmother's measured tone, describing the slight and its
effect more explicitly. She recalled that when Solomon asked if the

women could help, the men "came up with one answer, which was, yes. . . . They could be the hostesses. My grandmother was extremely vehement." This incident provoked her grandmother to establish a Jewish female-only organization "without any cooperation from the men."[23]

Like Anthony and Palmer, Solomon refused the token roles as hostesses that her male coreligionists recommended for women. She took her painstakingly compiled lists of potential female speakers and forged ahead with a Congress of Jewish Women to be affiliated with the Parliament of Religions. At the conclusion of this congress, the participants passed a resolution establishing the National Council of Jewish Women. Many years later, Rebekah Kohut vividly recalled the import of this event for women like herself: "at the time the Council was founded, participation by women in public life was still a new thing, and there was an excitement, a heady sense of independence, a thrill, a feeling that one was taking part in the best kind of revolution, even if it involved nothing more at the moment than parliamentary debates about hot soup and recreation for school children."[24] Although not affiliated with the Women's Congress, Jewish women acted in the same manner as gentile club women and suffragists. Both groups, originally bound together through Chicago clubwork, organized impressive displays of female aptitude. And both congresses precipitated a noticeable spike in female activism in the years immediately following the 1893 World's Fair.[25]

Although some historians have suggested that the early NCJW was not a feminist organization, Solomon and her contemporaries often presented Council's philosophy and accomplishments in terms that clearly conveyed their commitment to women's rights.[26] Like Kohut, contemporaries of the NCJW founders recognized the major steps taken by these generally well-to-do married women in pioneering new public roles for women. A 1933 history of Chicago Jewry credits Solomon with helping women break the "fetters that had kept [them] enslaved throughout the ages." Similarly, Solomon's granddaughter maintained that Council took "the Jewish woman out of her kitchen and . . . [gave] her an important role in society."[27] In 1937, at the request of a reporter for a message to her "sisters," Solomon responded, "let it be this—that, if women want to keep sane and sweet, let them see to it that they have an outside interest, many interests, outside of even their homes and their families. Seclusion is death—fellowship is life and life more abundant."[28] Council founders sought ways to augment women's traditional responsibilities for home and children, and they did so by employing a measured, somewhat accommodationist rhetoric regarding gender relations. This reformist position located the NCJW firmly within a centrist politics common to women of their class and political viewpoint, but it also served to offset any potentially negative, and perhaps obstructionist, reactions from male peers. In taking this stance, Council women did not differ greatly from non-Jewish women active in various women's clubs of the period.[29]

The social milieu in which the NCJW founders operated dictated the necessity of such a position. At best men could trivialize women's work; at worst they might condemn it. A full thirty-five years after the founding of the NCJW, an editorial in the *Reform Advocate* praised Solomon for her club work but in a such a way as to reassure readers that Solomon still maintained her qualifications as the consummate homemaker: "above all we have the happy thought that while she can make a good speech and handle matters of difficulty with ease and with poise and in the midst of distractions keep her head solidly on her shoulders, she can cook a good meal. . . . [They could verify this because she had cooked for them]. All in all we would say of Hannah Solomon she is the most all round Jewish woman—a mother in Israel—that we know."[30]

In a 1935 interview, Solomon reflected on this rather typical male attitude, exhibiting keen awareness of the way women like herself were received in the early years of the twentieth century. She told the reporter that back then to be a club woman meant "your ideas were too advanced for your own good or anyone else's. It meant you neglected your home, left your stockings undarned and your ice-box uncleaned. It meant, furthermore, you were busy about something besides your business, that you invited the censure of men, as well as conservatives of your own sex." She felt the support of the clubs gave women more "courage." In those days an "advanced woman," especially if she cut her hair, was regarded as a "dreadful creature"; indeed, many people considered such a woman to be "in the same category with long-haired men." Solomon laughingly added, "of course such a woman couldn't be trusted."[31]

Although middle- and upper-class women had the time and energy to devote to volunteer work outside the home, they still had to contend with negative conceptions about their "advanced" ideas. Women, especially those who were married, relied heavily on the support of their families to pursue their individual interests. Solomon, for instance, admitted that without the backing of her husband, Henry, including his financial support, she would have had neither the time nor the opportunity to participate in Council and other volunteer work.[32] Despite their stark socioeconomic differences, these women and those in the Arbeter Ring found themselves constrained to some degree by contemporary ideas regarding the proper behavior of married Jewish women. Yet both groups believed in helping women engage in public work together with men and thereby improve society at large.

Participants at the 1893 Jewish Women's Congress, seeking a compromise position between societal strictures on married women's activity and their own desire for personal actualization, created the NCJW, a national organization whose moderate program focused on "Religion, Philanthropy, and Education." They sought to initiate volunteer activities to promote the knowledge of Judaism and Jewish culture, to fight religious and other persecutions, and to involve women in social reform. By 1896 the NCJW had sections in more than fifty cities throughout the United States.[33] Like the International Council of Women, founded in 1888, the NCJW avoided political and religious issues that could potentially divide the membership, and both groups declined to take official positions on highly controversial topics. This policy notwithstanding, even before the NCJW was off the ground fissures appeared. The majority of members were middle- or upper-class women affiliated with Reform Judaism. Some Orthodox and Conservative women hesitated to join this organization, even though it was ostensibly committed to Jewish education and religion, because the majority of members held beliefs different from their own.

Henrietta Szold, the future founder of Hadassah, felt she could not support any group working to further religious goals; she believed these were fundamentally a private, individual matter. Although Szold delivered a paper to the Parliament of Religions as a representative of the Jewish Women's Congress, she refused to

join the NCJW. An adherent of Conservative Judaism, Szold anticipated friction between women like herself and those who were
affiliated with the Reform movement. Despite her position, women
from both the national office and the New York section tried to
recruit her to various posts. In 1900 Szold explained to Sadie
American, NCJW's executive secretary, that "the Council as a religious organization does and must arrogate to itself representative
powers, repugnant to me—equally repugnant if my peculiar religious views or any one else's are the object of its propaganda." She
felt that religion must remain a private matter and that an organization based on religion for "propaganda purposes is foreign, I
believe, to Judaism, and certainly to my nature."[34] Szold also alluded
to the potential class divisions that this body nurtured from its
inception. In a letter refusing the post as correspondence secretary
for the New York section, she commented that "as [the board of the
New York section] doubtless know[s] . . . I am not a woman of
leisure." She argued that she would only be able to give "rags and
tatters of time" to a position that demanded a woman's full attention, strongly implying that someone who did not have to earn a
living might be better suited to the job. Indeed, the NCJW relied
on women of means, especially married women, to staff leadership
posts. Unlike Szold, these women had both financial security and
freedom from all but the lightest household tasks.[35]

Despite Council's desire to involve as many women as possible, the homogeneity of most members' backgrounds and the manner in which they developed their organizational program curtailed
any significant participation from working—especially working-
class—women. Certainly not feminist in a radical sense, Council
women nonetheless did much to further women's religious education and public participation on issues critical to the Jewish community. Prior to World War I, Council emerged as the dominant
Jewish women's organization in the United States, closely tied to
the Jewish power elite but, like them, unrepresentative of the
majority of American Jews.

Daughters of Zion

The NCJW considered itself non-Zionist; as an organization it
neither opposed nor supported the establishment of a Jewish state.
In fact, like most Reform Jews of the period, Council members,

especially the leadership, tended to be anti-Zionists. Before World War I, the Zionist movement in the United States, represented by the Federation of American Zionists (FAZ), failed to attract a following of any significance, particularly among women. Yet pockets of support began to emerge in the early decades of the twentieth century as more Jews worried about the rise of antisemitism in Europe and the perceived decline of Jewish religious observance in the United States. Troubled by such developments as well as by female ignorance regarding Zionism, a small group of middle-class women in New York City formed a study group devoted to Zionist matters. In time they would transform this tiny circle into a highly effective national women's organization known as "Hadassah."[36]

The study circle was called the Hadassah Chapter of the Daughters of Zion—a group advanced by the FAZ as a means of bringing middle- and upper-class women into the movement. In the initial years of American Zionism, Daughters of Zion played only a minor role in its promulgation. Despite the FAZ's attempt to attract women through such chapters, many male leaders still believed that "the organization and propaganda of Zionism interest women less than men."[37] This attitude contributed to a generally lackluster record of female recruitment. One of Hadassah's founders, commenting on the men's stance, recalled that the FAZ had no program for women and "really no place for them."[38] Male leaders might concede that bourgeois women could raise money for educational and agricultural projects in Palestine, but many persisted in thinking that the larger issues of nationalist politics were of little or no concern to them. Because women were not deemed sufficiently serious about Zionist politics and ideology, less was required of them. Indeed, women in these early groups neither paid the *shekel* membership dues to the World Zionist Organization (WZO) nor sent representatives to the FAZ conventions.[39]

At least one prominent Zionist envisioned a more dynamic role for women in the movement. After a trip to Palestine in 1909, Henrietta Szold began to devise a plan by which ordinary women could assist in the "upbuilding" of Palestine through practical projects.[40] Szold's commitment to the Jewish people and interest in serving them through concrete projects began early in her life. Born in Baltimore, Maryland in 1860, Szold was the much-loved, first-born daughter of a respected rabbi from Hungary, who personally tutored her in a variety of subjects. As a young woman she helped found the Russian Night School, where immigrants could learn English. She and others at the school quickly realized the wider scope of immigrants' needs; they soon modified the school's curriculum to include instruction in sewing, carpentry, and plumbing. In 1893 Szold accepted a position as executive secretary to the publication committee of the Jewish Publication Society (JPS). Along with these duties she also served as a volunteer (unpaid) editor and translator for many of the society's publications. By the time she left the JPS in 1916 she had translated a dozen books and edited countless others.[41]

Szold's interest in Zionism arose in part through her close contact with Baltimore's Russian immigrant community. After speaking with them about Judaism, Zionism, and antisemitism, she began to consider Palestine a haven from both the violent anti-Jewish attacks in Europe and assimilation in the United States. Moreover, she believed that a Jewish state in Palestine could revitalize Judaism itself. To Szold, Zionism was both a secular and a religious phenomenon.[42] She made her first public speech on Zionism in 1896 before the Baltimore chapter of the NCJW, a month before the appearance of Theodore Herzl's influential work, *Der Judenstaat* (The Jewish state).[43] By 1910 she had become a leading American Zionist, having accepted the post of honorary secretary in the FAZ.

Several years before this, Rabbi Judah Magnes, then secretary of the FAZ, and his assistant Lotta Levensohn observed that the Daughters of Zion seemed to have little interest in substantive matters, displaying only "vague, romantic ideas about Zionism." Like prominent male Zionists, Levensohn noted that, lacking any serious work, the women in these groups "sooner or later lost interest and drifted away." Hearing these concerns, Magnes suggested that she invite Szold, already a prominent figure in the Jewish community, to participate in a study circle. The thought of communicating with such an eminent woman left Levensohn simply "dumbfounded," and it fell to Magnes to extend the actual invitation. Perhaps sensing the younger woman's propensity for hero worship or fearing adding new burdens to an already overloaded schedule, Szold accepted with the caveat that she be an ordinary member who held no special post.[44]

After her 1909 trip to Palestine, Szold reported to her study circle on the condition of Palestinian Jewish life. Her talk highlighted the lack of Jewish maternity services: the only hospital in Palestine at the time was run by Christian missionaries, who insisted on baptizing the babies born there. Szold also described the high rate of disease among children in urban areas, particularly of trachoma, a curable eye disease that when left untreated, ultimately results in blindness.[45] Her vivid descriptions led to two years' worth of serious discussions aimed at devising proposals to alleviate the abysmal state of medical care in Palestine. In January 1912 the women in the study circle finally concretized proposals based on the formulations they and Szold had been discussing since 1909.[46]

The plan that began to take shape involved helping women to become educated Zionists while at the same time launching a Palestinian program along the lines of the settlement houses started by Jane Addams and Lillian Wald. The group's initial program did not differ substantially from that of the non-Zionist NCJW. Both organizations, like so many others in the Progressive Era, highlighted education, service, and medical care—especially in urban centers. Since the WZO tended to neglect urban work, being more interested in national renewal through "improving" the countryside, the urban sphere of operation was wide open to be claimed by Hadassah. Yet rather than underscoring a deficiency in the world movement's activism, Hadassah founders proposed that their work would complement the men's.[47] Szold further maintained that urban public health initiatives would not only benefit the population of Palestine, they would also revive American Jewish women's spirituality. To Szold, Hadassah's work was not a form of benevolence or even nascent urban planning; instead, it was a critical component of Zionism itself, the upbuilding of *Eretz Israel* and the revitalization of Jews in the Diaspora.[48] In this way, she separated her group's work from that being pursued by the NCJW and gentile Progressives. A less lofty but more practical consideration drove Szold to push for a separate women's Zionist organization: having straightened out the FAZ's finances in 1910, she knew there was no way the men's group would have sufficient funds to get such a project off the ground and keep it running.[49]

While developing this program, Szold continually urged her cohorts to be pragmatists; Lotta Levensohn recalled how important Szold's sensible nature was to Hadassah's developing organizational ethos: "The dry-as-dust virtues of attention to detail and thoroughness—unromantic efficiency—took on a glamour as the whole design began to be apprehended." These ideas about efficiency, punctuality, and accountability fostered warm relationships between Hassadah and the men in the Brandeis faction of the FAZ. They would also rapidly bring the women's organization notable success.[50] By the first national convention in 1914 the organization represented 519 women in eight chapters and officially changed its name to "Hadassah, the Women's Zionist Organization of America."[51] By 1917 the women claimed 2,710 members in thirty-three chapters across the United States.[52]

The women worked diligently to attract recruits, even non-Zionists, by highlighting projects and methods especially attractive to women. Specifically, they argued that Hadassah should be "a philanthropic agency for those non-Zionists who can be interested in social work among women and children in Palestine." Shrewdly understanding the interest of club women and Progressives in "practical" work—work that resembled that of the settlement houses—Hadassah leaders used their projects as propaganda tools to attract others to Zionism. Drawing on the history of Jewish communal charity, they also asserted that American Jewish women would "embrace eagerly the chance of doing in a systematic way what they saw their mothers and grandmothers do in the haphazard way of the tin collection boxes (Pushkes)."[53] These methods quickly paid off. Despite the NCJW's officially neutral stance on Zionism, many of its members, including some major leaders, expressed interest in Hadassah's Palestine work. In March 1914 Janet Simons Harris, soon to be the NCJW national president, wrote Gertrude Goldsmith Rosenblatt that she was collecting donations for the Hadassah Nurses' Fund and that she had "stimulated similar work in Kansas City."[54]

This cooperation with non-Zionist women served a larger purpose in the Hadassah program than merely augmenting the membership. Following Szold, the leaders hoped to revitalize women's commitment to the Jewish people. Rose Jacobs explained the necessity of reaching those *Yahudim* (literally: Jews, but generally referring to Westernized or assimilated Jews) who behaved so differently than their Zionist counterparts. To her mind, such Jews were "calm and complacent. They went to Temple because it was proper, just as *goyim* went to church. They were not interested in the Jews as an entity. . . . Their children went to Sunday School. That was sufficient."[55] Another woman, commenting on the importance of Hadassah's work in Cleveland, stated that "it was a great success, and it attracted women of the Council . . . variety, who, for the first time, were spiritually awakened to the significance of Hadassah's task. The results were good. The 'aloofness' [or] 'looking down the German nose' vanished."[56] The Hadassah leadership wanted the NCJW to give up its "aloofness" to Jewish identity, to put aside what they considered its assimilative project, which here was associated with Americanized, middle-class German Jews. While many Hadassah leaders never seriously entertained the notion of emigrating to Palestine themselves, they felt that having a nation, a homeland, would strengthen Jewish identity in the U.S. They believed it would offset the drift from the tradition they perceived as endemic among the affluent and acculturated German-Jewish community.

The similarities in class backgrounds between NCJW and Hadassah members facilitated recruitment among the middle class. Yet attempts to recruit Yiddish-speaking, working-class women garnered less attention in organization publications, although evidence suggests that many rank-and-file Hadassah members came from Eastern European origins.[57] Despite Hadassah's potential contribution to the larger Zionist movement, both in terms of projects and numbers, its initially cordial relations with the FAZ soon disclosed larger tensions between the male leadership and the women. This occurred increasingly after Hadassah began to chart a course some men deemed too independent.

The women in the Arbeter Ring, NCJW, and Hadassah all expressed a certain amount of ambivalence regarding interactions with the men of the same class and ideological backgrounds. Each group of women wanted to pursue work that would further a particular cause, be it socialism, Zionism, or the inclusive, reformist program of the NCJW. Their social backgrounds, and especially their economic status, informed the way each group devised its organization and its program. Only the Arbeter Ring overtly focused on class politics, yet the unacknowledged similarity in the backgrounds among the founders of the other two groups created the potential for close relations between them right from the start. Early interactions between women of the NCJW and Hadassah occurred regardless of these groups' reticence on class politics and despite Council's refusal to take an official position on Zionism. Arbeter Ring women's commitment to socialism, their working-class status, their use of Yiddish, and their devotion to secular Jewish identity limited the interactions they had, or even wanted to have, with women in the other two groups.

Women in Hadassah and the NCJW also shared common ideas regarding gender, and this affinity further strengthened the ties between these two middle-class, female-only organizations. Although both the socialist and Zionist movements espoused gender equality, Hadassah, like the NCJW, opted to establish a separate women's organization, generally acceding political power to men. On the surface neither group seemed to present a threat to male authority or traditional gender relations. However, the three groups' organizational agendas in the years before the outbreak of World War I show that women in the Workmen's Circle, the most radical women, found their energy consumed by the struggle to find a place for themselves within their organization. They also show that those involved in the more rhetorically accommodationist groups rapidly developed programs that raised their groups' profiles and provided volunteer women entrance into the public world of social reform.

Gendering Membership

The earliest female members of the Arbeter Ring most likely had activist histories in a labor union, in the Bund, or in both. Fani Soloviov considered her own introduction to radical activism to be representative of the experiences of other women her age. In Russia, she maintained, a poor Jewish girl had only two options: to become a seamstress or a servant. Most girls assiduously avoided domestic service and, like Soloviov, opted instead to enter the garment trade. Like thousands of other immigrants, Soloviov left Russia for the United States in search of freedom and better living conditions but found only economic exploitation. This, she believed, compelled hundreds of women to join the union movement. It was not long before women like Soloviov also sought membership in the Arbeter Ring.[58] Other early members of the

Circle drew similar connections between women's activism in the labor movement or the Bund and their subsequent participation in the Arbeter Ring. These women gave particular credit to the socialists for leading women out of their kitchens, away from their so-called backwardness and into what they considered more productive work outside the home.[59]

In all likelihood, most of these young women were single during their sojourn in the labor force, since upon marriage Jewish women traditionally gave up paid labor outside the home. In 1911 only eight percent of married Jewish women were reported to be in the labor force, and a 1915 study found that eighty-three percent of female garment workers were single, as opposed to only fifty percent of their male coworkers. Labor historian Daniel Bender argues that, generally, male workers viewed their female colleagues as transients, in the paid labor force just until they found husbands. Because of this attitude, along with the age difference separating most "permanent" male workers from their "transient" female coworkers and the relative power male workers had over the women, sexual discussions, unwanted attention, and outright harassment were prevalent on the shop floor. Rose Cohen recounted in her memoir that the first English she learned was the phrase, "Keep your hands off, please."[60] Cultural traditions and the unpleasant nature of some work-sites contributed to many women opting to leave the workforce as soon as they could.

That many female Circle members were married seems likely in light of the numerous times domestic responsibilities were raised as impediments to women's taking on organizational work. Informally, as we have seen, married women relied on one another to help in times of need, but they seem to have received little support from male radicals. In 1904 members of Branch 1 of the Circle passed a resolution stipulating that once a week men should stay at home with the children while their wives attended meetings or lectures. Although the resolution reminded men that they could not "free one part of humanity and allow the other to be enslaved," the meetings to which the wives were "sent" by their husbands were not regular branch meetings but ones intended to build support for separate "ladies' branches."[61] At any rate, this is one of the few recorded instances of organized male support of any sort in the early days of the Circle.

Like the American socialists studied by Mari Jo Buhle, Circle members disagreed on whether women should join the same branches as the men, the "regular" branches, or form their own separate groups—"ladies' branches" and women's auxiliaries. Some, especially women of a more radical mind-set, insisted that they join the "regular" branches, disavowing any form of separatist organizing. Their desire for absolute equality did not materialize into prominent organizational posts for such women, and consequently there are few traces of them in the historical record.[62]

Others opted to join the ladies' branches where they might gain organizational skills and public speaking experience in an atmosphere many felt was more accommodating than in regular branches. Similar groups arose as early as the 1870s among German socialists in the United States and later among groups associated with the Second International. As in these groups, Circle women found that the separatist strategy did not lead to an equitable distribution of power nor did it solve their problems with men in the organization. Some men bluntly opposed allowing these groups to function as anything other than auxiliaries. They even argued that since women became ill more frequently than men, the ladies' branch insurance funds should remain segregated from the general fund. This insistence on women's physical difference as a barrier to their administrative equality guaranteed that the ladies' branches remained *hilfs-organizatsies* (helping organizations) only, separate but unequal. Members in these special branches initially received no benefits from the Circle and owed it nothing in return. Like other female auxiliaries tied to fraternal organizations, women in the ladies' branches earned benefits only through their husbands' memberships or through the limited sums raised by their own groups.[63] Nevertheless, ladies' branches sprang up in New York, Brooklyn, and a few other cities. Notwithstanding this initial popularity, however, many women still preferred to become members of a regular branch or remain in the auxiliaries, which demanded no financial attachments to or from the "regular" Circle at all.[64]

In 1906 the organization at last formalized the status of members of the ladies' branches by instituting a "second-class" membership for "wives of members, single women, or wives of non-members who were not working against the principles and interest of the Workmen's Circle." While this action officially inducted branch members into the order, the women still lacked voting privileges at conventions. This frustrating situation no doubt contributed to the fact that only four groups chose to become official ladies' branches at the 1906 Circle convention. Other women, having grown tired of battling the regular branches to recognize them as "separate but equal," finally opted to join them as individual members instead.[65] Many more women continued involvement in the informal auxiliaries, for which there are no membership statistics.

Despite their low numbers, ladies' branch members persisted in trying to equalize their status, and after 1906 they turned their attention to discriminatory aspects of the Circle's insurance coverage. In these struggles the tension between physical differences and a desire for membership equality is most starkly presented. The women's arguments with the central administration revealed how their position as mothers ultimately set them apart from the Circle's vision of the independent, autonomous, worker-member. In an organization based upon traditional family relationships, where single people carried their own insurance but husbands provided for their families, married women in the ladies' branches challenged the very model of membership. Their demands for equal inclusion, along with a benefit package that suited their needs, brought to the surface the inherently gendered, and until then virtually unquestioned, nature of Circle membership. While other socialist organizations offered women theoretical equality to men, they generally had little to do with the nitty-gritty world of health insurance provision. Circle members could not base their arguments solely on theoretical grounds; they could not ignore the practical differences in men's and women's medical needs. Even after the formal inclusion of the ladies' branches at a secondary membership level, women still did not receive coverage for conditions that men were not subject to. Yet women often confounded Circle medical personnel by requesting services routinely provided to men. In 1910, for instance, when a woman applied for admittance to the Circle's tuberculosis sanatarium, she "flabbergasted" the directors, who had not anticipated having any female patients.[66]

These obstacles notwithstanding, the ladies' branch members seem to have achieved an initial measure of success. The eighth convention in 1908 voted to allow class 2 members to upgrade their insurance to class 1, the class to which virtually all men belonged, although the convention still maintained different rules for funeral payments. Supporters of the measure argued that despite the stereotypes about women's health, statistically they made fewer claims than men. They also smoked and drank less and tended to work in less dangerous jobs. The only illnesses that affected women more frequently, they conceded, were those euphemistically referred to as the "special women's diseases." To the proponents of change this was not sufficient reason to vote against the measure.[67] Circle historian Maximilian Hurwitz later proclaimed that with the 1908 vote "the fight of the women members for equal rights in the Workmen's Circle had been won, gloriously and completely."[68]

Upon closer inspection, Hurwitz's declaration of victory for gender equality appears unwarranted. The ability to upgrade to class 1 membership did not entirely alleviate women's problems. Even though women theoretically now had coverage equivalent to men's, the medical particulars were far from agreed upon. Women still did not receive coverage for those conditions that deviated from the male life cycle. For instance, at the 1911 convention delegates struggled to define precisely which diseases the Circle insurance should cover. In the past women had been denied coverage for diseases unique to them, yet some members felt this policy should be overturned because the constitution did not mention exemptions based on specific diseases. Although the convention debated the issue, it failed to resolve the matter, which resurfaced in 1919. The Benefits Committee claimed that while everyone knew "women's diseases" did not warrant coverage, confusion still existed regarding precisely which diseases fit into this category. For example, some women had been denied medical benefits because they admitted to having tumors, an affliction apparently covered only if the tumors were not specifically "female" in nature. In order to clarify this muddled situation, the committee recommended that women receive benefits for all diseases not associated with pregnancy and childbirth.[69]

This issue of health benefits highlights women's awkward status in the organization. Equality with men seemed limited to those instances when their lives mirrored one another. In cases where women's lives diverged—be it through marriage, pregnancy, or leaving the workforce—they were deemed outside the Circle's protection. Like many mutual aid societies, it based its work upon the patriarchal construct whereby the husband was regarded as the primary breadwinner and therefore the "regular" member, while his wife maintained a dependent status. The U.S. Social Security Administration later embraced similar notions of male centrality and female dependence. The difficulty of challenging this male-centered model became even more evident when the ladies' branches complained about the distribution of funeral benefits. Benefits were routinely given to male members for their deceased nonmember wives, but frequently denied in cases where a ladies' branch member sought financial assistance in burying her non-member spouse. In 1908 the National Executive Committee ruled that women whose husbands were not members could not file a claim for funeral coverage. Two years later, delegates from Ladies' Branch 102 urged that the funerals of nonmembers, regardless of sex, be paid for on the basis of their spouses' coverage. Women in Branch 102 continued their advocacy on this issue well into the next decade. A cartoon in a 1925 convention publication depicted a rather strident looking ladies' branch proponent, Besi Alinski, pounding her hand on a podium and demanding "equal rights for women" on behalf of ten ladies' branches.[70]

With their energies focused on achieving membership and insurance benefits that were equal to those already provided to men but that also addressed their particular needs as women, Arbeter Ring women did not develop the types of programs initiated prior to World War I by the NCJW and Hadassah. Unlike these women, those in the Arbeter Ring chose to pursue equality within the same group as their husbands and coworkers. Yet even in light of this commitment, some women in the Workmen's Circle did not feel that gender equality precluded a certain amount of separatist organizing at the branch level. Such women endeavored to find a means by which to be equal to men without ignoring the way that gender affected their lives. Yet whether they joined the regular branches or struggled for recognition in the ladies' branches, all Circle women initially found their energies consumed by the struggle to find a place for themselves in their socialist brotherhood.

NCJW and Social Welfare Work

Although the NCJW considered itself primarily a religious organization, the group soon undertook charity work on the local level, particularly in trying to serve segments of the population overlooked by existing Jewish organizations. To them, services for women and children, especially single immigrant women, was the area of most glaring inadequacy. After the 1913 formation of the National Federation of Temple Sisterhoods (NFTS), which focused on the religious sphere, Council increasingly turned its attention to philanthropic matters. This shift away from religion came in the wake of rabbinical aversion to Council's religious agenda. From the start rabbis dissuaded women from taking too large a part in religious education and theological discussions. In light of the rabbis' obstinacy and the appearance of the NFTS, Council women entered a field where power, at least for the time being, was not quite so contested.[71]

Council leaders had long expressed a special interest in social welfare work with women and children. A 1897 NCJW publication announced that "women's work ought first to turn toward the condition of women and children, the two most helpless classes among [the "delinquent, defective and dependent"]."[72] The Department of Immigrant Aid, organized in the first year of Council's existence, protected vulnerable young women as they made the trip from Europe to the United States. In order to shield them from the dangers of traveling alone, particularly of being lured into prostitution, the department distributed leaflets in Europe warning young girls about the hazards they faced on their way to the United States. The department also stationed volunteers at Ellis Island to greet the newcomers and help them adjust to their new home. To aid in the transition, Council offered the immigrants guidance on the citizenship process and referred them to established Americanization programs.[73]

Their experiences at Ellis Island alerted Council leaders to the need for direct female involvement in port work. From the outset, Council volunteers noticed that Jewish men's groups often neglected the unique problems faced by young girls. The NCJW leaders tried to raise men's awareness of this deficiency but, according to Sadie American, "the men shrugged their shoulders and said:

'Why cannot men do all the things that are necessary; why do you need women to look after the girls; what is it that the girls need that they do not get? Prove it to us.'" American asserted that men, due to their "conservative" nature, simply could not understand what it was that made young girls' situations so different from that of boys, or why women needed to be actively involved in this sort of work.[74]

In building her case, American provided examples of the problems confronting girls at the entry ports. Although her intention was to illustrate the difficulties men had in communicating with young women, her stories ultimately reveal the more general language and cultural barriers separating port workers from their immigrant charges. In one instance a doctor, testing immigrants to make sure they were not "feeble-minded," asked a young woman what she had worn for clothing in her homeland. The new arrival replied, in English, "paper"—a response that led the physician to suspect her of being mentally deficient. It took some time, and questioning of other people from her country of origin, before the NCJW volunteers discerned that the young woman was using an English translation for a Russian word denoting both "paper" and "cotton rags." Another young woman similarly replied in a such a way as to raise suspicion about her mental fitness. Upon being asked by a doctor to count backward from twenty, she responded with a simple, "Warum?" (Why?). Council women eventually convinced her to answer all the physician's questions, no matter how silly, and thus saved her from being sent back to Europe.[75]

In addition to port work, Council fervently sought to counter Christian proselytizers who, like their fellow missionaries in Palestine, attempted to convert Jewish immigrants, under the pretext of providing health care services either at their own centers or through individual home visits. Council started its own program of "friendly visiting" aimed at improving children's health and expediting the acculturation of their parents. Although these visits took place among coreligionists, stark differences in class and culture ensured a certain degree of tension.[76] Despite the friction, the NCJW proved instrumental in furnishing a host of necessary services to the immigrant community. In addition to health care, Council also dispensed information and legal advice on the citizenship process, advocated secular education—including sex education in the public schools—supported private religious training for girls, and initiated programs for the often forgotten rural Jews. The NCJW leaders felt it was their duty to help immigrants maintain a strong religious identity while at the same time teaching them how to become patriotic U.S. citizens. Americanization efforts intensified following the passage of the Nineteenth Amendment in 1920, at which time Council assumed responsibility for training immigrant women to become well-informed voters.[77]

At the same time that women in the settlement house movement shifted from being volunteers to social work professionals, Council too began to reconceptualize its work as something more than charity. As early as the group's founding meeting in September 1893, Sadie American suggested that the organization could avoid some of the negative stereotypes associated with middle-class women's benevolence by referring to their work as "philanthropy" rather than "charity."[78] Forty years later Hannah Solomon reflected on this perceived difference between lady volunteers and professionals. She asserted that "Lady Bountifuls had tried to disburse [charity] with hearts alone and undervalued planning," and that they feared partisans of rational methodologies who were "devoid of sympathy." Council, Solomon argued, was among the first to institute a program where both "heart and brain worked in harmony together." Reflecting the importance of the settlement movement to her own group, Solomon singled out Jane Addams for praise. By the turn of the century, Solomon proudly remembered, Council women occupied an important place in the developing field of social work, and she linked the NCJW accomplishments to those of Jane Addams and her followers.[79]

Despite their endorsement of professionalization, Council leaders did not abandon their conviction that all women, even volunteers, had a natural aptitude for social welfare work. They remained committed to the idea that women should participate in such endeavors whether they had professional training or not. To some extent, this attitude resembled the "female dominion" arising among Jane Addams's proteges. Julia Lathrop, head of the Children's Bureau in the early twentieth century, relied on her connections to the world of female voluntarism to further her government work. Arguing that women could better understand and deal with the problems of women, Lathrop and other former volunteers cut a new professional path for women like themselves.[80] Additionally, by employing language quite similar to that used by reformers like Lathrop (as well as Hadassah), Council leaders proposed a vision of complementary gender roles. In this view, men and women performed distinct tasks that proved equally vital to the overall success of a project. At the 1914 Council triennial, Sadie American outlined this concept of interrelatedness:

> We women have time in the daytime to come together, and the men have time in the evening to come together, and the time will come when we will fully realize that each needs the other, for advice, for their different points of view, male and female, the men contributing that which is virile, if you please, but the womanly influence equally valuable, equally necessary; . . . we women [are] not looked upon as simply doing women's work, but [both men and women] cooperating for progress.[81]

By the time of the First World War, Council had become extremely attuned to the ways that male-led social welfare agencies could overlook the special needs of immigrant women and formulated their own programs to address those needs. Though cognizant of how immigrant women were neglected in the programs of other welfare groups, Council made no significant effort to create a cross-class or even cooperative relationship with the women they aimed to serve. Still, their advocacy on behalf of these women resulted in the NCJW articulating a distinct need for women's public work and convincing their male contemporaries not only of the necessity for such work but of women's natural aptitude for it.

Creating a Gendered Zionism

Hadassah's commitment to a specific ideology, movement, and activist program, along with its distinct separation from men, ensured that it would not have to experiment in its early years as much as did women in the NCJW and Arbeter Ring. From the very start, Hadassah focused its energy on providing medical services to the Palestinian population, and from the outset it considered this work especially suited to American women. Hadassah's programmatic and ideological foundations seemed secure, yet its semi-independent status soon led to friction with the established male-led organization, the FAZ. In the process of dealing with the doubts of male Zionists regarding their capabilities, Hadassah women formulated a gendered Zionism that celebrated what they perceived as women's natural propensity for social welfare work.

Initially larger and more powerful, the FAZ quickly clashed with the upstart Hadassah. Much of the FAZ leadership considered Hadassah a collection agency, a philanthropy, or, worst of all, an insignificant charity, despite the fact that raising funds and distributing them was precisely the role the men had planned for a national women's Zionist's organization. Henrietta Szold and her fellow board members rejected such characterizations. They quickly moved to ensure a degree of autonomy for the women's group while at the same time distancing their work from that of traditional charities. In 1915 Szold told the Zionist publication *Maccabaean* that Hadassah was decidedly not a charity: "We go to Palestine equipped as American Jewish women particularly are, with philanthropic and social work, with the purpose of bringing to Palestine the results of American healing art."[82] Not unlike the FAZ men, Szold believed that American women were more interested in practical projects than ideological discourse; however, unlike those men, she thought of this as a virtue, not a flaw, in women's nature. Still, many male Zionists criticized Hadassah's focus; FAZ leader, Louis Lipsky, contended that because men involved themselves in "all phases of Zionist development" they found Hadassah's narrow interest in social welfare alone "curious."[83]

This Zionist condemnation of "charity" was not merely a quirk of certain male leaders. It manifested itself on several interlocking levels. First, the FAZ disparaged charity and philanthropy on grounds that it did not further the Zionist program of reclaiming Eretz Israel. In this paradigm one important aspect of Zionism was the creation of the New Jewish Man: to transform the sickly, weak, European ghetto Jew into a healthy, strong, Palestinian farmer. This required attention to agricultural projects, physical labor, and "improvement" of the land—creating farms and orchards from the desert.[84] In a letter Hadassah's 1921 convention, Henrietta Szold noted that at its founding the group "was contemptuously charged with being, not practical—that would have been kindly censure—but philanthropic, which, from a Zionist point of view, was the last word in malice."[85] Beyond this Zionist element the urban work reminded men of *halukah*, or charitable giving to support those people, generally the elderly, who chose to live out their days in Jerusalem not from any Zionist motivation but simply because they wished to die in the land of Israel. Zionists wanted to distinguish their work of modern nation-building from alms-giving to the destitute, religious elderly.[86]

It is also important to note that Hadassah originated at a time when social work generally, but particularly Jewish social work, was in the process of federation, specialization, and professionaliza-tion—all of which, for the Jewish community, often meant that organized male-led initiatives superseded women's independent work. Practitioners of the developing field of social work also dis-missed the work of untrained, though well-meaning, volunteers as unproductive at best and harmful at worst. Many advocated replac-ing amateurs with social workers trained to handle the needs of the sick and the poor with more professional objectivity. While this tended to reduce the numbers of female volunteers, many women ultimately did receive training and entered the professional field of social work.[87]

Hadassah women, then, perceived as untrained volunteers concerned only with social welfare issues, operated within a milieu that designated them selfish amateurs disinterested in the larger questions of ideology and politics. If they sought equality with men in the movement on male terms—intense debate and unceasing "wrangling"—the men still dismissed them as mere women, better suited to fund-raising and charity.[88] When they moved, finally, to accept the notion of separate, complementary spheres and took on the responsibility of pursuing "philanthropic" goals, they again met with male resistance: in the men's view, such work remained mun-dane charity pursued by amateurish ladies, not professionals and certainly not true Zionists. As Szold later noted, "there has been constant criticism because [Hadassah] was not political enough, or because it was too political[,] either it didn't think or it thought too independently." She questioned whether it was possible that male leaders simply wanted large numbers of new "recruits" but "not their minds."[89] The Hadassah leadership, Henrietta Szold in partic-ular, remained undaunted by this conundrum and created a means by which "amateur" Zionists could promote social welfare in Pales-tine. The contribution of these female "amateurs," they believed, could be every bit as important as that of their male counterparts.

Hadassah sent two visiting nurses, Rose Kaplan and Ray Landy, to Palestine, supported with funds donated by philanthropist Nathan Straus and non-Zionist supporters from Chicago. This non-Zionist benevolence did not improve the perception of the Hadassah mission in the eyes of the FAZ. The nurses, however, proved effective in lowering maternity and infant mortality among the population of Jerusalem. In 1913 Jane Addams and Rabbi Stephen Wise both visited the nurses' settlement and gave favorable evaluations of the work being done there.[90] The local population, however, initally had little faith in Hadassah. The nurses—proponents of modern, scientific methods—clashed with those who believed in "myths and magic," as a later Hadassah pamphlet characterized them. This propaganda piece described the people in Palestine as practicing "ancient rites . . . [including] conjurings, smearings, amulet-wearing, weird incantations and the application of hot irons to affected portions of the body." Not unlike Progressives struggling to Americanize immigrants back home, the authors of this pamphlet claimed that Hadassah arrived in Palestine to face "this medieval setting . . . with the latest scientific ideas." Despite the initial cultural clash, over time the community began to trust the nurses and, through them, Hadassah in general.[91]

Along with the nurses' program in Palestine, Hadassah embarked on an educational plan for American women. Articles and announcements in the first several years of the *Bulletin* reveal keen interest in educating members in the "Hadassah plan" and in Zionism generally. Early issues contain suggested reading lists, including the writings of such Zionist luminaries as Theodore Herzl, Leon Pinsker, and Ahad Ha'Am.[92] Like their counterparts in the NCJW, Hadassah leaders wanted their work understood within the context of professional Jewish social welfare work. Yet Hadassah women also desired to show that their contributions were an integral part of the Zionist mission as well.

Hadassah initially allowed non-Zionist women interested in their Palestinian projects to become associate members. Over time the group would do away with this type of membership and also insist upon only one chapter per city. Both initiatives resulted from the need for Hadassah to become a streamlined, efficient, and purely Zionist organization. These reform measures also served to bring together Jewish women from a variety of backgrounds, on an equal basis, to pursue their interest in Palestine and Zionism.[93]

Hadassah's membership, like that of the Zionist movement in general, would began to grow significantly only after the outbreak of World War I. Yet the organization laid important groundwork in the early years of its existence. The leadership instituted a definite program of action, one that enabled American women to take the lead in an area of work neglected by other Zionists. In assuming responsibility for the medical needs of Palestine, especially the urban centers, American Zionist women found a means by which they could assert some degree of independent authority. Publicizing the success of their efforts would be a basis for increasing their membership in the ensuing years. Moreover, the often negative interactions they had with male Zionists, who perceived their work as being more like traditional benevolence than Zionist nation-building, led them to formulate a positive, gendered understanding of their work. In explaining to themselves and others how their work actually did serve the Zionist program, Hadassah leaders relied on a rhetoric similar to that of NCJW leaders. But unlike those other middle-class reformers, Hadassah characterized its work as part of the general plan to upbuild Palestine and create a homeland for the world's Jews. During and especially after the war, Hadassah would begin to reconceptualize its Palestine projects as laying the foundation of a haven for the world's persecuted Jews. As the women's desire to protect Jews intensified so too would their use of maternalist language and imagery to describe their unique contribution to the Zionist enterprise.

On the Eve of World War I

At the turn of the century, Jewish women, like their gentile contemporaries, embraced a move toward the public sphere. Women from across political and class spectrums joined organizations or formed their own during this period. The shape and nature of the groups Jewish women founded depended to a great degree on their own life experiences, not the least of which included interactions with men of their class and ideological viewpoint. While the women in all three organizations believed they had much to contribute to their movements and to society in general, each group forged its own path, devising unique ways of negotiating societal strictures and male expectations of women's capabilities. In doing so, Jewish women created a variety of means by which to enter the public sphere, provide for the community, and further their own ideals.

Despite their differences, women in all three groups discovered that a certain amount of separatism from men afforded them more independence and autonomy over their own actions. Their attempts, though, met with stiff opposition from those men who felt women should subordinate themselves to masculine leadership and, at the other end of the spectrum, from those people who believed true gender equality prevailed only when women acted like men and thus ignored the significance of gender in their lives. This opposition notwithstanding, all three groups maintained close affiliations with and dedication to the Jewish people. During the war women would find that meeting the urgent needs of the Jewish "nation," variously defined by each organization, would necessitate putting gender politics on the back burner.

The Crisis Years

Jewish Women and World War I

The First World War had a profound impact on the American Jewish community despite the fact that the United States did not directly involve itself in the conflict until mid-1917. Following the outbreak of hostilities in August 1914, American Jewish organizations immediately turned away from their individual projects to join large-scale international relief endeavors. The intensity and scope of the crisis impelled American Jews to act in concert, cooperating to a degree unknown before the war. Women's groups, like other American Jewish organizations, responded to the plight of European Jewry and united in the national effort to coordinate raising relief funds and distributing them.

Despite women's heightened involvement, the war years seemed to exacerbate male attitudes against which women had fought for years. Women from the NCJW, Hadassah, and the Workmen's Circle discovered that after the outbreak of the war their opinions were sought even less frequently than before, their leadership rarely summoned. In an effort to respond effectively to the crisis, Jewish women willingly joined with men's groups to facilitate the speedy distribution of relief funds. But this cooperation soon resulted in a near total subordination of their plans to those devised by men. In some cases, like the Workmen's Circle, discussion of gender issues virtually disappeared as men and women turned their attention to their "brothers and sisters" in Eastern

Europe. Women's experiences in the wartime relief campaigns would soon challenge their faith in men's commitment to gender equality; cooperation, they found, rarely resulted in recognition of women's significant contribution to these efforts. Jewish women were not unique in facing such barriers. Women in both the peace and preparedness movements also encountered resistance from men. At the same time, these women were strong advocates of the idea that women brought unique contributions to the public world.[1]

Jewish women's cooperation and continuing, if muted, conflict with men similarly reinforced a strong sense of gender identity. By 1920 members of all three organizations spoke forthrightly and proudly about their own accomplishments and capabilities. Not only did women experience a growing sense of gender consciousness, they also began to reexamine their ideas regarding Jewish identity. The war uncovered fissures in the normative Jewish identity propounded by elite American Jews. Although all the major organizations rallied to the call to save the "Jewish people," the definition of what precisely that meant was increasingly complicated by gender, class, ideological, political, and religious differences. By war's end divisions within the American Jewish community that many people had previously left unexamined could no longer be ignored.

The Plight of Jews in Eastern Europe and Palestine

When the nations of Europe went to war in August 1914, American Jews viewed developments with intense anxiety. The vast majority of the world's fifteen million Jews lived in those areas of Europe most directly affected by the onslaught of war: Germany and the Russian and Austrian-Hungarian Empires.[2] As members of the most recent wave of immigration, a majority of American Jews felt a visceral connection to the events in Europe. Although they expressed great affinity for those they left behind, few American Jews, if any, worried about Russia's tsarist regime, which was responsible for some of the worst persecutions of Jews in modern times. Therefore, when war broke out between the Central Powers and the Allied nations, including Russia, most American Jews refused to lend support to the tsar's war effort. At best Jews hoped that France and Great Britain might pressure their ally to change governmental policies affecting that empire's Jewish subjects.

44

Within a few short months even these faint hopes died when it became all too apparent that the war had intensified the plight of Jews, especially those in the Pale of Settlement, where most Russian Jews lived. In the fall of 1915, as German forces advanced quickly into Russian territory, the Russian military laid the blame for their losses on Jews and other non-Russian populations, calling them conspirators, traitors who loved Germany more than Russia. This attitude served, in some areas, to inflame local antisemitic fervor, which not infrequently resulted in pogroms or other anti-Jewish actions. The Russian government ordered the expulsion of large numbers of Jews from the Eastern front, not to protect them from the violence of their neighbors but to prevent any further "sabotage." During the rest of 1915 the government forcibly relocated some 600,000 Jews further east, sometimes with only the briefest of warning, providing Jews with little or no time to pack their belongings or put their affairs in order. The tremendous growth in the urban population, especially in the Pale, put an onerous burden on communities. Disease and hunger ran rampant in cities such as Vilna (Vilnius), which sheltered some 22,000 refugees. Given the authorities' attitude toward the Jews, state-sponsored aid was meager at best. The Central Powers' military successes offered a bit of relief to the fleeing Jews: by late 1915 most of the Pale of Settlement lay under their control. In their swift advance the Germans overtook some two-thirds of the refugees, thus enabling many to return home. This did nothing to raise the tsar's opinion of the Jews, nor did it significantly improve their physical distress; one estimate places the value of Jewish material losses at $400,000,000.[3]

Jews were no safer outside the boundaries of the Russian Empire. Russian soldiers carried their antisemitic beliefs across the border into Galicia, a portion of the Austrian-Hungarian Empire inhabited by large numbers of Jews. While all Galicians suffered tremendously as the various armies battled back and forth across the territory, Jews alone faced the special enmity of Russians who believed they preferred Germans over Slavs. Thousands of Jews fled the area rather than suffer persecution at the hands of the Russians. Consequently, the refugee population in the Austrian-Hungarian Empire rivaled that of the tsar's lands. Perhaps as many as half the population of Jewish Galicia, or nearly 400,000 people, fled westward to escape the invading Russian army. In all areas where the Jewish refugees congregated, food shortages and inflation soon followed. Although both were typical occurrences during wartime, gentiles often laid the blame for these conditions on the Jewish refugees.[4]

In the fall of 1914 the Ottoman Empire entered the war on the side of the Central Powers. At this point the small Jewish population in Palestine, many of whom had only recently moved there from Russia, faced a fate similar to that of their relatives in Eastern Europe. Turkish officials considered these Jews, along with citizens of other Allied nations, a threat to military security, and in December 1914 they ordered the expulsion of Russian Jews from Jaffa. Within a year some 11,000 Jews were in Egypt, many of them in refugee camps. In April 1917 the Turkish authorities ordered the remaining Jews in Jaffa, some 9,000 people, to leave that city. As in Europe, disease and starvation ravaged the refugees in Egypt as well as those who remained behind in Palestine.[5]

The war exposed the uniquely tenuous position of Jews living in the warring nations. Unlike most other national groups, Jews inhabited areas on both sides of the conflict and were therefore readily subject to accusations of treason or sabotage. Antisemitism, easily inflamed by wartime exigencies, magnified the already precarious position of Jews in Russia, Palestine, and the Austrian-Hungarian Empire. Local populations in Galicia and elsewhere blamed the economic devastation not on their leaders but on Jewish merchants who had played a large role in local economies before the war. While Russians believed that Jews felt closer to the German invaders than their Slavic neighbors, Ottoman officials thought Russian Jews living in Palestine retained an allegiance to their homeland and therefore would seek to undermine the Central Powers' war effort. Jews in the United States immediately recognized the dangers facing Jews trapped in the war zones, and they quickly mobilized to provide whatever aid they could.

American Jews Respond to the War

In October 1914 the Orthodox community founded the Central Committee for Relief of the Jews Suffering Through the War (known as the Central Relief Committee or CRC). Later in that same month the elite, generally non-Zionist American Jewish Committee (AJC) called a meeting of some forty Jewish organizations to set up a united body for relief collection and distribution: the American Jewish Relief Committee (AJRC). Prominent Jews from across the ideological spectrum, including representatives from the CRC, participated in the formation of this new organization. When it became clear, however, that the elite AJC men, most of whom were Reform Jews, would dominate the AJRC, the Central Relief Committee opted to retain its autonomy. In order to maintain the highest efficiency possible in getting relief to the needy, the leaders of the AJRC and CRC worked out a compromise that called for distinct fund-raising efforts but a unified distribution. In November 1914 the two groups established the American Jewish Joint Distribution Committee (JDC) to dispense funds to Jews in the warring nations. In August 1915 a third collection entity, the socialist People's Relief Committee (PRC), began contributing to the JDC.[6] All the major Jewish organizations participated in one way or another with these three committees. The NCJW formally joined the AJRC while the Workmen's Circle affiliated with the PRC. Hadassah contributed to AJRC and, like other Zionists, also raised funds for the Palestine Emergency Fund.

Council women, who had many ties to the non-Zionist leadership of the American Jewish Committee, participated in the AJRC's founding conference. The sole NCJW delegate quickly noticed the dearth of women at that gathering and "made a plea in the name of Jewish Womanhood" that more women be included.[7] Despite this mild criticism, publicly the NCJW expressed unqualified support for AJRC efforts. Privately, however, certain board members voiced reservations about the unified relief effort. Some feared that the relief funds would never reach the most needy. Others worried that targeting relief to Jews alone would send the wrong message to gentiles both at home and abroad. "It shows a certain narrowness," one woman argued, "for the Jews of this country to specify simply Jews as the people to help."[8] These women worried that a focused initiative might lead some people to question American Jews' loyalty to the U.S. Countering these apprehensions, Evelyn Aronson Margolis relayed the confidences of a Red Cross acquaintance who insisted that targeted relief was an absolute necessity. This person, she asserted, believed that general aid funds "would never, never reach the Jews, at least in Europe." Arguing that antisemitism was so intense that it led national and local governments to channel their relief funds to gentiles alone, her Red Cross contact asserted that European Jews were desperate for American assistance. Moreover, Margolis contended, participating in the AJRC would do more than help the starving Jews abroad. It would also heighten Council's prominence in the arena of American Jewish organizational life: "I do think that if we want to show ourselves a really big National body of Jewish Women, now is the time to show it by a contribution," she concluded. In the end her position won out, and Council became an active contributor to the AJRC.[9]

This argument about whether to target relief funds would not become an issue of vehement contention in the Arbeter Ring until the postwar period. Initially the Workmen's Circle, like other American Jewish socialist organizations, uniformly reacted to the outbreak of hostilities by asserting that the war would help capitalists and therefore should be opposed. This position reflected the working-class, internationalist mind-set of the prewar socialist movement. But where socialists in Europe quickly joined in the nationalist fervor of their homelands, American Jewish socialists continued to reject the war because they ardently opposed the alliance with Russia. Indeed, not a few Eastern European immigrants expressed hope for the tsar's demise and openly rejoiced at each Russian military defeat.[10]

The Workmen's Circle also expressed annoyance at the lack of attention given to the predicament facing Eastern European Jews. In 1915 Circle leadership criticized the obvious discrepancy between the sympathetic and effusive American media response to the Belgian victims of German atrocities and the relative lack of reporting on the plight of Jews in Eastern Europe. The leaders argued that, unlike the Belgians, Eastern European Jews faced violence not only from invading armies but also from their own nation's military forces and sometimes even from their neighbors. Questioning how many American Christians even knew of the Jews' distress, much less contributed to relieving their misery, Circle leaders concluded that the crisis demanded "Jewish help for Jewish victims."[11] Along with raising questions about Americans' general commitment to caring for Jewish war victims and about unqualified Jewish allegiance to Germany, the Circle's position also signaled a distinct break from other socialists' Marxist internationalism, which focused on the working class regardless of national or ethnic attachment, and a shift to something decidedly more nationalist in tenor. Following the war some communist members of the group would question whether funds should be sent solely to Jewish workers or to working-class people regardless of their national origin, but during the years of active fighting the more nationalist position predominated.

Reflecting this ever growing commitment to cultural nationalism, the Arbeter Ring assisted in establishing an organization to work for Jewish individual and national rights in Eastern Europe. The Jewish National Workmen's Committee on Jewish Rights (NWC), included the United Hebrew Trades, the Jewish Federation of the Socialist Party, the Forverts Association, and the Labor Zionists.[12] The NWC undertook to inform the public about the Jewish condition in Eastern Europe and to appeal to the U.S. government, the International Congress of Socialists, and the postwar peace conferences to guarantee equal rights for Jews. Due in part to the presence of a very vocal Zionist contingent the Arbeter Ring did not play a central role in the NWC. Circle members wanted the NWC to focus its activism for Jewish rights on Europe, while the Zionists were, in the words of one Circle member, "interested above all in the question of *Eretz-Israel*." Despite its major role in relief campaigns, some members felt the Workmen's Circle was "pushed aside into a corner" in matters of NWC policy.[13] Still, the war's impact on Jewish life in Eastern Europe led Circle members to reevaluate their stance on Jewish nationalism, even as the organization remained, for the time being, firmly opposed to Zionism.

When war broke out in 1914, Zionists, like socialists, found themselves on both sides of the conflict. The World Zionist Organization (WZO), headquartered in Berlin, had in its upper echelon men from both Allied and Central Power nations. In light of this, the WZO quickly turned to the United States to request that this segment of the movement take over the management of Zionist affairs for the duration of the war. In August 1914 the WZO established the Provisional Executive Committee for General Zionist Affairs (PEC), based in the United States under the leadership of Louis Brandeis. In conjunction with the crisis atmosphere brought on by the war, the relocation of Zionist headquarters resulted in the dramatic growth of the American Zionist movement. At the start of the war, the Federation of American Zionists (FAZ) had a membership of only 7,000, yet by 1918 the organization claimed nearly 150,000 adherents.[14] Individual Zionists contributed to the AJRC while Brandeis and other Zionist leaders actively raised money through speaking tours and other events. But this cooperation soon grew strained. Certain wealthy donors to the AJRC, for example, began to stipulate that they would give money for Palestine relief only if they could be assured that the funds would not go toward any Zionist institutions. The final straw came when the AJRC took credit for sending a relief ship, the USS *Vulcan*, to Palestine, to which Zionists felt they had contributed the bulk of the supplies. Despite their anger at the AJRC, Zionists acknowledged that they were unable to raise adequate funds for Palestine on their own. In the end, they utilized the JDC to distribute their funds, but they took responsibility for raising the aid themselves. This situation did not lead to total peace between Zionists and their opponents. The Zionists shortly began to complain that the JDC refused to divert to Palestine its fair share of relief.[15] The unity symbolized by the JDC could not entirely mask the divisions growing between the various segments of American Jewry. While all American Jews sought to aid relatives and coreligionists overseas, they disagreed on several issues: the best way to achieve this goal, which Jews constituted "the most needy," and what should happen with the Jewish minorities in Europe and Palestine after the war.

Forging Gender and Ethnic Bonds

Despite emerging divisions, coalition work proceeded apace. In the process of contributing to the relief campaigns, women in Hadassah, the NCJW, and the Workmen's Circle established relationships with other organizations espousing goals similar to their own, both Jewish and non-Jewish, single and mixed-sex. The alliances they made and the degree to which they cooperated with these other groups depended a great deal on each organization's ideological stance, its immediate goals, and, perhaps most importantly, the class status of its membership. Although Circle and NCJW members occupied opposite ends of the class spectrum and held widely divergent views regarding the political economy, women in both groups continued to identify strongly as women, thinking of themselves as having much in common with non-Jewish women of their own class.

Zionist women, on the other hand, pursued a singular course by centering their attention on Jews alone and using relief work to promote the Zionist ideology more effectively at home. One Hadassah leader, reproaching members who had neglected the organization in order to focus on more generalized war relief efforts, commented that "Zionism affects [Zionist women's] poor sisters, and for that matter, their rich sisters in America as much as it does their sisters over seas, and until they come to a realization of this fact they cannot be considered true Zionists."[16] Interactions between Hadassah members and non-Zionists in the American relief campaigns presented Zionists with a wonderful opportunity to convey their message to potential recruits. Through such efforts as sewing circles, where women gathered to prepare clothing and other items for Palestinian children, Hadassah members successfully drew some non-Zionist women into their sphere of activity. During this period two non-Zionist groups in Chicago and Pittsburgh organized Palestine Welfare Societies, expressly devoted to assisting Hadassah's work, though they retained their distance from the group's ideology.[17]

Some Hadassah leaders thought that the brutality of the war and the way that it exposed the precariousness of Jewish life in Europe would convert American Jews to the Zionist cause. Shortly after the outbreak of war, Henrietta Szold, in a letter to a supporter in Cleveland, asserted that the war might serve a useful purpose by encouraging the restoration of the Jewish nation:

> I have been repeating to myself all these weeks since the war began that this is our supreme test and our supreme opportunity not only for us Zionists, but for the American Jew in general. It all depends upon us now whether the Jews shall remain a gypsy nomad people, in spite of the fact that four hundred thousand of us are fighting at the front, or whether we shall become a nation in every sense of the word.[18]

Several months later Szold made similar remarks to Augusta Rosenwald, whose husband, Julius, opposed Zionism. She told Rosenwald that although she believed the war was a disaster, she thought it had helped clarify the "anomalous situation" of Jews around the world. "It is a miracle," she wrote, "that, though we Zionists were not hitherto able to bring many to our way of thinking, nevertheless many in these days of stress think with pity of our little sanctuary." Some of these non-Zionists, she believed, would eventually begin to support the "little sanctuary" as a palliative response to devastation befalling European Jewry, a tragedy she believed would one day be described as the third *Hurban*, or catastrophe, following the destruction of the first Temple by the Babylonians in 586 BCE and the second by the Romans in 70 CE.[19]

Hadassah's powerful commitment to the Zionist movement limited the energy its members expended on interactions with non-Jewish organizations. In a rare occurrence, several leaders briefly joined the pacifist People's Council for Peace and Democracy, an organization that the Zionist Judah Magnes helped found. In September 1917 members of Hadassah's Central Committee, including Henrietta Szold, enrolled in the organization that had grown out of a mass meeting held by the American Conference for Democracy and Terms of Peace. Attendance at this initial meeting, like membership in the later People's Council itself, consisted primarily of gentiles such as Eugene Debs, Norman Thomas, and Oswald Garrison Villard. Louis Brandeis, leader of the PEC, expressed great irritation that some of his followers had participated. He felt it was imperative that Zionists maintain political neutrality in order to avoid potential setbacks in achieving their ultimate goal. The People's Council was considered by many to be not merely a peace organization but a seditious group espousing unpatriotic, socialist attitudes.[20]

Henrietta Szold and Jessie Sampter were called in to meet with the PEC leadership and were informed that, if they insisted on remaining in the People's Council, they should resign their Hadassah posts. Brandeis told them, "When a person who is as conspicuous as Miss Szold . . . takes a position and is known, then the injury that is done is obvious." Within a month, Szold yielded to Brandeis's wishes and withdrew from the group, and it is likely that other members of the Central Committee quickly followed her lead.[21] Her biographer feels that Szold's actions were motivated by her commitment not just to the Zionist movement but more specifically to Hadassah itself. Fearing what her resignation would mean for the organization and for her own professional life, Szold chose Zionism over pacifism, even though she refused to denounce her beliefs.[22] This brief cooperation with a non-Zionist, predominantly gentile, peace organization proved to be a singular and short-lived experience for Hadassah's leaders. The women's involvement in the group was entirely individual and did not reflect an official, organizational position. After this, Hadassah focused its energies solely on relief work; they continued to reach out to non-Zionist Jewish women but curtailed activism outside the realm of Jewish politics. In choosing to do so, the leaders not only signaled their privileging of Zionism over pacifism, they also exhibited behavior not unlike that of Council's leadership—namely, withdrawing from a movement deemed too controversial for many mainstream Americans, including the foremost male leaders of the Zionist movement.

Jewish socialists were far less inhibited than the Brandeis-led Zionist movement about expressing their opinions on the war and potential U.S. involvement. At the same time that the Circle as an organization was strengthening its already close ties to other Jewish working-class groups and deemphasizing any lingering socialist internationalism, the group's paper *Der fraynd* (The friend) printed the inaugural of a woman's column, "Iber der froyen velt" (About the women's world). Unlike other sections of the paper or other organizational publications, these columns rarely, if ever, referred to Jewish identity. Usually authored by Adele Kean Zametkin, the columns focused on issues affecting working women regardless of ethnicity or religion.[23] Zametkin, born in Russia in 1869, emigrated to the United States in 1888 and became the personal and professional partner of the prominent Jewish socialist and *Forverts* cofounder Michael Zametkin. During the war, her columns featured topics of interest to women such as suffrage, wages, and maternity benefits, and in each case she stressed the centrality of class to these issues. Although the columns do not shed light on the grassroots activities of Circle women during the war, they reveal Zametkin's and her editors' beliefs that working-class Jewish women should be well-informed on a variety of gender-related issues. As the Circle itself embraced ever more strongly a program of secular, cultural, Jewish identity centered on the Yiddish language, Zametkin's columns urged Jewish women to forge bonds with working women across ethnic lines.

An even stronger gender consciousness arose among leaders of the NCJW who affiliated with non-Jewish women's organizations even as their own members collected money for Jewish war victims. According to Barbara J. Steinson, gentile women "threw themselves into war relief with a zeal born of the conviction that they served a uniquely noble cause."[24] Prior to the U.S. declaration of war in April 1917, American women's organizations, Jewish and gentile, ran the gamut of opinion; some endeavored to promote peace while others worked for military and national preparedness. Jane Addams and other feminists founded the Woman's Peace Party, while Lillian Wald and her allies created the American Union against Militarism. After April 1917, large numbers of women activists continued to support various relief efforts, but a far greater number of women embraced patriotic initiatives than persisted in the peace movement; to take just one example, the Woman's Committee of the Commission for Relief of Belgians transformed itself into the Woman's Section of the Movement for Preparedness. From right to left, women found that participation in war relief, peace, or preparedness gave them a sense of confidence in their own abilities.[25]

Having been the Jewish organization most integrated with gentile women's activism prior to the war, the NCJW now took center stage as Jewish women's representative in the worlds of mainstream American relief and female political organizing. In the first years of the war Council established ties with a wide array of associations promoting both relief and peace. President Janet Harris served on the executive committee of the National Committee for Relief of Belgians, while Hannah Solomon joined the Women's Belgium Committee. Local NCJW chapters assisted the work of the Red Cross, and Council raised $205,000 for war relief.[26] The NCJW's Peace and Arbitration Committee, established in 1908, cooperated with the peace initiatives of other women's groups. In 1916, at Jane Addams's request, the committee sent a message to President Wilson asking him to call a conference of neutral nations, the aim of which would be to create a mediation court to

solicit settlement proposals from the warring nations and ultimately bring about permanent peace. In response to an invitation
to become a member of the Women's Department for National
Preparedness that same year, Harris advised her board to decline as
she thought participation in an organization for "preparedness"
would appear inconsistent with Council's peace agenda. So long as
Council worked for peace, she said, it should avoid assisting any
movement "that seemed to accept war."[27]

Despite Harris's position, and unlike their contemporaries in
the Woman's Peace Party, many NCJW leaders actively supported
the war effort once the United States entered the fray in April
1917. Rebekah Kohut proudly recalled helping Dorothy Straight,
New York society matron and cofounder of the *New Republic*, to
make "war-workers of hundreds of New York debutantes." Kohut
also served as the industrial chairman of the National League for
Women's Service and was appointed by John D. Rockefeller, Jr., to
represent Jewish women on the United War Work campaign. Nevertheless, other leaders maintained their dedication to peace even
as they muted their fervor during the war. For instance, after con-
cluding her service as Council president in 1920, Janet Harris
moved on to active involvement in the Women's International
League for Peace and Freedom.[28] The diversity of Council women's
response to the war reveals their continued ties to women of their
own class—ties that remained strong despite differences in religious confession and political beliefs. Yet soon enough the plight of
European Jewry would lead a number of them to rethink their conceptions of Jewish identity, which prior to the war had downplayed
secular or ethnic constructions of Jewish nationhood.

In the end Hadassah, the Arbeter Ring, and the NCJW all
expressed great concern for Jews in Eastern Europe and Palestine.
The distinct vantage points of the organizations regarding religious
or ethnic identification, gender consciousness, and class status
informed not only how they responded to the war but also their
concrete efforts to provide relief. In helping Jewish men in these
endeavors women frequently took a backseat and relinquished
national leadership. Yet although they conceded their secondary
status in male-led relief initiatives, this did not result in a total suppression of gender as an issue nor of women as a force in Jewish

politics. Women intentionally cooperated with Jewish men, all the while continuing to pursue their own agendas and laying plans for postwar initiatives.

The JDC's Gendered Appeals for Relief

With organizational structures in place, the American Jewish community turned to the critical task of gathering and distributing relief funds. Regardless of women's absence from the top leadership of Jewish relief agencies, images of women continued to figure prominently in organizational publications. The AJRC and JDC both relied heavily on representations of women to convey a feminized vision of European Jewry and its plight. These images attempted to personalize the crisis in order to compel American Jews to give as much as they possibly could. All the Jewish relief drives relied heavily on a rhetoric of family to drive home the need for giving. But where the socialists and Zionists most often spoke only of their "brothers and sisters" overseas, the well-to-do men of the AJRC and JDC portrayed a European Jewry that was frail, fearful, and feminine.

Representations of European Jews in JDC publications frequently presented them as bedraggled women with starving children at their sides. In one depiction American benevolence appears as a statuesque, healthy woman extending her arms across the sea to help her starving European sister in a drawing curiously titled "All Israel are Brethren." Such illustrations served to feminize European and American Jewry, symbolizing difference in material wealth through the physical bodies of women. Typically, however, only European Jews underwent such a feminization, and this, in turn, underscored their helplessness. The textual exhortations appealed directly to potential donors, reminding them of how close they were to those living abroad: "Had this World-War occurred twenty years ago we might be pleading FOR you instead of TO you." American Jews were encouraged to think of the victims as their very own relatives: "Have American Jews become callous to the sufferings of their brothers and sisters, fathers and mothers in the war zones?" Yet in creating this international Jewish "family" the relief organizations most frequently employed female images to show the despair of European Jews, especially as the war progressed. One solicitation, centered around the image of a tired old woman without food or support, declared boldly, "Tired of Giving? You Don't Know What Feeling Tired Means!" Another focused on the suffering of "Jewish babes, Jewish mothers, Jewish boys and girls and the Jewish aged," raising the specter of families struggling to survive without fathers and young men. Another appeal directly referred to the greater potential for female suffering. "The first to bear the brunt of conditions for which they are in no wise responsible will be our brethren," it reminded readers, "and to an even greater extent than the men, the women and children—the most helpless and defenceless among the entire populations."[29] In formulating their pleas in this manner, both the ARJC and the JDC posited the existence of "family" bonds between all the Jews of the world. The images entreated American Jews to do their part to aid the helpless victims of the war—the Jewish aged, children, and especially women bereft of male protection.

These exhortations, based on conjuring up images of persecuted and oppressed women, merged together neatly with the pre-war concerns of the Jewish middle class that young women might be lured into "white slavery." Before the war a number of organizations in Europe and America, among them the NCJW, diligently sought to help young women avoid prostitution.[30] Because Jewish involvement in prostitution had already figured as a central concern of middle-class American Jews prior to the war, the feminized visions of European suffering only served to exacerbate these anxieties. Reports from Russian relief workers alerting American Jews to the general demoralization of the Jewish population brought on by starvation and want did little to ease these fears. For instance, the prominent Yiddish writer S. Ansky believed prostitution had become widespread because so many Jewish refugees lacked even the most basic necessities of life.[31]

The focus on prostitution also served to displace and silence fears about the rape of Jewish women by soldiers. Although many people feared for women's safety during wartime, distress about Jewish prostitution, rather than rape, became the central element in the larger appeal to the international Jewish family. Rabbi Judah Magnes told a large audience at Carnegie Hall that young women in Eastern Europe struggled to maintain their "purity" in the face of poverty and the influx of soldiers into their shtetlekh: These virtuous women tried to sell flowers to avoid having "to sell them-

selves to the handsome officers and soldiers that fill the streets."
Still, Magnes assured his listeners, "the great mass of our Jewish
womanhood has remained steadfast, has remained loyal and true
to our high traditions of chastity, to our noble heritage of family
purity."[32] While rape went unacknowledged, sexual dangers arising
from the war, and admitted to only in the form of prostitution,
nevertheless threatened to destroy the Jewish family, both nar-
rowly and broadly defined. The JDC was not alone in maintaining
silence regarding sexual violence perpetrated against Jewish
women; the women's groups also failed to discuss the issue in their
wartime publications or even in private meetings. Yet the reluctance of JDC men to broach the topic of rape continued well after
the war. In preparation for the World Congress of Jewish Women,
held in 1923, Bertha Pappenheim of Germany urged the NCJW
to obtain JDC reports on atrocities committed against Jewish
women during the war. Although President Janet Harris requested
the information, she was denied access to the material, which the
JDC deemed "strictly private and confidential."[33]

In the conceptualization of the major relief entities, vulnerable women needed the assistance of their able, strong relatives in
the United States to ensure that they did not succumb to starvation
and moral impurity. This focus proved quite successful; during the
war years alone the JDC distributed approximately $15 million to
Eastern Europe and Palestine and processed some $10.5 million in
private claims (money sent to a specific individual or family) from
1914 though 1921.[34] The NCJW, the Workmen's Circle, and
Hadassah all participated in the major fund-raising effort, often
utilizing similar tactics to galvanize their memberships. Yet each
organization had its own unique focus; while all the groups worried
about their "family" abroad, they conceptualized that family from
distinct perspectives. The prewar agendas and ideologies of the
groups, along with the alliances they made during the early years of
the war, influenced how the three groups reacted, which Jews they
sought to aid first, and what methods they believed would prove
most effective in achieving their aims.

Women's Work: Aiding the Jewish Family Overseas

Of the three organizations, the Arbeter Ring's wartime publications
mentioned the group's actual fund-raising methods the least, and

they revealed little of the precise nature or extent of female members' contributions. As we have seen, initially the Circle was preoccupied with recipients' class status and how quickly the funds could make it to victims. At a special conference in 1914 one member urged that whatever method the group employed to transmit aid, the money should go first to those in most dire need. In 1915 the Circle leadership sent a $20,000 check to the AJRC with the proviso that the money go to the workers' committees in Galicia and Russia.[35] This dedication to the working class eventually led the organization to amend slightly its anti-Zionist posture. Early in 1916, despite official opposition to Zionism, the Arbeter Ring announced that it would help Jewish war victims in Palestine along with those in Europe. The policy change was explained as a war measure only, one in concert with the Circle's dedication to Jewish workers worldwide, and definitely not an official endorsement of Zionism.[36]

Despite attempts to limit aid to the Jewish working class, some Circle members maintained very close ties to their European birthplaces and longed to assist the people back home regardless of wealth. This was particularly the case with the *landslayt* branches (those branches behaving like *landsmanshaftn* through affiliation with a specific shtetl in Eastern Europe). These branches contributed to general fund-raising but also raised money for their individual hometowns. Lubliner Branch 392, to take just one example, prided itself on acting swiftly once news of Lublin's distress reached the United States.[37] Such intimate ties between Circle members and the Jews "back home" further influenced the Circle's movement toward a more Bundist cultural nationalism.

The Circle raised significant sums of money for the AJRC and later the PRC. Local branches organized concerts, picnics, musicals, and the sale of relief "stamps." Arbeter Ring members participated in "Flower Days," "Tag Days," and "Jewish Relief Days." President Wilson himself declared January 27, 1916, "Jewish Day"—dedicated to raising funds for Jewish war victims.[38] Typical of such endeavors was the Arbeter Ring's "Tag Day for Jewish War Victims" held on Washington's Birthday in 1917. Some 1,000 volunteers went door to door and collected over $22,000. A little coercion helped motivate the volunteers: Branch 367's leaders declared that any member not taking part in the campaign would face a one-dollar penalty. The Circle continued to hold special collection days for the duration of the war, even changing an old staple, "Sanatorium Day," into one for war relief. While the Circle never raised the astounding sums of money brought in by the upper- and middle-class associations, they consistently reported impressive amounts in the range of $20,000, no small feat for people earning far less than the average member of the NCJW or AJRC.[39]

It is hard to discern the level of women's contribution to the Arbeter Ring efforts given the cursory nature of reporting on the fund-raising campaigns, yet evidence suggests women were an important element in many local efforts. Atlanta members recalled how Circle women throughout the state of Georgia helped in assembling clothing, holding picnics, arranging balls, and participating in the PRC fund-raising. The JDC also reported that at a "People's Relief Committee Bazaar" held in New York City in 1916, "women in all stations in life vied with one another in their lavish expenditure of time and effort to aid the cause."[40] Generally though, women's complete cooperation with men in these campaigns resulted in the submergence of their presence during the war years. In just a few years this would change. By the final years of the war immigration restriction combined with male service in the armed forces led to growing anxiety about sustaining membership, and in the fall of 1917 the leadership inaugurated the first of many membership drives. A year later the Circle announced a campaign specifically targeted at women, particularly the wives of members.[41] Such campaigns would contribute significantly to the revitalization of women's activism in the 1920s.

Hadassah women, with an organization and publication of their own, left a much more detailed record of wartime activity. The women utilized a variety of fund-raising tactics, including house-to-house collections similar to those of the Workmen's Circle and the donation of old gold and silver. From 1915 to 1916, at a time when Hadassah's total membership numbered just over 1,000, such campaigns brought in nearly $11,000, or one-eighth of the total collected for the Palestine Emergency Fund. This work was an essential factor in the movement's ability to send a relief ship full of food and medical supplies to Palestine in 1916. Aside from money, Hadassah members, often with the help of non-Zionist women, assembled a variety of materials, including medicine and clothing, for this shipment.[42]

Yet Hadassah did not abandon its own Palestine program. The war had forced the closing of the nurses' stations, but the group quickly formulated new plans to broaden its mission upon conclusion of the hostilities.[43] Setting the tone as she so often did, Henrietta Szold urged members to look forward to a time when they would be able to contribute to the "reconstruction of communal Jewish life in Palestine." In 1916 Hadassah announced plans to send an American Zionist medical unit to Palestine. The group would continue sending contributions to the Emergency Fund while at the same time raising an extra $25,000 to underwrite the proposed Medical Unit.[44] Members worked diligently to come up with this additional funding, even foregoing streetcar rides so as to donate the money saved on fares to the unit, but in the end the task proved beyond the resources of the still small membership, and the group had to turn to the JDC for the bulk of the unit's initial funding.[45]

Despite obvious enthusiasm for the new project, political and military realities forced a two-year delay in the unit's departure for Palestine. The American declaration of war precipitated an outright denial by Turkish authorities to any requests that the Medical Unit be allowed to enter their territory. By the time the unit had permission to sail, after British forces took Jerusalem late in 1917, Hadassah and its allies had assembled an impressive store of equipment and goods: 400 tons of hospital equipment; several hundreds of cases of drugs, medicine and bandages; six autos; and over one hundred large cases of clothing, food, and dental materials.[46] At the last minute the reserved Alice Seligsberg was nominated to serve as the unit's administrative head. Seligsberg had considerable experience, having founded and then administered the Fellowship House, a New York agency for orphans, from 1913 until 1918. Under her lead, the unit halted the spread of epidemics, opened hospitals in Jerusalem, Jaffa, and Safed, and began to work on various medical and sanitation projects throughout Palestine.[47] Hadassah's wartime collaboration with the Brandeis-led Zionist movement and the JDC provided the fledgling organization with practical experience in fund-raising and membership recruitment. It also gave members the opportunity, through the Medical Unit, to put into practice their beliefs about women's potential to contribute to nation-building in Palestine.

The collaboration that characterized Hadassah's relationship with the American Zionist movement paralleled Council's experience with a host of men's groups, including the AJRC, the fraternal order B'nai B'rith and the Jewish Welfare Board (JWB), an entity ministering to the religious needs of Jews in the armed forces.[48] Yet unlike the Hadassah leadership, at the height of the war some Council women worried that their group occupied an unequal status vis-à-vis these men's organizations. One reason for this, according to Rebekah Kohut, was that many prominent men tried to dissuade women from embarking on their own programs. "Our work was lauded," she maintained after the war, "but we were asked to serve under these organizations. So the Council. . . [,] suppressing the identity of its own organizations, took part in the Jewish Distribution Committee."[49] Kohut was correct to note that Council failed to achieve a position of equality in the JDC, but this did not mean there was a total abdication of the NCJW's prewar program. Regardless of men's wishes, the group continued its work in the United States while at the same time envisioning a day when this work could become international in scope.

From 1914 until the U.S. declaration of war in 1917, the NCJW proceeded with its work on Ellis Island, assisting nearly 4,000 Jewish girls and young women through its Department of Immigrant Aid.[50] The heightened tension between the United States and the Central Powers worsened the already deplorable circumstances of would-be immigrants and added urgency to the NCJW project. In the fall of 1917 Helen Winkler, DIA chair, reported that growing numbers of Jewish women had attempted to immigrate to the United States over the last three years. Like most refugees, the majority of these women were destitute. When the United States severed relations with Germany in February 1917, thousands of refugees found themselves stranded in neutral European port cities with no means to travel abroad. As the likelihood of immigrating became ever more precarious, these refugees, lacking the means to sustain themselves, succumbed to hunger and disease. Their debilitation rendered them "unfit" and thus ineligible for entry into the United States even if they managed to procure proper documentation. Finally, Winkler noted, where a hardy few somehow managed to avoid disease, the newly instituted literacy requirements raised yet another, for many decisive, barrier to admission.[51]

America's declaration of war in April 1917 transformed German immigrants held at Ellis Island into enemy aliens overnight. According to Helen Winkler, about 2,000 people languished at the new detention camp established on the Island, which was horribly overcrowded and disease-ridden. In May the U.S. government forbade nearly all visits to the island. NCJW women lobbied the Bureau of Immigrant Aid to allow Council to return to its previous work at the newly established detention center. Success in this effort meant that Council was the only women's organization allowed in the area. Its work here was important not only because it continued a valuable project and kept the NCJW in the spotlight, but also because it laid critical groundwork for an expanded international program after the armistice. Hannah Solomon later recalled that NCJW women were "made guardians for all the women and girls and children who arrived at Ellis Island during the war," and Council would use this as a model in assisting refugees in European port cities after the war.[52]

In November 1917 Rebekah Kohut proposed sending a small coterie of women to Europe to investigate how best to institute a postwar reconstruction project. As the JDC was embarking on a similar initiative, Kohut approached its leadership to discuss the women's plans. Although she received JDC support for her postwar vision, she decided that Council should begin European work as soon as possible, even before the war was over. To do so would require the approval of the Jewish Welfare Board, which refused to allow women to travel overseas during wartime. In opposition to the generally accommodationist posture it took throughout the war, Council now resolved "to do reconstruction work under our own auspices after the war." Kohut, in particular, expressed annoyance at the women's treatment: "What a pity that an organization of women as representative as the Council should not have been *welcomed* to do its appropriate work!"[53] Women like Kohut began to appreciate the fact that all too often cooperation with men's organizations resulted in the subordination of women. Women might be tolerated in their position as helpmates to men, raising money and organizing teas, but they were not supposed to become too involved in designing their own projects.

Men and women collaborated to a great degree in the collection and provision of wartime relief. Yet the relationships between men and women, particularly those in different organizations, could be difficult. Women voluntarily accepted the fact that they would more often follow rather than lead the national initiatives. They conceded to this arrangement out of concern for those abroad and with the belief that unity would produce the most efficient results. Interactions between men and women during the war reveal that seemingly effortless cooperation flourished where women acceded to their secondary roles, as they evidently did in the socialist and Zionist movements. But when some women grew frustrated with their status in the major male-led relief endeavors, significant conflict arose. Although the most overt battles, especially in the Zionist movement, would come in the inter-war period, evidence of women's growing ambivalence toward male programs and frustration with masculine attitudes began to surface even in the war's final days.

Gender Dynamics in War: Cooperation and Conflict

The crisis atmosphere and the proliferation of relief activities had awakened in many women a heightened sense of their own ability, and some men, notably Louis Brandeis, made public note of women's important contributions, acknowledging the great debt they owed to women for their commendable service. David A. Brown, a major leader in the AJRC, was one of the few men aside from Brandeis to note the centrality of women to successful fund-raising efforts. He was especially grateful for the work Council women did in the Michigan relief drive he led. Brown's account of his experiences not only shows in what high personal regard he held Council women, it also reveals the far more typical male reaction to female input. Brown decided that recruiting a women's committee to coordinate fund-raising among the female population would make the 1915 Michigan campaign more effective overall. To his surprise his colleagues responded quite negatively to the idea. "They thought I was going a bit too far," he remembered, "and indeed, that it would be a waste of effort." Ignoring their position, Brown put the local chapter of the NCJW in charge of the women's committee. The special women's campaign attracted a great deal of press coverage and proved extremely successful; not only did the women meet their quota of $25,000, they raised an extra $6,000 above their goal.[54]

Brown's success in Michigan caught the eye of JDC chairman Jacob Schiff, who requested that Brown head the 1917 national campaign for $5 million. Once again Brown insisted on setting up a women's committee. This time Schiff himself opposed the plan, "saying this was a man's job and questioning the possibility of women raising money from women." Refusing to relent on the matter, Brown finally persuaded Schiff to reconsider by allowing him to name the women's committee chair himself. Schiff chose "that champion of women's champions," Rebekah Kohut, who, according to Brown, "did her job with her women associates as thoroughly and as effectively as any men's organization with which I have ever been associated."[55] The cooperation between Brown and the NCJW shows the importance of male allies in assuring that women received the recognition they deserved, including leadership positions in mixed-sex settings. Without such male support, even the most energetic and effective women leaders were pushed to the sidelines. The interactions between Brown and the NCJW or Brandeis and Hadassah, however, are exceptional. Far more men held opinions about women that resembled those of Jacob Schiff.

Perhaps in response to such attitudes and the subsidiary roles they were generally expected to play, many women grew less enthusiastic about men's initiatives as the war progressed. Women's general indifference to the founding of the American Jewish Congress highlights the change in women's reactions. Unlike the creation of the relief committees in 1914, the battles over the Congress just a few years later, a battle that consumed men's attention during the last years of the war, seemed to have had little effect on women in the three organizations. Overall they remained uninvolved and, as reflected in their publications, largely disinterested in the drive to form a representative body of American Jews.

American Zionists first spearheaded the movement for a democratically elected national body of Jews that would work for American Jewish representation at postwar peace conferences, fight for Jewish rights as a national minority in the newly created Eastern European states, and advocate the creation of a Jewish state in

Palestine. The wealthy opponents of Zionism who headed the AJC and the JDC opposed the Congress movement from the start, considering its demands far too nationalistic. Such men adhered to a conceptualization of Jewish identity grounded in religion alone, and they rejected the idea of a separatist movement among American Jews. Moreover, they refused to consider nationalist solutions to Jewish problems abroad, desiring instead the creation of governments in Eastern Europe modeled on the liberal Western democracies. In response to the Congress movement, the AJC men organized a counter-movement more in line with their own perspective on these issues. The battle between these two sides led to an odd alliance between the patrician AJC and the anti-Zionist socialists of New York's Lower East Side. By late 1916 the leaders of the disparate factions entered into more serious negotiations on convening a single Congress.[56]

Privately, NCJW leaders expressed great reluctance about the Congress from the outset, echoing the concerns of their male allies that such an organization would promote Jewish nationalism. In the autumn of 1915 the AJC selected Council as one of several organizations invited to participate in a conference aimed at challenging the Zionist-led Congress plans. Council leaders accepted this invitation without notable deliberation. Yet later, in the spring of 1916, when proponents of the Zionist-dominated Congress invited the NCJW to a preliminary conference, board members voiced more open division. Hannah Solomon maintained that although Council could easily support the stance of the proposed Congress relative to securing religious and civil rights for Jews abroad, "we would hesitate to endorse" the sections dealing more explicitly with Jewish nationalism. Reviving arguments first heard in the debates over relief distribution early in the war, Helen Winkler argued that during a time of intense U.S. patriotism, when the nation demanded its citizens' loyalty and support, it would do Jews more harm than good to organize into a distinct political body. If American Jews wanted to secure rights for those abroad, she asserted, they needed to work together with other Americans and avoid putting up "new walls of separation between ourselves and other peoples." Other women agreed with her, particularly since they felt that the Congress was "distinctly identified with Zionism." Executive Secretary Ernestine Dreyfus thought that if Council were to join the Congress, "I think we passively, at least, endorse [the Zionist] movement." In the end the national board passed two resolutions: one declining membership in the Congress and the second expressing Council's support of actions aimed at securing civil, but not national, rights for Jews abroad.[57]

When the AJC and Zionist leaders reached a compromise later that year, thereby uniting the Congress movement and its shadow opposition, Council briefly joined the consolidated assembly, although it withdrew in 1917. One reason may have been the minimal representation at the Congress accorded to the NCJW. The greatest number of seats went to the largest or most powerful male-led organizations such as the American Jewish Committee and the Federation of American Zionists, each of which received six seats, or the Workmen's Circle, which was given three. Even *Poale Zion*, a socialist Zionist group begun in 1905 and counting fewer members than the NCJW, had two seats at the Congress. Most groups, including the NCJW, received only one seat apiece. This surely galled some NCJW leaders as their group was the largest Jewish women's organization in the United States at the time. In explaining the withdrawal from the Congress, President Janet Harris informed members that the costs were prohibitive. To her mind, the head tax of $245 for "one lone woman" to serve as a delegate was not an efficient use of organizational resources. She and others also believed that, by altering the dynamics of Jewish politics in Eastern Europe, the Russian Revolution in March and America's entry into the war in April had rendered the Congress unnecessary.[58]

Although Hadassah was a Zionist organization, its leaders also exhibited a certain detachment regarding Congress preparations. Publications from that time contain only a few, brief articles about the Congress, written by Dr. Dora Askowith, the national director of the Women's Organization for an American Jewish Congress.[59] Askowith reported in 1917 that Hadassah had been generally supportive of the Congress movement in some cities, even running their own members as potential delegates.[60] She proudly alerted the women to the Congress movement's support for equal suffrage, informing readers of the Zionist publication the *Maccabaean* that due to the war "the Jews of America where equality of rights is enjoyed, became the trustees of the Jewish people throughout the world, and the American Jewish Congress the medium of expression." Women, she argued, must now "stand shoulder to shoulder" with Jewish men and take an active part in the Congress movement.[61] She failed to explain why a movement so firmly committed to women's equality required a separate entity focused on drumming up support among women, Zionists in particular. No doubt the relatively cool official reception on the part of Hadassah's national leadership played no small role in the development of an organization specifically geared toward garnering women's support. Despite Askowith's exhortations, Hadassah's leadership did not fervently embrace the Congress. One reason for this might have been that Henrietta Szold and other leaders had close ties to the men of the AJC and would be reluctant to take a position that might potentially damage their ability to raise funds from wealthy non-Zionist AJC members. On the whole, Hadassah, like the NCJW, reported little about developments in the Congress movement.[62]

In keeping with her own and the Circle's overriding interest in general suffrage and labor issues, Adele Kean Zametkin also neglected discussion of the Congress in her "Iber der froyen velt" columns. Given the Circle's organizational stance against Zionism, there was little reason for her not to do so. Once the compromise was reached between the AJC, socialists, and Zionists, the Workmen's Circle's main editorial page began to express more interest in Congress developments. The women's column, however, remained silent; no equivalent to Dora Askowith emerged from the ranks of Circle women. At the May 1917 Circle convention, delegates protested the Congress election process, which they believed lowered the representation of groups such as the anti-Zionist socialists. The Jewish National Workmen's Committee on Jewish Rights, of which the Arbeter Ring was a member, briefly withdrew from preparations in the spring of 1917 but ultimately participated in the final Congress, held in December 1918.[63]

The Congress situation reveals that while the women's organizations might not openly challenge their male counterparts in major national endeavors, they did not blindly or uniformly follow men's lead in every matter. Women's ambivalence about participating in the Congress debates, particularly Hadassah's indifference on the national level, shows that women determined what was best for their own organizations even in a period of widespread cooperation. Still, women's protest over these matters during the war was most frequently expressed in private with public disapproval rendered through silence and organizational indifference to men's grandiose plans. Dedication to helping Jews abroad was surely a major reason why the women avoided any semblance of disunity, even as men openly bickered about the makeup of the American Jewish Congress and other matters. But ideological commitments might also have played a role in suppressing overt female opposition to their treatment.

Hadassah, for instance, found itself ever more tightly bound to the male Zionist movement by the end of the war. Although the women's group had dramatically increased its membership and budget—and by late 1918 had embarked upon a major new enterprise in Palestine—this independent status was curtailed when the Zionist movement adopted a plan formulated by Louis Brandeis to create a more efficient organizational structure. In 1918 the FAZ became the Zionist Organization of America (ZOA), and its leaders urged all American Zionist groups to adopt its "district plan," which placed smaller groups into regional sections led by district committees reporting to the national ZOA. The ZOA, in turn, would be the sole American entity in contact with the World Zionist Organization (WZO). Proponents argued that this plan would reduce duplication, administrative costs, and inefficiency. Hadassah's Central Committee became an advisory body working in concert with the ZOA's Bureau for Propaganda Among Women. The women lost direct responsibility for their Palestinian projects; while they continued to raise money, the funds would be channeled to Palestine through the ZOA and WZO.[64]

Hadassah leaders accepted the reorganization but not without some reservations. At the 1918 convention Szold assured members that Hadassah would still play a unique role in the movement. "Propaganda among women will always require special means, special methods," she asserted, "and I believe that the propaganda for Zionism will always have to be put before women as a series of special, concrete purposes." Nevertheless she urged members to maintain their loyalty to the Zionist movement. She could not, however, seem to resist reminding men of their historical ineptitude at organizing women:

> As we were ready to take up the work [among women], we are going to be selfless enough to lay down the work when we are no longer the proper agents. We introduced the sex line into Zionism when it had never existed there before. If the time has come to break it, let us do so. You know that in Zionism that woman's vote is equal to the man's vote. We only gathered ourselves together because it seemed that the men who had been existing for sixteen years had not been able to get the women in.[65]

Szold promised members that this was yet another stage in the growth of the Zionist movement, and that given women's equality to men in the movement, any unification plan could not undermine women's participation. Privately, though, Szold was less sanguine about Hadassah's future. In a letter to a friend and fellow leader she confided that since the reorganization plan so completely divided up Hadassah's work she doubted whether the group would be able to maintain its independence. Szold feared that Hadassah's Central Committee would have only "illusory" advisory powers, and these fears soon proved to be well founded. In only a matter of weeks Szold wrote to Alice Seligsberg to tell her that Hadassah's Central Committee was not even being consulted in the promised advisory capacity, complaining that "up to this time [it] has not been called into consultation by the other [ZOA] departments which are now dividing its work among them."[66]

Hadassah leaders willingly submitted to a reorganization plan that resulted in the group's near dismantling as an independent organization. They did so in the spirit of Zionist unity and in the belief, soon invalidated, that a movement guaranteeing equality between the sexes would ensure women's continued activism. Yet only the rare woman achieved prominence in the ZOA. Szold held a major post as secretary of education, and two other women headed ZOA departments, but both of these reported to men. Moreover, one of these appointments was to Hadassah's rival, the Bureau of Propaganda among Women, over which Louis Lipsky, no great friend of Hadassah's, had final authority.[67] Hadassah members quickly learned that complete correspondence to the dictates of the larger movement did not always best serve women's interests, no matter how theoretically committed the movement was to gender equality.

As a result of their various interactions with men, women in all three groups found their sense of gender consciousness heightened during the war years. Consequently, as the war reached its conclusion, each group expressed a stronger commitment to promoting women's suffrage and the right to engage in the public sphere. By 1918 some women began to look forward to a period of renewed, independent, female activism. Not all men were happy with this awakening self-confidence and revitalized desire for autonomy. As the NCJW and Hadassah in particular began to exert themselves more forcefully on the national and international stages, growing opposition arose among those who felt more comfortable when women's organizations behaved as mere auxiliaries to men's groups.

Growing Support for Women's Rights

Before the war few Jews had participated actively in the suffrage movement, and no Jewish organizations existed that were primarily concerned with achieving the vote for women. No doubt this was due, in part, to the fact that in the late nineteenth century some leaders of the woman's suffrage movement expressed pointedly anti-Jewish opinions, and when the wave of Eastern European immigrants arrived on U.S. shores many suffragists openly embraced social antisemitism. But by 1915 the tenor of the suffrage movement had changed as younger activists reached out to neglected constituencies in order to attract greater support for a constitutional amendment. Jane Addams, Florence Kelley, and Maud Nathan resisted making the sorts of nativist and racist arguments used by the previous generation of suffragists. Even Carrie Chapman Catt, who early in her career made nativism a central component of her beliefs, modified her language after the founding of the International Woman Suffrage Alliance and her travels abroad. As the U.S. suffrage movement stepped up its lobbying efforts, Jewish women took more interest now that the movement did not seem as antagonistic as it once had.[68]

Of the three organizations, Hadassah commented the least on the struggle for the vote, even though it firmly supported this right. Any notice the group took of the issue was placed within a framework of women's status in the Zionist movement or the new settlements in Palestine. In 1918 Hadassah sent a telegram to President

Woodrow Wilson urging him to support the federal amendment for women's suffrage, proudly pointing to the fact that women already had equal suffrage in Zionist congresses and conventions as well as in Palestinian Jewish villages.[69] Like Hadassah, male Zionists took for granted that women had already achieved total equality in the movement: "It is noteworthy that equal suffrage is characteristic of the Zionist organizations throughout the world. Women are so prominently identified with the movement that their right to vote at the International Congresses and at the national conventions is taken as a matter of course," the *Maccabaean* proudly intoned.[70] In time, Hadassah leaders realized that Zionist statements about gender equality did not resemble practice, either at home or in Palestine. In these conflicts within their movement in the inter-war period, Hadassah leaders would begin to advocate ever more strongly for women's rights. Yet for the duration of the war Hadassah, a still relatively new and numerically weak organization, more frequently extolled the virtues of Zionism rather than criticize that movement's treatment of its female members.

The NCJW vocally supported women's rights, not infrequently employing the term "feminism" to characterize its dedication to female equality. As early as December 1914 prominent Kentucky suffragist Madeline McDowell Breckinridge addressed the Council Triennial on the topic of "The Feminist Movement," offering a historical overview of the women's rights movement with a particular focus on recent the battle for the vote.[71] As the war progressed, such messages appeared more frequently and in ever more forceful tones. A speaker at the 1917 triennial told delegates that since the outbreak of the war Jewish women had become involved in "every phase of that world-wide movement of revolt against artificial barriers, which we call feminism." Such women, she averred, had once satisfied themselves with work related only to their homes and families, but the war, particularly the "cry of persecuted mothers and children," forced many of them to look beyond their private lives. She explicitly connected women's new agenda to "the wisdom of those earlier martyrs of feminism, whose dream is now in the dawn of realization." While the war work that had drawn them from their homes centered around serving the needs of Jewish women and children, the ultimate result was, according to this speaker, to strengthen the ties between Council and adherents of the feminist movement.[72]

Notwithstanding the rhetoric regarding their commitment to all Jews and women, Council's feminism had a decidedly elitist tilt. It did not unite NCJW women with the "persecuted mothers" of their concern, but rather enabled them to serve those women better. Moreover, despite their sensitivity to expressions of anti-semitism, Council feminists could themselves express a certain degree of racism not uncommon for suffragists of the period. The 1917 Triennial speaker, for instance, argued that since "the negro" had been given the right to vote, there was no reason why (white) women should be made to prove themselves any further before they too attained suffrage.[73] Regardless of their unmistakable support for feminism and equal suffrage, the majority of Council members were still reluctant to endorse the platform officially. The same 1917 convention ultimately defeated a resolution favoring women's suffrage. While supporting women's rights in the abstract, the group's aversion to controversial issues led it to take a moderate stance even as its some of its most vocal members grew ever more devoted to feminism.[74]

The Arbeter Ring, so unwelcoming to women in its earliest years, now engaged in the most public discussion of women's issues in the three groups. Although the organization passed a resolution in favor of women's suffrage at its 1917 convention, it had not always supported the amendment. In April 1915 Adele Kean Zametkin reported that the Socialist Party and the Arbeter Ring were actively discouraging support for women's suffrage. This was not unusual. Following the ethos of the Second International, American socialists refrained from endorsing the middle-class suffrage movement, criticizing that movement's dedication to maintaining the economic status quo. Socialists could support women's suffrage so long as they pursued their goal in concert with class-based organizations. Indeed, in the months following Zametkin's editorial, the Socialist Party in New York under the direction of activist Theresa Malkiel vigorously worked for passage of the 1915 state amendment.[75]

Regardless of the Socialist Party's shifting position on the topic, Zametkin and other female columnists for *Der fraynd* never wavered in their support for a woman's right to vote. From its inception, Zametkin's column provided instruction in the history of women's rights movements around the world and sought to influence socialist women's opinions on key issues. Along with short lessons in women's history stretching from the Roman Empire to the Seneca Falls convention, Zametkin constructed powerful arguments for women's suffrage based on the needs of wage-earning women. She argued that consistently lower wages made it imperative that women gain the right to vote in order to effect positive change in their own lives.[76] Like her feminist NCJW counterparts, Zametkin claimed that the war had facilitated women's entrance into the public sphere, especially through taking jobs they had never held before. She repeatedly asserted that it would be impossible for men to continue to deny women the right to vote in light of how capable they had proven themselves recently.[77] Stressing the centrality of class to all political questions, Zametkin cautioned against simply joining the women's movement without contemplating whether suffrage activists had working women's best interests in mind. She was particularly cognizant of the political games played by suffrage supporters, observing that Theodore Roosevelt once opposed women's enfranchisement because he felt that women themselves were "indifferent and related coldly to the whole question. But now that it is 'warm' he has nothing against it. He figures that women's votes will come in useful to him on election day."[78] She urged her readers to avoid acting like middle-class suffragists who did not understand that the vote must be part of a larger struggle for women's full liberation: "An observant, thoughtful woman worker can even now glimpse how the rich ladies, the 'high ladies,' the leaders of the suffrage party throw loving glances at the two ruling parties. For them there is no difference between the Democratic and Republican parties, [they are only concerned that they] get the right to vote through them."[79] Yet like most women of her time, including those in Hadassah and the NCJW, Zametkin's advocacy of women's issues failed to include an analysis of gender relations in the private sphere; her articles rarely, if ever, discussed male-female interactions or men's role in maintaining the home and raising children.[80]

Rather than pressing for reform in the private sphere, Zametkin, like other socialists, advocated that the government address women's domestic concerns. Her very first column in March 1915 called attention to women's need for state-funded maternity insurance, a benefit not provided through the Circle. She also believed that the state should help women whose children were designated "illegitimate." In August 1915 she sarcastically commented on English anxiety over the potentially large numbers of "war babies." The "capitalist morals" of the English, she noted, were torn in two by children who would force the government to decide whether they were "kosher" or not. Zametkin believed that the state needed to care for unwed pregnant women since, to her mind, private charities would never be able to provide for them adequately. In her opinion, charitable donations usually wound up in administrators' pockets rather than in the hands of the needy.[81]

Compared to the women in the NCJW or Hadassah, Zametkin espoused the most broadly developed program for ameliorating women's inequality. Like other socialist women, her politics were solidly class-based, and she did not see much room for cross-class female cooperation; indeed, she more frequently expressed downright suspicion of upper-class, comfortable women. The topics of her columns suggest that Arbeter Ring women, especially those who had fought for equality in the organization prior to 1914, did not entirely abandon their interest in these questions as they turned their energies to raising funds for war relief. Her work foreshadowed a burst of female activism in the Circle, one which the most radical women, along with the male leadership, would strive to keep centered on class-based, not gender-based, politics.

To a greater or lesser degree, Hadassah, the NCJW, and the Workmen's Circle all expressed growing interest in women's rights, and by the end of the war each became more vocally committed to gender equality. Hadassah and the Circle both positioned the issue of women's rights within the larger context of their ideological paradigms: Hadassah expressed satisfaction that the United States was catching up with the venerable Zionist tradition of equality, and the Workmen's Circle concerned itself not with women per se but with working-class women in particular. Hadassah was the organization least concerned with class politics and its impact on women's advancement. Arbeter Ring and Council both expressed their commitment to women's equality as a function of their class;

Adele Kean Zametkin did this expressly, Council women through implication and omission.

Poised for Future Action

As they struggled to assist Jews in other lands over a period of several years, American Jewish organizations utilized language and images that conjured up feelings of kinship to Jews overseas. By the end of the war American Jews felt a profound connection to Jews in Europe and Palestine, and they struggled to find an adequate solution to the "Jewish Problem" in these lands, most notably in the emerging nations of Eastern Europe. Yet the united "family" of world Jewry also showed signs of division as gender, class, and ideological concerns began to pull family members apart. American Jewish women participated in discussions regarding the future of European and Palestinian Jewry. Despite the fact that women often took the lead from their male contemporaries, particularly in the opening days of the crisis, by the November 1918 armistice much about women's lives had changed. A growing interest in women's rights and an increasing penchant for associating themselves with the movements to achieve those rights had led women in all three groups to greater confidence regarding their abilities. Yet by the beginning of 1919 women in only one organization, the NCJW, seemed poised to set off in a new direction, to cut a path independent of the their male allies. Socialist and Zionist women still remained closely tied to their movements; however, even they would soon begin to express their desire for an equality that was more than rhetorical.

At least for a time, the crisis atmosphere dictated that organizations cooperate toward their common goal. For women in the three organizations this meant an increased awareness of their connection to Jews from around the world, but also, and more immediately, that they followed male directives. This was most notably the case in the Zionist and socialist movements, where (competing) visions of Jewish peoplehood were more fully theorized than among the middle-class German Jews of the NCJW. Yet while overt discussion of gender inequality or other conflicts may have been suppressed for the duration of the war, women did not entirely abandon their prewar struggles. Rather, their experiences in the war relief campaigns profoundly influenced the shape of their postwar activities and strengthened their resolve to aid the Jewish people, battle for women's equality, and promote the value of women's work, however each group defined these concepts. Participation in war work and the temporary suppression of outright confrontation over questions of gender would give way to a postwar flourishing of Jewish women's activism.

CHAPTER 3

The Move Toward Autonomy

The NCJW and Hadassah
in the Postwar World

N ancy Cott and others have argued that after World War
I and the attainment of suffrage, many American women
turned away from separatist organizing and other forms
of the nineteenth-century "woman's rights movement," acknowledging instead a diversity among women and experimenting with
newer modes of feminist activism. Others, most notably those in
the international women's movement, continued to embrace separatism despite the difficulties this sometimes posed in attracting
new members, especially those of a younger generation.[1] In the
1920s Jewish women in the NCJW and Hadassah followed the
model of the international movement. After years of cooperation
with men, prominent leaders in both Council and Hadassah
reasserted a strong organizational and female presence, demanding
recognition from and parity within the larger relief and Zionist
movements. While other women optimistically embraced equality
with men in the public sphere, Jewish women's experiences in the
war years and immediately thereafter had shown them that true
equality was an illusive goal. In separatist organizing they rediscov-
ered the female networks, space, and resources that provided them
with greater opportunities to achieve power. This renewal of prewar strategies enabled Jewish women in both organizations to
claim a larger role in their respective movements as well as among
their female peers.

Some historians have argued that despite the wartime move into the public world of preparedness, peace, relief, and paid labor, in the final analysis the war brought very little substantive change to most women's lives. Others have asserted that women's lives changed irrevocably, especially in terms of sexual mores, dress styles, and ideas about gender roles; young women in particular were, in the words of Birgitte Soland, "becoming modern."[2] Although decisions by the leadership of the NCJW and Hadassah to reassert their organizational autonomy by separating from men might appear to be somehow resistant to modernity, the women themselves claimed that, to the contrary, these strategies represented an actual advance for women, one that was quite in concert with a modern perspective on gender relations. Indeed, some proponents of separatism insisted that the distance was necessary in order to ensure their groups' very survival. They declared that if the groups wished to avoid becoming mere women's auxiliaries of the JDC or the ZOA, their groups would have to reassert their autonomy. Postwar gender separatism, then, was not a step backward for these organizations but a strategy consciously utilized by the leadership in order to facilitate and enhance women's participation in the modern political realm.

The JDC in the Postwar World

With Europe ravaged, the U.S.S.R. and surrounding lands in turmoil, and the doors to the United States effectively closed to immigration, American Jews realized that their duty to those overseas would neither end with the armistice nor with the final peace treaty. Relief activities would have to continue in an atmosphere suffused with antisemitism both at home and abroad. The era of "100 percent Americanism" and the postwar Red Scare negatively affected the Jews of the United States and had even worse consequences for those wishing to emigrate from Europe. The not uncommon antisemitic association of Jews with capitalist excess and radical extremism intensified following the Bolshevik Revolution of November 1917. Many Americans believed that Jews in Russia had been central to that event and that American Jews were tainted by a similar radicalism. Authorities in Chattanooga, Tennessee, for instance, refused citizenship to several Jews simply because they held membership in the Arbeter Ring, an organization deemed foreign and on the fringes of acceptable political behavior.[3] Fear of Jewish radicals was not limited to the South; in 1920 Henry Ford's newspaper, the *Dearborn Independent*, printed an article titled "The International Jew: The World's Problem." This piece reiterated the major themes of the *Protocols of the Elders of Zion*, a forgery circulating in Europe since the late nineteenth century that purported to have uncovered a secret cabal of Jews intent upon gaining control of the world. Ford's newspaper continued to print scurrilous attacks against Jews well into the decade.[4]

The fear of Russians generally, and especially of Russian Jews, along with widespread nativism led to the passage of laws severely limiting the number of immigrants allowed into the country each year from Eastern Europe and elsewhere. Without relatives in the United States who could vouch for them, few Eastern Europeans could hope to gain entry. From 1919 to 1920 nearly 120,000 Jews immigrated to the United States, but of this number only a paltry 689 arrived without being able to claim relatives already residing in the country. The most prominent American Jews, wishing to avoid more undue attention being drawn to their community, urged that Jews keep a low profile in this and other public debates. In 1924 Louis Marshall went so far as to request that the JDC assist refugees in Europe rather than lobby against the restrictive immigration measures recently passed in Congress. All these factors combined to put a virtual end to European Jewish immigration to the United States: in the years 1907–1914, 656,000 Jews entered the country, but from 1924 to 1931 that number plummeted to 73,000.[5]

Jewish refugees in Europe did not heed this sea change in U.S. policy. Thousands had flooded the major European capitals during the war, and these refugees were in no hurry to return to their Eastern homes once the war ended. West European port cities like Rotterdam filled to bursting with Jews hoping to obtain the documentation that would allow them to travel to America. The situation in the East was even worse. In Poland alone approximately one million Jews were left homeless by the war. Starvation and disease ravaged these desolated communities. Widespread sickness, violence, and family dislocation contributed to a tragic rise in the number of orphans, both those whose parents had perished in the war and those who were abandoned in the hope that someone else might provide for them. Polish and Ukrainian officials reported having some 275,000 such children within their borders.[6]

The creation of new, independent states in the East as a result of the Central Powers' defeat also contributed to the turmoil experienced by Jews. The chaos and panic generated by competing groups within these new nations all too often led to violent pogroms against local Jewish populations. The overthrow of the tsar and the prospect of national independence did not halt the antisemitic fervor of certain groups in these nascent countries. Pogroms broke out across Eastern Europe, reaching a furious and violent peak in the summer of 1919. In Ukraine especially, the anti-Communist White Army and those allied with it exploited the popular stereotype of the Jew as Bolshevik to their brutal advantage. Ultimately some 35,000–100,000 Jews perished as a result of the Ukrainian pogroms, and as many as a quarter of a million were affected overall.[7]

Jewish groups involved in the JDC struggled to address these emergencies, but inter-group disagreements that arose during the war continued to plague postwar efforts. The socialist People's Relief Committee felt that the JDC leadership had too great a commitment to relief work and paid scant attention to the reconstruction of Jewish life in Eastern Europe. Communist PRC members in particular criticized the JDC for providing only minimal funding to labor unions and other worker organizations.[8] Zionists, on the other hand, complained that Palestine was receiving far less than its fair share of the overall JDC funds. They asserted that of the $60 million the JDC raised between 1916 and 1926, only $7 million, or 12 percent, was sent to Palestine. JDC officials countered that their organization based aid distribution on need alone, and therefore Palestinian Jews had received a fair amount. This did not appease Zionists, who felt that Palestine was being neglected by the non-Zionist dominated JDC. To augment what they saw as a paltry JDC contribution, during the 1920s American Zionists forwarded an additional $20 million to Palestine.[9]

Despite these disagreements, Zionist leaders and prominent American non-Zionists actually grew closer over the course of the decade. Palestine underwent sustained growth in the 1920s but also witnessed an upsurge in violence between the Arab and Jewish populations. At the San Remo conference, Great Britain officially received the mandate over Palestine, which was formally approved by the League of Nations in 1922. In the years immediately following, a number of riots broke out across Palestine, leading the British to curtail further Jewish immigration. Following these incidents, Zionists and some non-Zionists who were opposed to a political state but not to Jewish settlement in Palestine began to unite. The British Mandate allowed for the creation of a Jewish Agency to oversee Jewish matters in Palestine, and, spurred by Chaim Weizmann's desire for non-Zionist funding of Palestine endeavors, the two factions worked together to create this agency by decade's end.[10]

Aside from internal ideological conflict, the JDC also faced complications in its initial relations with the U.S. government. At the conclusion of the war, Felix Warburg requested permission to send a Jewish commission to Eastern Europe for the purpose of providing relief. The federal government denied his request, informing him that all relief coming from the United States for those areas formerly occupied by Germany should be sent through the American Relief Administration (ARA). The JDC decided to funnel money through the ARA, choosing to distribute goods to non-Jews as well as Jews in the hopes of offsetting antisemitic reactions against its work.[11] Ultimately the JDC contributed $3.3 million toward the $100 million ARA effort. Because it agreed to cooperate with the ARA, the JDC was eventually allowed to send workers overseas to begin aid missions to the Jews.[12] Jewish contributions in the years from 1919 to 1921 reached $33.4 million. Much of this money went toward founding soup kitchens, maintaining hospitals and orphanages, and bringing food to people starving in the countryside. The JDC also set up a tracking bureau to help people locate lost relatives. In time, it established a more orderly provision of services, moving beyond the emergency stage of its relief program. In February 1920, Boris Bogen headed up the first JDC Overseas Unit, which cooperated with local populations to establish more permanent social welfare provision. The next year the JDC ended its emergency relief but proceeded with the general reconstruction program. Throughout the decade the organization provided services to children and orphans, promoted medical care, established schools, and loaned money to the destitute for business start-ups.[13]

Working with the ARA immediately after the war paved the way for more extensive cooperation between the two groups. Invited by the ARA to participate in its mission to the U.S.S.R. in 1920 and 1921, the JDC eagerly took on this new project. American Jews were very concerned about Soviet Jewry, particularly following the wave of pogroms in Ukraine during the Civil War. Having little experience as farmers and crowded into small towns and cities, Jews in Soviet-controlled areas suffered acutely during the drought and famine of the early 1920s. Boris Bogen, the JDC representative for Eastern Europe, worked with the ARA to distribute some $4 million in relief funds for Soviet Jews through 1922. The ARA pulled out of the U.S.S.R. that year, but the JDC continued its own activities through a special agreement with the U.S. government. Seeking to ameliorate Jews' precarious economic status in the U.S.S.R., some JDC leaders suggested Jewish colonization and training as farmers. In July 1924 the JDC, in conjunction with several Soviet agencies, founded the American Jewish Joint Agricultural Corporation, or Agro-Joint. Between 1924 and 1928 Agro-Joint resettled nearly 6,000 families in Ukraine or in the Crimea. By 1928 there were 112 Agro-Joint colonies in Ukraine and 105 in the Crimea, some having decidedly Zionist names, such as Tel Hai.[14] Like other American Jewish groups, Hadassah and the NCJW contributed to these JDC endeavors, with Hadassah benefiting greatly from JDC investment in its Medical Unit. Soon, however, leaders of both groups began to question whether their current involvement afforded them the access to organizational power and financial investment that they believed they deserved.

Breaking New Ground:
The NCJW and International Work

Following the war, Council members still comprised only a tiny minority of the delegates at JDC meetings. At a 1921 meeting in Chicago, for instance, NCJW representative Alma D. Cowan discovered that she was the "only woman with delegate privileges" in a room of 150 men. Even though she had gone to the meeting with no other goal than to listen to the deliberations, this stark evidence of women's absence compelled her to agitate, however benignly, for greater female representation. When the meeting's agenda turned to planning for a study commission to Europe, the men failed to mention a single female for possible inclusion. Cowan then took the floor and politely requested that at least one woman be asked to serve. Later, reporting back to her own board, she admitted to serious doubts regarding the success of her small effort, but she was glad that Council's position was at least put on record.[15]

This modest step was repeated the following year, when Council women again sought representation on the overseas commission. At the "Victory Conference," convened in the spring of 1922 to discuss the Jewish situation in Russia, delegates proposed sending a commission of prominent, respected community leaders overseas to gather information on the condition of Russian Jewish life. The primary purpose of the commission was to convey to the American Jewish community the urgent need for sustained fundraising. Louis Marshall spoke eloquently in favor of the endeavor, referring to the ways the war had forced Jewish Americans to develop "a consciousness of duty and a brotherhood of obligation. . . . We no longer, in our philanthropic life, in our active life, draw lines by geographical boundaries. It is no longer a question as to whether a man's parents came from England or France or Germany or Poland or Russia, but as to whether or not he is a Jew."[16] Once again women were excluded from the vision of universal Jewish brotherhood, both rhetorically and in actuality—not a single woman's name arose as a possible commission member. At least this time one male delegate noted the dearth of possible female commission members. However, he quickly added "never the less, it does not matter whom we send abroad on this Commission except that they must be big men."[17]

Council's representative to the Conference, Rebekah Kohut, refused to let women's participation in a major relief campaign slip through her fingers without at least voicing her frustration, especially since her own organization had just embarked upon a reconstruction plan for Europe itself. Arguing that women numbered among the most experienced social workers in the United States, she maintained that female skills, both instinctive and acquired, were indispensable to the proposed commission. Unlike male social workers, she asserted, women were not preoccupied with "cut-and-dried scientific methods." Reiterating themes Council women had been espousing since the 1890s, Kohut stated that women "have an understanding of certain things that you men have not."[18] Her passionate defense of women's capabilities won her a round of applause, but it did not significantly change the status of the NCJW in the larger movement. As many other American women were finding in the days following the passage of the suffrage amendment, Kohut's experiences showed her that formal political equality in the nation did not necessarily translate into equality in women's organizational, professional or personal lives.

When it became evident that the JDC men would persist in their foot-dragging when it came to gender issues, Kohut and others concentrated their attentions on the Reconstruction Unit they had devised in 1917 and launched in 1920. Rather than waste their energy attempting to change the minds of men in the JDC, or begging for a solitary slot on a study commission, women like Kohut opted to turn their considerable talents to their own projects and to devising new ways by which women could serve their "brethren" overseas. Still, the tasks before them were significant. They had to establish a program, make connections with women in Europe, and, most importantly, obtain the necessary funding. As they had in the years prior to the war, Council women relied on separatist strategies to achieve their goals. Rather than working with men, and risk being lost in the shuffle or reduced to the role of fund-raisers who could never hope to rise to national leadership, Kohut and her colleagues returned to the methods that had made their organization a success in the years before the war broke out.

Rebekah Kohut was well-suited to the job she willingly shouldered. Born in Hungary in 1864, the third child of a Conservative rabbi, Kohut grew up in the United States, living in both the South and West. In 1887 she married the widowed, Hungarian-born rabbi Alexander Kohut and, at the age of twenty-three, became stepmother to his eight children. She devoted herself to public work while caring for her husband and family. Yet it was not until after his death in 1894 that she stepped into the national limelight.[19] She traced her devotion to international relief to the conversations she had with her mother years before about women's efforts to rebuild the South following the Civil War. Reflecting on those conversations, Kohut imagined that similar, though far worse, conditions confronted European Jews, and she believed it was imperative that American women come to their aid.[20] Acknowledging that her passionate commitment to volunteer work with women and children had led some people to mock her, she remarked in old age that "because I felt miserable about them and spoke solemnly about them, and the need of doing something, I know I was looked upon by some as that ridiculous thing—a professional do-gooder. Oh yes, I was the funny humanitarian type—just made for caricature and burlesque."[21] Kohut did not allow such opinions to dissuade her from her primary goal. While laboring to help refugee women and children, Kohut also vigorously opposed those who belittled the voluntary contributions of American women to public life.

In April 1920, well before the Victory Conference, Kohut headed a Council mission to major European cities in order to study the refugees' situation and assess how best to meet their needs. Accompanied by her personal secretary, Estelle Frankfurter, Kohut traveled throughout Europe and was alarmed by the destitution she found there.[22] Their first stop was Antwerp, where she and Frankfurter encountered a large number of Polish Jews who had fled their homeland. Because many had been smuggled across numerous borders in their desperate journey west, they usually could not produce documentation of their births and resident status. American officials prohibited such people from traveling to America without first presenting a Polish passport and applying for a U.S. visa, an impossible request for most of these destitute refugees. Kohut observed similar conditions in the Hague and Rotterdam—large numbers of would-be immigrants forbidden to travel abroad due to lack of proper documentation. In each city, she was struck not only by the refugees' poverty but also their inactivity, which she felt only intensified their feelings of hopelessness.[23]

As she moved east, the Jewish plight was visibly worse In Berlin Kohut learned that some 70,000 Polish Jews had recently entered the German nation; most of these people hoped to make it to Holland and from there emigrate to the United States. Bertha Pappenheim, the head of the Jüdischer Frauenbund (League of Jewish Women), and other well-known German-Jewish social welfare activists discussed with Kohut during her stay in Berlin how American women might help in Europe and contemplated the usefulness of convening an international congress of Jewish women in the near future. In Vienna Kohut met the distinguished Zionist and social welfare activist Anitta Müller-Cohen, who had worked tirelessly throughout the war to aid the great number of Jewish refugees flooding into that city. After the war Müller-Cohen established canteens, nurseries, day care facilities, and trade schools for girls, all of which received funding from the JDC and the American Relief Administration.[24] European women like Müller-Cohen were doing what they could to ameliorate the plight of the refugees, but Kohut saw that the problems clearly outweighed their ability to attend to them sufficiently.[25]

Later in her trip, Kohut once again met Bertha Pappenheim. During this meeting Pappenheim, sounding very much like her American counterpart, "strongly complained of the hindrance the men place[d] on women's work through their control of the financial end."[26] Increasingly Kohut and other Jewish women were coming to understand that if they wanted to run their own projects they would need greater access to and control over relief funds, especially the funds raised by their own membership. Cooperation predicated upon women simply following male directives held little appeal for these women now that the war was over. Council leaders found their European allies more willing partners than American men in developing and actuating their visionary plans. The reinstatement of overtly separatist organizing strategies was not a mere holdover from the past, something that an older generation of women's activists clung to and was reluctant to abandon. Instead, as Hannah Solomon had done in 1893, NCJW leaders eagerly turned to separatism when integration with men offered them less than the amount of power and control they felt was their due.

On her return to the United States in November 1920, Kohut urged the NCJW to embrace a cooperative reconstruction program in Europe advising Council to work in concert with European women to help refugees rebuild their lives in Europe rather than emigrate overseas. A certain amount of nativism is apparent in her suggestion that it might be better to assist Poles and Russians in their own nations instead of ruining "our" country with undesirable immigration.[27] She also scolded the men's organizations for their treatment of the NCJW during the war years. Reiterating a common theme, Kohut recommended that the JWB and JDC entrust work among female immigrants to the NCJW, who better understood their "special needs." Going one step further, she called attention to the "relatively unimportant recognition and opportunity to function" women had received in recent years from the JDC and JWB. She especially criticized the JDC for attempting to subvert Council's autonomy during the war years even though the NCJW had "set aside its own desires and needs in order to be helpful in the larger and more important program of the Joint Distribution Committee." She argued that the JDC should now consider Council an equal, rather than junior, participant. She recommended that her group ask for "no less than" $100,000 in JDC funds to start its own reconstruction program.[28] Kohut pressured her group to demand that their work be accorded the same respect and monetary investment as the projects of other JDC constituent organizations.

The first Reconstruction Unit sailed for Europe at the end of 1920. Its small group of committed social welfare activists found that the precarious situation of the refugees had not much improved since Kohut's visit earlier that year. Not only did refugees face poverty and disease during the long wait for proper documentation, they also had to contend with the anti-immigrant, and often antisemitic, attitudes of government officials, including those from the United States. Unit workers reported that several U.S. government representatives referred to the potential emigrants in Dutch ports as "scum of the earth," "dregs of humanity," and "carriers of disease." In late 1920 the U.S. government ordered that emigrants bound for the United States be quarantined to prevent typhus outbreaks. This regulation was interpreted variously in different port cities, but in all of them it seriously curtailed refugees' freedom of movement away from the ports and thus their ability to obtain employment during the waiting period.[29] Council representatives sought to keep the refugees' minds active during the quarantine and assist them in learning skills needed to find employment. Although immigration restriction severely reduced the number of Jews who would be allowed to enter the United States, Council leaders also wanted to ensure that those who did manage to gain passage held the "right spiritual attitude toward America." Unit workers sought to "spread the gospel of bodily cleanliness" among potential immigrants, no doubt to counter suggestions that Jews were filthy and diseased. They also began Americanization classes and taught English to those refugees interested in learning. In all its endeavors, the unit cooperated with Dutch and other European women, training them to take over the work themselves one day.[30] Although still an American organization, the NCJW believed that it could create European national groups in its own image, groups committed to social welfare work and vehicles for Jewish women's voluntary contributions to public life. A second unit arrived in Europe in the spring of 1922 followed by a third in spring of 1923. Where the first unit centered its attention on Western European port cities such as Rotterdam, subsequent units expanded further east, working with local groups to set up services akin to those begun in the West.[31]

Believing as they did that women themselves were critical for the success of these projects, Council leaders trained others to eventually take over program administration. Unit women strove to create European councils of Jewish women in each of the cities where a Reconstruction Unit was stationed, as well as in other locales, and by 1925 eleven councils had formed in Europe and Australia.[32] This aspect of the reconstruction program suggested that the NCJW might one day spearhead an international organization similar to its ally, the International Council of Women, a development with which not all members were entirely comfortable. Yet the growth of international Councils demonstrates the success of the NCJW's bid to revive female separatism as a means by which to build organizational power and heighten their own group's effectiveness. Just as in its early years, Council leaders of the inter-war period struggled to negotiate their Jewish and gender identities—to find a space that would allow them to promote simultaneously Jewish and women's interests without neglecting either one.

Publicly the NCJW embraced its bold move on to the international stage; privately, some members voiced concern that the organization might be overextending itself. As early as 1921, as Council prepared to send another unit to Europe, several board members asked their colleagues to consider whether it was wise for the group to expand so quickly. They worried that the international work, added to their already substantial expenditures on the Department of Immigrant Aid, would deplete funds earmarked for other domestic programs. President Rose Brenner tried to soothe these fears by telling members that the proposed International Congress of Jewish Women would address this very issue, namely how much longer the American Council could continue to fund projects in other nations. In the future, she assured the board, the European councils would deal themselves with problems arising in their nations. Yet the prospect of an international Jewish women's umbrella organization troubled one board member, Evelyn Aronson Margolis, who expressed reservations about Americans launching "an international Jewish organization of any description whatsoever, even a thing as harmless as the Council of Jewish Women." Alluding to antisemites who envisaged malevolent, international Jewish conspiracies in the most benign of gatherings, she added, "Do you get my point?" Her intimated worry met with cries of "yes," and the board agreed that any conference organized with European women should explicitly be identified as an informal gathering only, not an "international Jewish group."[33]

Despite certain members' apprehensions about taking an active role in founding an international Jewish women's organization, the NCJW's postwar work among refugees and in establishing European councils of Jewish women significantly advanced movement in this direction. Within a couple of years Council began to reassert its prominence among American Jewish organizations by loosening its ties to the JDC and other male-led relief organizations while at the same time strengthening alliances with Jewish women's groups in Europe. Rebekah Kohut and others involved with the Reconstruction Unit used gendered characterizations of their work to argue that, just as it had before the war, the NCJW offered necessary services to women and children that the male-led organizations failed to provide. While not abandoning all ties to the JDC, Council women determined to take a firmer stand, asserting their presence in both the American and European Jewish organizational worlds.

Hadassah and Palestine: "A Joyful Mother of Children"

Hadassah found itself in similar straits as the war drew to a close. International in scope from its inception and more directly tied to the Zionist men's organization than the NCJW ever was to the JDC, Hadassah women devised other means by which to assert their independence. While both Hadassah and the NCJW argued that voluntary efforts were still necessary in the postwar world, their attitudes toward the financial support of these efforts differed somewhat. Where the NCJW argued that it was as deserving as other groups receiving funds from the JDC, Hadassah fought for total control of its own finances, which by the early 1920s comprised a significant portion of the general American Zionist coffers. This difference arose from the fact that control over Council's finances was never in doubt; while the NCJW contributed to the JDC, it still managed its own discrete budget. On the other hand, after the war Hadassah found itself in the position of raising funds that were turned over almost entirely to another Zionist entity, which then disbursed them to the projects developed (and underwritten) by Hadassah members. It was only a short time before the group's central leadership began to oppose this arrangement.

Before these troubles arose, Hadassah women seized the opportunity to increase services to Palestine even as they feared they would no longer be able to rely on the non-Zionist funding they had received in the past. Reflecting larger tensions between the JDC and the Zionist movement, early in 1922 Hadassah leaders voiced their suspicions that the JDC planned to stop funding the Medical Unit in favor of a "so-called reconstruction program" in Europe.[34] Despite several threats throughout the early 1920s to discontinue the financing of Hadassah projects, the JDC carried its support through 1927. Nevertheless, even in the face of this potential monetary decline Hadassah expanded its program of medical services in Palestine, opening a school for nurses in November 1918, the same month that the Medical Unit moved into the Rothschild Hospital in Jerusalem. Within ten years the nurses' school produced 135 graduates and instituted course work for male orderlies, who were needed in areas inhabited by large numbers of traditional Jewish and Muslim men who refused to be seen by a female nurse.[35]

The extent of disease and malnutrition in Palestine after the war compelled the women to broaden the range of Hadassah's medical services, especially to children. During the 1920s, Hadassah involved itself in anti-epidemic work, including an antimalarial program funded by Louis Brandeis. The women's organization assisted with land reclamation projects, such as reforestation, aimed at lowering recurrences of malaria. By the time the Mandate government stepped in to take over the routine extermination of mosquitoes in 1931, it relied solely on the professionals trained by

Hadassah to assist in this work.[36] Hadassah also opened additional hospitals in Safad, Jaffa, and Haifa, and founded several infant welfare clinics, first in the Old City of Jerusalem and in fifteen other areas by 1926. Under the leadership of public health nurse Bertha Landsman, Hadassah sponsored a milk distribution program called *Tipat Halav* (Drop of Milk) stations. Landsman was so horrified by the high rates of infant mortality that she committed herself to improving conditions for mothers and children by producing and distributing the first pasteurized milk in Palestine. When too few mothers made use of the program, Landsman devised a means by which to bring the milk to them personally: the Donkey Milk Express. Parents who could afford the milk were assessed a fee to cover the costs of free distribution to the poor. One young woman whose husband balked at paying this assessment managed to convince him to change his mind by abstaining from the *Mikveh* (ritual bath, in which religious women must immerse themselves before resuming sexual relations following their menstrual periods and after childbirth). "I absolutely *refused* to go until he gave me the money for milk. He won't refuse again," she confidently told the nurses.[37]

Hadassah's interest in the welfare of children led it to initiate such diverse services as school lunch programs and health exams, a variety of aid to orphans, and even a children's mental health clinic.[38] The leadership's commitment to helping local populations regardless of religious confession also spurred their involvement in activities designed to foster better relations between Arabs and Jews through children's recreational activities. In 1925, while traveling in Europe, Bertha Guggenheimer, the aunt of Hadassah leader Irma Lindheim, decided to open playgrounds in Jerusalem for all children, and requested that Hadassah administer the project. Hadassah accepted the proposal in 1928 and subsequently expanded the program further.[39]

By the time that the JDC, along with the *Keren Hayesod* (Foundation Fund) and ZOA withdrew financial support from the Hadassah Medical Organization in 1927, thereby making it Hadassah's responsibility alone, the women's organization had positioned itself as central to the maintenance of health care throughout Palestine. Reflecting on the change in HMO status and in Hadassah's general program, Henrietta Szold commented in 1929 that "The

Hadassah Medical Organization came into the country as a war relief organization and remained in the land as a peace organization."[40] The expansion of medical services would have been impossible had not the organization so successfully recruited new members and developed funding sources back home. As early as the 1924 convention, Henrietta Szold alerted delegates that the group's achievements in Palestine demanded ever larger financial contributions. At that convention delegates resolved that "each Chapter form a committee to enlist the interest and cooperation of other organized groups of Jewish women in their respective communities."[41] For years Hadassah women had considered it their mission to reach out to their non-Zionist sisters in the United States. Now the organization made this standard policy. Szold and other leaders had long believed that because women differed from men, their understandings of Zionism diverged as well. She told members that "it is the women's Zionist spirit that we mean when we speak of the Hadassah spirit. It is the women's interpretation of Zionism—deep service in which the individual loses himself [sic] in the cause, in which the cause comes directly to the individual."[42] Hadassah leaders now urged their members to take that message to other American Jewish women, to relate to them the "women's interpretation of Zionism," one that closely resembled the "interpretations" of other inter-war women's groups.[43]

Beliefs about Haddasah's special, feminine contributions colored members' perceptions of their mission in Palestine. Certain leaders, for instance, argued that Hadassah's medical work, attending as it did to both the Jewish and Arab populations in Palestine, would facilitate better relations between the two groups. In 1921, when Arab hostility resulted in violent attacks against Jews in Jaffa, Szold urged members to see the connections Jews had with Arabs and counseled that all Jews work to remove "every possible admixture of injustice" from their designs on that land. "We shall ally ourselves with the best of our Arab fellows, to cure what is diseased in us and in them. *Arukat bat Ammi*, and also *Arukat ha-Goyim!* The healing of the daughter of our people, and the healing of the nations."[44] Upon returning to the United States in 1923, Szold asserted that Hadassah's medical work was the "best missionary work [Jews] could do in the face of our relations to the Arabs" and that it would be a "political blunder" to halt it.[45] Such gendered constructions of Hadassah's mission found increasing expression as the decade wore on. In 1926 Irma Lindheim, then national president, told convention delegates that

> heretofore in this man-run world of ours, men have gone into a country to conquer it. . . . The women have said this colonization is unlike any other colonization and that is why Zapotinsky [most likely Vladimir Jabotinksy, the founder of the Revisionist movement] is wrong. When other people have gone they have gone to possess that country; they have gone to take advantage of the natives, but when we went into Palestine Hadassah went in with her hand outstretched, Hadassah went in with a healing, kindly humanitarian spirit and said it did not make any difference if they were Hebrew, Arab or Christian children.[46]

Szold and the Hadassah leadership regarded their work as a means not only of nurturing a healthy population and upbuilding Palestine but also of curing what threatened to divide the Arab and Jewish populations. Women in the international women's movement made similar claims for the female ability to heal the world after the Great War. In 1918 activist Mary Sheepshanks asserted that "men have made this war; let women make peace—a real and lasting peace." More than a decade later Huda Sha'rawi stated that "if men's ambition has created war, the sentiment of equity, innate in women, will further the construction of peace." Even female colonial adventurers were believed to differ from men when it came to dealing with local populations. Writing about traveler May French-Sheldon's encounter with a tribe of Africans, Fannie C. Williams contended that "they had learned to fear the white man, and to expect nothing from him save oppression and cruelty, but with a woman it was different."[47]

In the late 1920s Henrietta Szold extended her commitment to peace by joining a small group of men and women in *Brit Shalom* (Covenant of Peace), an organization devoted to the creation of a binational Arab-Jewish state. Although Brit Shalom failed to attract the support of most Zionists, Hadassah leaders continued to champion their own organization's potential to ease conflict between the two populations through medical work. This stance on Arab-Jewish relations exemplified the leaders' belief that their general program of social welfare and medical work, their "womanly" contributions to nation-building, helped advance the general Zionist program.[48]

In devising and promoting this vision of a gendered Zionism, the leadership employed candidly maternalist rhetoric. One Hadassah leader, Nima Adlerblum, linked women's interest in maintaining life directly to Hadassah's own work: "It is the beauty of Hadassah that it conceived life from its very inception . . . for Hadassah translates itself in creation, production and self-development."[49] Henrietta Szold urged that Hadassah as a whole "devote ourselves to motherhood work." She suggested that if the first aim of the group was the development of Palestine, "let our second aim be to make our land 'A Joyful Mother of Children.'"[50] The leaders believed that women's biological potential to give life, together with their traditional responsibilities of caring for children, led them to be more pragmatic than men. These women felt that Zionist men often took up but failed to follow through on specific projects. The special nature of women, born of their responsibility to nurture and care for infants and children, enabled them to be more steadfast than men. Hadassah's Central Committee, for instance, informed the male Zionist movement that the woman "generalizes from experience. It is true that women are more minutely practical than men, with an eye constantly alert to detail, because they are kept close to the facts of life, birth and bread and shelter and disease."[51]

Without this direct maternal commitment Hadassah leaders feared their entire medical and social welfare project in Palestine would fold under the mismanagement of Zionist men. Szold elaborated on this attitude, advising Hadassah members not simply to persevere in the face of male opprobrium but to affirm forthrightly the sensible, feminine element inherent in their work. At the 1924 convention she urged the delegates to contrast Hadassah's plans with those undertaken by the male-led organization:

> What our lords and masters do not seem to understand is that true pedagogy, a wise insight into psychology, means waiting for results. They want you to utter promises and pious wishes that cannot be carried out. I am not a man-hater, but I would like you, for instance, to compare our resolutions with the resolutions that have been

adopted by the men's convention; and you will find that we have uttered no pious wishes, that whatever we have resolved upon is practical and can be carried out, and that it is thoroughly Jewish.[52]

She and other leaders believed that this maternal desire to create and nurture life in Palestine had a distinctly Jewish and explicitly Zionist component. Women's work, while perhaps not consumed by abstract ideology and international power politics, produced results and contributed significantly to the overall Zionist mission. The projects supported by Hadassah, the leaders argued, were always completed and managed efficiently. Far from being the group of unorganized volunteers derided by professional Zionists, these women considered themselves more realistic than their male colleagues and every bit as Zionist.

The connection between Hadassah's ideals and those of the international women's movement was set forth explicitly in a *Newsletter* article about Hadassah's interaction with another major Zionist women's group, the European-based Women's International Zionist Organization (WIZO), formed in the early 1920s. Hadassah's leaders sent greetings to the new organization at its founding convention in Carlsbad and took the opportunity to explain why women's concerns were so critical in peacetime. They mentioned the women's international organizations that were working toward "conciliation" in the postwar world and alluded to a comment made by Carrie Chapman Catt about the work of the International Woman Suffrage Alliance: "it was left to women to seat those of French with those of German birth at one and the same Conference table, as happened in Rome in the early months of the present year." Hadassah's leaders concluded that Jewish women's organizations played an even more critical role because Zionists sought not only conciliation but also creation—of Jewish settlement in Palestine but also the re-creation of Diaspora women through their commitment to Zionism.[53] The ties between Zionists and international activists were not merely rhetorical. Rosa Welt-Straus, whose daughter Nellie was a major Hadassah leader in Palestine, founded the Palestine Jewish Women's Equal Rights Association, which was comprised solely of Jewish women and later affiliated with Catt's International Woman Suffrage Alliance.[54]

The same *Newsletter* issue describes an interaction between

Hadassah and a group of Zionist women in Lithuania in the 1920s, an incident that provides further insight into Hadassah leaders' ideas regarding women's attributes as well as the sentiment that women's participation in Zionist causes contributed to their overall success. The article reported on the formation of a new Hadassah chapter in Yanishik. Apparently, local Zionist men had included women in a fund-raising project that was quite successful. After the fund-raiser it once again became difficult to raise money, leading the men to resolve "to draw women into the work." Disregarding the men's renewed interest in their capabilities, the women opted to support Hadassah's work in Palestine rather than to raise more money for the local group. The women sent £16 to Hadassah and contacted the regional Zionist headquarters in Kovno for further guidance. This office never responded to their solicitation for propaganda material on Hadassah's work; indeed, they seem not to have replied to the women at all. After this the Yanishik women turned directly to Hadassah offices in New York, asking that they be considered a new chapter.[55] In responding to the Yanishik women, Hadassah leaders urged them to think of fund-raising "as the measure of moral responsibility," and told them that to take up a project and follow it through to completion was to "apply the mother-feeling to a social task." Rather than have the women continue forwarding money to Hadassah, they advised them to decide on a specific Palestine project that would then become their own.[56] To Hadassah leaders the sustained funding of an enterprise amounted to more than mere philanthropy; such financial responsibility for the care of others was an expression of women's maternal instincts on a societal or national level. This incident revealed to Hadassah leaders how attractive their work was to women from around the world, leading some to question why they occupied such a subservient role in a movement in which they were a central component. Throughout the 1920s, as Hadassah expanded its overseas program, its leaders sought to regain organizational independence, to break out from under an arrangement that more often than not, to their minds, amounted to submission rather than equal partnership.

Hadassah's Struggle for Independence

Hadassah's emphasis on practical projects and use of maternalist language had made it a success, but this also brought the group into conflict with the FAZ and later the ZOA. As described in chapter 2, following the war Hadassah became part of the ZOA, according to the plan formulated by Brandeis, and the organization lost direct responsibility for its Palestine projects. Despite the obstacles this presented to its sustained autonomy, Hadassah's membership increased throughout this period, while that of the ZOA declined; as early as 1921 one of every three members of the ZOA was a "Hadassah lady." In 1920 several key Central Committee members began a struggle to break free of the ZOA.[57] In this battle each side in the dispute used gender to support its arguments and underscore its vision of how the complementary nature of men's and women's Zionism should work in practice. The decade-long struggle reveals that Hadassah's form of separatism, one that granted leaders little real control over administration, did less to promote women in the movement than the separatism embraced by the NCJW in the 1920s. Financial autonomy was crucial in order for women to gain the benefits that separatism had to offer.

The larger context for this gendered conflict was the battle that split the movement between those who followed Louis Brandeis and those whose commitment was to Louis Lipsky, a man perceived by many to be controlled by the European Zionist movement, especially its leader, Chaim Weizmann. A host of issues divided the two factions, including relations to the British Mandatory power and the role of American non-Zionists in the proposed Jewish Agency. The issue of most immediate concern, however, centered on financial management and the Keren Hayesod, designed to facilitate development and settlement in Palestine. Typically the Europeans had less interest in the Progressive standards for efficiency and organization advanced by Brandeis and his followers. Brandeis believed that the funds feeding this entity, investments and donations, should remain separate. He also maintained, similarly to Hadassah, that Americans should retain a certain degree of control over the funds they raised. Initially, the Brandeis faction claimed success, winning a resolution against the "commingling of funds" at the ZOA's 1920 convention in Buffalo. Weizmann arrived in the United States in the spring of 1921, ostensibly to work through a compromise with the American group, yet he managed to increase support for his own vision of the Keren, aiming to defeat the Brandeis group at the next ZOA convention.[58]

Hadassah shared many of Brandeis's concerns about the Keren Hayesod and the WZO's financial management. When the ZOA began to transmit Hadassah funds for the Medical Unit through the WZO's London office after the war, the women and the unit complained that the distribution had become sloppy and irregular. Henrietta Szold, in particular, felt that Menachem Ussishken and other European Zionists in Palestine cared more for politics than for public health.[59] Yet Hadassah leader and later president Rose Jacobs believed that the problems between Hadassah and the ZOA grew acute only with Weizmann's trip to the United States. According to his plan, the women's group would raise funds for the Keren and it, in turn, would oversee the financing of Hadassah's medical services. In essence, the women's group would be turned into a fund-raising entity.[60] After years of trying to counter this perception of their work, many Hadassah women realized that their function in Zionism had changed little in the eyes of the male establishment.

The potential change in Hadassah's relationship with the ZOA and the WZO led some women on the Central Committee to reassert their organizational prerogatives. A showdown occurred when Louis Lipsky commanded Hadassah's Central Committee to raise funds for the Keren. Seven members refused, and Lipsky immediately requested their resignations. When they again resisted a ZOA directive by refusing to resign, Lipsky had the women expelled and dissolved the Central Committee. However, the seven women denied the legality of this expulsion, stating that only Hadassah members had the right to discharge their leadership committee.[61]

It soon became apparent to these leaders that something more than financial management was at the heart of Lipsky's actions toward them. Rose Jacobs asserted that although Lipsky made his "formal" charges against the recalcitrant women in writing, other, more damning, charges were conveyed to them verbally:

> It was charged that we were philanthropists, not Zionists, that we were seeking power and position, that we were reckless, that we were indifferent to the needs of the Jewish People, that we lacked appreciation for Zionist accomplishments, that we did not have a

proper sense of how to evaluate the contribution to Zionism that had been made by the European Zionists.[62]

Other Hadassah leaders voiced similar assessments of the battle with the ZOA. Like Jacobs, these women considered the struggle for financial control as inseparable from negative estimations of women's Zionist commitment and administrative capabilities. Irma Lindheim, for example, believed that both the 1921 and the later struggle in 1928 centered around financial and administrative issues that were manipulated by certain male leaders interested in maintaining control of the women's group: "These were all basic issues, yet in the hands of those interested in political maneuvering, they were made into an attack on personalities and a battle of the sexes, a struggle between women and men for domination."[63] Years later Jacobs bluntly asserted that Lipsky wanted to eradicate Hadassah's independent status. "Mr. Lipsky's attitude toward Hadassah was unnecessarily harsh," she remembered. "Many times he was ready to destroy it. That arose, I think, from a kind of immaturity. To him it was part of a game—a game of employing a political machine to attain a desired result."[64] Much united the Hadassah leadership's position with the Brandeis faction in these disputes, and Lipsky used similar words to criticize both, yet it soon became clear that gender played a central role in the ZOA's attack on the women's group. Lipsky fought to maintain control over the American Zionist movement. To his mind, this meant not only keeping the Brandeis group out of power but also ensuring the continued dependence of women.

Attempting to put his political machine into action, Lipsky arrived at the 1921 Hadassah convention with a "strong men's delegation" in tow, intending to sway the delegates to his way of thinking. The men gave the convention chair, the reserved Alice Seligsberg, a hard time. Rose Jacobs, seeing Seligsberg's difficulty in maintaining control over the proceedings, felt obliged to take it over herself. Far less timid than Seligsberg, she "shouted and gesticulated until order was restored, an executive session was ordered, Mr. Lipsky was compelled to leave and the day was saved."[65]

Left to their own devices, the women continued to argue among themselves. Both those who desired autonomy and those who wished to uphold the present arrangement with the ZOA used arguments that interwove ideas about gender, finances, and aptitude to bolster their respective positions. Diligently trying to persuade the opposition to accept the leadership's position, Pearl Franklin told reluctant members that "since the purse strings meant power to do good, why shouldn't we hold those purse strings instead of turning them over to a group in which we had less confidence than we had in ourselves?"[66] Others agreed with Franklin's viewpoint and expressed frustration that men, in the end, did not consider women capable enough to manage their own projects. A delegate from Chicago pointed out that women had been trying to achieve some sort of equality in the Zionist organization for nearly twenty years and thus far had utterly failed:

> We have dissipated our energy on anything from preparing the dinners at functions, selling things, and we haven't had a definite purpose, women must apply themselves to something definite. It is the sob-stuff that has made HADASSAH what it is in America, and we want to retain that part of the sentimental work that only women can do and we must maintain that definite work, not that vague thing.[67]

Contrasting Hadassah's work with the "vague" formulations of men, she affirmed Hadassah's mission, albeit in tones suggesting women's propensity toward the sentimental. Women, she argued, needed a definite project on which to set their sights; fund-raising for no clear and immediate purpose would not serve to build the organization and the movement in the same manner as the methods devised by Hadassah itself.

Delegates in opposition to secession also used arguments regarding gender and administrative proficiency to support their case. Such women opposed autonomy because they felt Hadassah was unable to maintain the Zionist character of its organization without ideological leadership from the ZOA. Some of these women reiterated a common ZOA complaint about Hadassah by stating that "perhaps the largest number of Hadassah members are really not at heart Zionists" but simply philanthropists. Despite the leadership's attempts to present Hadassah's work as women's brand of Zionism, as philanthropy in service to the developing nation and thus a legitimate form of nationalism, some women and like-minded men continued to devalue the Zionist element of women's contributions.[68] They strongly implied that since so many women were not true Zionists, they must continue to be led by the more knowledgeable men.

Delegates countering these presentations of women's work quickly leaped to the defense of Hadassah's "philanthropic" nature. In one woman's opinion, Hadassah's success had resulted from its focus on raising funds for social welfare projects in Palestine—the philanthropic "sob-stuff" mentioned by others. Conceding that the ZOA needed to be supported, this delegate stressed that it already was supported—"by men." Why, she queried, should women undertake to finance both the men's organization and their own work?[69] These debates reflected the longstanding, uneasy position of women in the American Zionist movement. After nearly ten years of very successful fund-raising, membership promotion, and the initiation of countless services in Palestine, women continued to feel it necessary to defend their work as inherently Zionist and to reiterate their right to equality in the movement's ranks. The internal debates of the 1921 convention show that not all women were convinced of the leadership's articulation of a woman's Zionism distinct from philanthropy. While proponents of women's autonomy envisioned a Zionist movement predicated upon separate, complementary, yet equal spheres of influence, opponents agreed with ZOA leaders who felt that, left to their own devices, the women's Zionism would devolve into middle-class, female benevolence. The maternalist rhetoric that had served the leadership so well in building the movement could also limit their independent action when some men and women advanced different understandings of how this complementarity should work in practice.

Hadassah's membership was clearly divided, yet the seven leaders and their followers could boast of solid organization and many successful projects. Even pro-ZOA Hadassah members most likely feared pushing this effective coterie of leaders out of the organization entirely.[70] Such fears would not have been unfounded. At the 1921 convention, Alice Seligsberg circulated a confidential memo to key women proposing a secret meeting to discuss the possibility of Hadassah members paying their dues to the WZO but refusing to fulfill their obligations to the ZOA. The letter also urged recipients to speak privately with other members who might be interested in creating a new women's Zionist society.[71] Whether or not Lipsky was aware of this memo, he stopped short of forcing the seven out of the ZOA. His desire to hold on to as many Hadassah members as possible ultimately led him to compromise with the stubborn women. The agreement they reached kept Hadassah within the ranks of the ZOA and gave it the right to be the sole Zionist organization working to recruit American women. Hadassah also won direct representation at the World Zionist Congress for the first time. Finally, the WZO agreed to pass the medical work back to Hadassah, thereby restoring it control of its own projects.[72]

The leadership's success in this first battle was due in no small part to the group's dramatic achievement in attracting new recruits to Zionism. Hadassah sustained successful recruitment efforts well into the 1920s, relying on its ideas about women's Zionism and the interrelated spheres of influence for men and women to increase membership. In 1924 Henrietta Szold wrote her family that she believed "our lords and masters were rather stunned by our appearing [at their convention] with a paid up membership of 16,500." But despite a reduction in overt tension between the men's and women's groups, conflict simmered just beneath the surface.[73] Late in 1925 the United Palestine Appeal (UPA) was founded to coordinate American fund-raising efforts for the Keren Hayesod and *Keren Kayemeth L'Yisroel* (Jewish National Fund). Hadassah agreed to participate in the UPA's first campaign, and Henrietta Szold served as one of the its vice presidents. Under the new agreement, reminiscent of the earlier unsuccessful accord, all funds raised by Hadassah would be transmitted to Palestine through the UPA. Almost immediately Hadassah leaders expressed dissatisfaction with the UPA's high administrative costs and complained that too much money was being diverted from their Palestine projects.[74] Frustrated with the management of the men's groups, Hadassah leaders soon called for a review of both the UPA and the ZOA administrations.

At the twelfth convention in 1926, delegates were lobbied by several UPA representatives, who had nothing but praise for the women. Emanuel Neumann, for instance, called Hadassah the backbone of UPA fund-raising drives.[75] Despite the acclaim, some

Hadassah members insisted that women's efforts be rewarded with more than flattery. Like their counterparts in the NCJW, these leaders demanded greater recognition for women's support of male-led fund-raising. In particular, they asserted that Hadassah's contributions to the UPA should be credited to them as an organization rather than as individual ZOA members. Sounding themes reminiscent of Rebekah Kohut's demands of the JDC, Pearl Franklin contended that if Hadassah were to persist in fund-raising for male-led entities it must at least do so as an organization and receive appropriate recognition for its efforts. Some delegates quickly objected that such demands sounded overly aggressive and too much like a renewed call for total separation from the male-led organizations. Franklin countered that without a certain degree of autonomy, women in the Zionist movement would never be as active as they might be and once had been. Championing themes common to proponents of separatism from a host of movements, Franklin insisted that a well-defined women's Zionist organization had to exist in order to provide less assertive women, those who refused to speak at even the smallest mixed-sex meetings, with a safe forum to voice their opinions and gain leadership skills. Hadassah's major contribution in this regard, she asserted, was its ability "to understand the psychology of the women, which the men, bless them, do not always understand."[76] As in 1921, discussions of administrative and financial matters were laced with references to gender. Some women argued for autonomy on the basis of women's unique needs but, as happened earlier in the decade, others used this same argument to discredit women's aptitude for leadership.

In 1927 Hadassah's leadership began to express trepidation about the continued growth of the UPA. By this point Hadassah members constituted a majority of the overall ZOA membership, and some leaders feared that the UPA would soon overshadow the ZOA, further subverting women's power in the movement. The board worried that the UPA presented a significant threat to Hadassah's autonomy because its further expansion could transform the group into a mere auxiliary. Consequently Hadassah leaders determined to reassert ZOA primacy over the UPA and at the same time expand Hadassah's own power within the ZOA itself. Trying once again to reconcile demands for both separation and integration, Hadassah's national board urged members to become more directly involved in ZOA administration, especially since Hadassah shared in all actions resulting from ZOA decisions, both positive and negative.[77] Delegates to the 1927 convention pressed for a resolution calling for a reorganization of the ZOA that included the creation of a committee to oversee fund-raising. Although committee members would act as Zionists, not as representatives of their home organizations, the Hadassah proposal called for one-half of the committee seats to be allotted to its own members since they comprised more than one-half of the ZOA membership.[78]

Leading the charge in the drive to reorganize the ZOA was Irma Lindheim, who acted not only in her capacity as Hadassah's president but also as a ZOA vice president who served on both the executive and administrative committees. Henrietta Szold had previously held these same positions in the ZOA, but Lindheim felt Szold had been too easy to ignore, given her frequent sojourns in Palestine. Resolving to make Hadassah's voice equal to its numbers in the making of ZOA policy, Lindheim asserted that her organization would "be a token one no longer." Having witnessed the earlier struggle between the two groups, Lindheim held few illusions about the real source of tension between the ZOA and Hadassah. She later recalled that "from the point of view of the men, most impertinently the tail was trying to wag the dog. A clash of personalities and methods developed which was costly in time, energy, and effectiveness, a result not unique at the time, when any organization of women sought to enter territory hitherto controlled by the men."[79] As in 1921, Hadassah leaders found that while their criticisms of Lipsky and the ZOA closely resembled those of other Brandeis allies, the arguments arrayed against them quickly devolved into gendered attacks on women's capabilities.

When the UPA was forced to rely on a bank loan in order to cover its expenses, Lindheim decided the time had come to put a stop to the poor management of both that entity and the ZOA. She counseled her board to refuse to cosign for the loan and then relayed to Lipsky that if the ZOA wished Hadassah's continued involvement in the UPA a thoroughgoing reorganization would need to take place. On March 31, 1928, a piece in the *New York Times* summarized Lindheim's views on recent events. Despite her insistence that she spoke for herself alone, Lipsky interpreted the article as a very public attack on him by Hadassah as an organization. He demanded that Hadassah's board repudiate their president, they opted instead to give her a vote of confidence. Furious about this turn of events, Lipsky attacked his opponents in the *New Palestine*. Seeking to paint Lindheim and the board as a bunch of meddlesome women who failed to understand their suitable role in the movement, he accused them of having fallen away from Henrietta Szold's exemplary model. Szold, he maintained, "recognized the proper role of women within the ranks of the ZOA," insinuating strongly that the current leadership did not.[80]

The crisis came to a head during Hadassah's convention in June 1928. Lipsky tried to have the convention postponed until after the ZOA met, even though traditionally Hadassah's annual meeting was held first. Lipsky also attempted, by a questionable administrative ruling, to lower the number of Hadassah delegates eligible to attend the ZOA convention. As in 1921, during the women's convention major debate revolved around the relative merits of autonomy versus continued allegiance to a ZOA headed by Lipsky. Arguments not settled earlier in the decade reemerged as proponents of restructuring defended themselves against attacks that they were not true Zionists. In the estimation of some, the proper expression of Zionist commitment for women could be realized only by following the lead of the ZOA. Anything else was evidence of their underlying desire for "power," for playing politics—and playing it badly at that.

Lindheim sent greetings to the convention (she could not attend herself due to illness), urging delegates not to allow a complete submergence of Hadassah into the ZOA. If Hadassah were to do that, to accept ZOA standards of administration and lose its own identity, then, she wrote, one could easily say of the Zionist movement, "divided they stood, united they fell."[81] Lipsky could not keep away from Hadassah's convention. As he had back in 1921, he arrived once again with a delegation of men who appealed to the women to support his position. Alluding to the actions of the Brandeis faction, he contended that "the Zionist movement has gone through two years of hell" as a result of what he called guerrilla tactics used by people who would not face him in public. But his assertion that he came to the convention solely as a neutral party drew laughter from the audience.[82] In light of Lindheim's absence, Zipporah (Zip) Szold, wife of Henrietta's cousin Robert, acted as chairperson of the board; Alice Seligsberg served as convention chair, despite her mild manner, since Rose Jacobs refused to do so, citing her great animosity toward Lipsky. Zip Szold later reported to Henrietta that although applause broke out upon his arrival, soon "the men started to make a demonstration designed, I believe, to break up our Convention." As they had in 1921 the women promptly moved to make the session an executive one in order to clear the men from the hall. This proved to be no easy task, but the women prevailed and were able to carry on with their business free from outside agitation.[83]

Pearl Franklin reiterated her argument from 1921 that Hadassah's greatest achievement had been to interest such large numbers of women in Zionism. Reminding delegates that she was first and foremost a Zionist, Franklin told them that on purely practical grounds she did not think Hadassah would have been so effective had it not been a separate women's organization. A mixed-sex group could never have attracted 37,000 women to the Zionist message. Women, she asserted, did their best work on their own, free from male intervention.[84] Other women vehemently opposed any move toward what they characterized as the leadership's "separatist policy."[85] Vice president Ida Silverman, who had been closely involved with the UPA, even went so far as to resign her post. Rose Jacobs, in speaking out against Silverman's position, took the opportunity to chide her for holding un-progressive views of women and in the process turned the contemporary assessment of female separatism on its head. "We are living in the twentieth century," Jacobs boldly declared. If women supposedly had equal rights to men why do men "all of a sudden" resist women's efforts? "When women want to assert those rights," she asked, why are they told by men that "they have no right to do so?"[86] For years the Zionist movement had proclaimed its respect for equal rights, touting its stance on women's suffrage. Now women like Jacobs insisted on holding the movement to its word, especially since American women had gained the right to vote at home. Yet at the same time, Jacobs was calling for an assertion of equal rights in a context of gender separation.

Although much of this controversy was presented as only a skirmish in the larger war between Brandeis, Lipsky, and Chaim

Weizmann, privately Hadassah leaders did not mince words about what they thought was the Lipsky faction's true complaint about their organization. Leaders clearly believed that these men opposed any substantive input from women regarding the management of the American Zionist movement. Women's contributions were admired so long as they remained in the realm of social welfare and fund-raising, even if such activities were also commonly dismissed as insufficiently Zionist in character. When women sought to affect the course of the movement at large (and particularly once they made up the larger part of that movement itself), male leaders like Lipsky openly renounced this female intrusion into "politics," defined as a male preserve. In April 1928 Irma Lindheim wrote Henrietta Szold that Lipsky felt that "Hadassah after all was only an auxiliary, and had no right to express itself or have any voice in the policies of the organization."[87] Other leaders heard similar assessments of the relationship between the ZOA and Hadassah. Nellie Straus Mochenson wrote to Alice Seligsberg from Palestine to tell her that she was "appalled" by what she heard was going on in the United States between the two groups. "The hatred and malice, the vulgar and stupid tone of the inferiority-complex inspired articles in the New Palestine were beyond belief," she wrote. She maintained that nowhere had she seen a point that "Hadassah could well have made—namely that the Z.O. had decided to crush it as much as a year ago, and was seeking a casus belli." She added that she had seen Joseph Cowen in Palestine and he had told her "very casually 'Hadassah is going in for politics now, and we must crush it.'"[88] Hadassah's own *Newsletter* bluntly reported the fact that certain men challenged the organization's equal status in the movement and sought to deny women the right to make policy and administrative decisions, to engage in "politics." One article cited the Zionist and Yiddish press as having accused Hadassah of "'sullying its skirts with dirty politics.' . . . This all sounds very much as though the gentlemen were in the habit of saying to their wives: 'There, there dear, run along to your knitting and don't trouble your pretty head about these things. These things are men's work.'"[89]

The stress of this conflict, no doubt exacerbated by the personal nature of the attacks and the fact that the battle coincided with the death of her husband, nearly drove Irma Lindheim to a nervous breakdown. Yet even in the midst of personal and public turmoil she calmly gauged the nature of Lipsky's anger. According to Lindheim, he so resented the challenge women presented to his authority that he referred to their efforts as "diaper Zionism." She told a friend that Lipsky persisted in maintaining that he had tried to cooperate but, in her words, he felt "it has been impossible to work with Hadassah, that they are arrogant, that they nag, that they interfere in things which are none of their business." Men like Lipsky, Lindheim felt, refused to consider women able to step outside their ordained sphere, to engage in public work on an equal basis with men: "The dignified exercise of Hadassah's right of suffrage is called 'politics' by the ZOA, in order to put it in bad repute; and the women of Hadassah are being told to go home and tend to their tea parties and leave the affairs of Palestine to the men."[90]

Prewar attitudes about gender behavior that associated men with the public world of politics and women with the private world of the home lingered on in the Zionist movement. Kristi Andersen has noted that although women had long engaged in activities that would commonly be referred to today as "politics," in the early twentieth century that term most commonly referred to partisanship and to issues pursued by men out of self-interest. Building on older notions of female activism, women were supposed to be nonpartisan and disinterested, working for the general good rather than individual advancement. In the days following women's formal entrance into the ranks of voters, however, American women and men of all stripes came to reinterpret the meaning of the "political." The American Zionists's struggles over financial control, separatism, and women's relative power in the movement reflect these broader reassessments taking place in American culture. In the end, Hadassah's leadership prevailed a second time. After acrimonious debate they, in alliance with the Brandeis faction, eventually forced Lipsky to accept reforms in the administration of the ZOA. Hadassah won a reduction in its payment to the ZOA and a higher delegate allotment to ZOA conventions.[91]

Women such as Rose Jacobs, Pearl Franklin, and Irma Lindheim recognized that without control of its organizational agenda and finances, Hadassah women would remain in secondary positions within the movement, no matter how large a membership they delivered to the ZOA. The battles of the 1920s reveal their desire to be taken seriously in the movement, to achieve a voice comparable to their numbers while at the same time persevering in the development of their special brand of Zionism. The women's Zionism advocated by Hadassah proved an effective tool for raising membership, but the battles of the 1920s showed that such gendered strategies could also be used to limit women's activism by those men, and women, who, unlike Brandeis, only reluctantly supported equal rights for women in the Zionist movement.

Benefits and Limitations of Separatism

As World War I drew to a close and American Jews looked to the future of their coreligionists in Europe and Palestine, they anticipated the need for sustained relief well into the foreseeable future. Women in the NCJW and Hadassah also recognized the necessity for further monetary investment in those regions, and they looked for ways to expand their own programs abroad. Both groups sought to claim for themselves the special preserve of social welfare work targeting women and children specifically, and each utilized a highly gendered language to justify their heightened involvement in these areas after the war. Meeting no small resistance to their renewed activism, women in the two organizations realized that they needed to break from JDC and ZOA control over their programs, future agendas, and finances. The NCJW, which had always entertained greater organizational autonomy than Hadassah, moved to expand its overseas work through the establishment of a Reconstruction Unit of its own and fought for this unit to achieve respect (and therefore funding) comparable to the projects of similar male groups in the JDC. Hadassah, on the other hand, having dramatically augmented its membership and the scope of its Palestine work, turned to the ZOA requesting greater representation as an organization. Facing stiff resistance from men in Louis Lipsky's faction, key Hadassah leaders twice allied with Brandeis's group in an effort to break Lipsky's control over the movement and, more immediately for them, to attain a modicum of independence for women.

Both groups relied upon gendered characterizations of their abilities to explain why they should be involved in certain types of work. By utilizing such justifications the women found themselves arguing for equality while at the same time maintaining forcefully that men and women were at heart different. Women advancing this viewpoint soon learned that many men, and not a few women, accepted their notion of complementary spheres but rejected the idea that these spheres were equal. Particularly in the Zionist case, their opponents argued that if these differences existed, then men, who in their minds held a greater capacity for ideological thinking, should be allowed to lead. Using their own arguments against the women's rights activists, opponents contended that women's special nature rendered them unsuited to participate in "politics"—a word whose definition became increasingly vague, conveying foremost those activities related to the traditionally male sphere of public activism. Leaders in both Hadassah and the NCJW repeated arguments about women's natural aptitude for social welfare work among women and children, but they often found that these arguments, rather than elevating female volunteers to a place of equality with professional and more ideologically inclined men, led to a devaluation of their contributions.

The struggle to obtain respect for the work of their organizations and the difficulties they faced led women in the NCJW and Hadassah to turn their attention ever more intently toward other women. At the same time that they distanced themselves from the control of men's groups and affirmed women's proclivity for social welfare work, they also reached out to other women in similar predicaments. The NCJW appealed to middle-class Jewish women worldwide to build an organization modeled on the International Council of Women and also deepened their involvement with other U.S. women's groups. Hadassah, on the other hand, made a concerted effort to augment its organizational base by contacting middle-class American Jewish women and urging them to support the Zionist cause.

CHAPTER 4

Women Organizing Women

Gender and American Jewish
Identity, 1920–1930

I n breaking some of the bonds tying them to male-dominated
organizations, Jewish women in the 1920s strengthened their
own groups. At the same time they built alliances with other
women, both Jewish and gentile, nationally and internationally.
The NCJW and Hadassah shared with others a continued interest
in women's and children's issues, concerns that had motivated them
since their inception, and both groups employed gendered and
maternalist rhetoric. Like other American women's organizations,
these two Jewish women's groups also struggled to find a place for
themselves in a world where "politics" referred to issues deemed
self-interested, perhaps controversial, but always masculine. Male
Zionist leaders had hoped to dissuade Hadassah leaders from
involving themselves in the movement's administration by labeling
the women's assertion of influence a selfish drive for political
power. During the 1920s NCJW leaders designated certain issues,
especially Zionism, as "controversial" or "political" and therefore
outside organizational parameters. At the same time, however, they
embraced equally controversial issues such as peace and disarmament that were regarded as more in concert with their gendered,
organizational mission, one that they shared with many other
American women's groups.[1]

While Hadassah and Council leaders moved closer together in
rhetorical and organizational style, their fundamental disagreement
over Zionism resulted in their presenting similar, yet ultimately

competing models for how to be an American Jewish woman. Where the NCJW forged many bonds with others interested in a host of issues associated with postsuffrage women's activism, Hadassah women focused their energies ever more intently on the Jewish world. Council leaders stressed the American-ness of their organization, its similarity to other women's organizations of the period, in the process highlighting acculturated Jews' resemblance to their non-Jewish sisters in other organizations. Hadassah, on the other hand, sought ways to create a Jewish American identity that coincided with its feeling of connection to Jews throughout the world, moving toward what Michael Berkowitz calls in relation to Western European Zionists a "supplemental nationality." Like their counterparts in Europe, Hadassah women did not perceive a contradiction between firm allegiance to building a nation-state in Palestine and being a patriotic citizen of one's land of birth.[2]

Yet the methods by which Hadassah leaders chose to pursue their goals reveal that even though they committed themselves to an ideology unpopular with many acculturated American Jews, and irrelevant to most gentile Americans, they nevertheless adhered to many ideas held in common with other middle-class American women. Both Hadassah and Council women engaged in similar projects and employed comparable language. The commonality with the NCJW in method and rhetoric enabled Hadassah to present itself as the more Jewishly-identified equivalent of the NCJW. By linking Hadassah's work to that pursued by Council, and by extension other American women's groups both at home and abroad, Hadassah was able to recruit large numbers of women to the American Zionist movement, sustaining and building it during a period more commonly characterized by precipitous decline.

Growing Diversity, Common Problems

In the postwar era both Hadassah and the NCJW expanded their organizational agendas, and thus required greater funding and more dues-paying members. Stressing their interest in mothers and children, the inherent maternalism of all women, and belief in female practicality proved effective for both groups. Yet as they grew in size and geographical scope, Hadassah and the NCJW faced similar problems in trying to maintain unity among an increasingly diverse membership. During the 1920s both faced new

divisions surfacing in their ranks over language, generational discord, and the regional origin of national leaders.

Some of the problems confronting the groups were relatively
simple. As these large organizations spread into small towns and
rural areas, their top leaders grew more aware of the distinctive
issues facing women in such places. For instance, in 1926 a woman
from Springfield, Ohio, writing to the "Section Problems" column
of Council's the *Jewish Woman*, pled for help for her *Kleinstadt*
(small city). When local leaders excluded certain members from
their dinner parties, she observed, major feuds evolved, which often
culminated in the rebuffed members resigning from the organization or at the very least refusing to participate any further in group
activities.[3] Human dynamics, which surely played a role in large
city sections, became accentuated in small towns, where a meager
Jewish population ensured that a membership loss of even one or
two would be keenly felt.

As the founding members grew older, age played a noticeable
role in complicating intragroup relations. Both Hadassah and the
NCJW sought to attract younger women by forming youth groups
affiliated with the nationals. In 1920 Junior Hadassah was established for women in their teens and early twenties. The Council of
Jewish Juniors had been founded much earlier, a year after the
NCJW's inception, in 1894. Upon marriage Council Juniors were
supposed to move into a "Senior" section, although in small towns
Juniors and Seniors often combined resources.[4] Both Junior groups
were meant to serve as a training ground for future members, not
constitute a permanent affiliation. Yet as the leadership aged and
clung to outmoded ideas, the more modern, younger women grew
disenchanted with their elders. Sometimes tension could build over
such seemingly trivial issues as dress length and hairstyles.

Hadassah members found that young women did not always
abandon their youthful ways and style of dress when they graduated
from the Juniors. As more young women joined the Senior ranks in
the 1920s, some older Hadassah women complained about the
fashionable clothing these young women wore at meetings and
conventions. While modish dresses might be appropriate for the
Juniors, the leaders thought that upon graduating to the Senior
ranks women should attire themselves in something more befitting
their age and marital status. Chiding these older members, a

Newsletter article concluded that if Seniors persisted in clinging to their old-fashioned ways young women might opt to remain in the Juniors forever. Hadassah depended on maintaining an exuberant growth and needed to attract young women. If these new members chose to wear clothes that did not convey the matronly air of days long past, then, the author suggested, older women would simply have to adapt.[5]

Perhaps because the NCJW had dealt with the Junior-Senior divisions for a longer period of time than Hadassah, this sort of controversy arose much less frequently there, or at least less publicly, in the 1920s. Both groups, however, faced problems related to language usage. Although many leaders and long-term members were conversant in French and German, few, if any, spoke Yiddish. As more immigrants and their daughters gained the wherewithal to join voluntary organizations after the war, Yiddish-speaking women became an ever larger presence, albeit as rank-and-file members only. Hints of a growing awareness of the Yiddish contingent appear in the groups' publications, but both seem to have done little substantive work to recruit actively in the Yiddish-speaking community or to groom Yiddish-speaking women for leadership positions.

Hadassah leaders, especially Henrietta Szold, urged their followers to learn Hebrew, but they did little to reach out to women who spoke Yiddish. Nevertheless, Yiddish-speakers appeared at Hadassah meetings, though they were hardly a vocal presence. For instance, in 1925 a delegate addressed the convention in Yiddish asking for more propaganda about Hadassah in that language. Presumably, she utilized a translator to get her point across to the crowd, but since the organization itself did not employ a transcriber familiar with Yiddish, her speech was reduced to no more than a brief notation in the official record. No discussion followed her report that might have shed light on what she actually said. Despite this official silencing, her presentation had some impact: the convention unanimously passed a resolution committing itself to producing more Yiddish material and enrolling more Yiddish-speaking members.[6] Yet, at least in terms of its own *Newsletter*, Hadassah failed to achieve the first goal. Between 1914 and 1929 only one Yiddish piece appeared in Hadassah's monthly publication.[7] Because it was a Zionist organization, it is not surprising that

Hadassah showed so little interest in promoting Yiddish; the group's primary focus relative to language was to encourage American women to learn Hebrew. Still, the leaders' limited interest in producing Yiddish propaganda is striking given the large number of potential recruits to be found among that community in the United States. As a basically middle-class organization, tied to such elite men as Louis Brandeis, Hadassah constructed through language an image of itself as a distinctly American, acculturated, and English-speaking Zionist organization.[8]

Council's Yiddish problem had a different cast to it than Hadassah's. Not ideologically opposed to the use of Yiddish the way some prominent Zionists could be, Council leaders nevertheless had little direct knowledge of Yiddish themselves. Yiddish was the language of Council's clientele; very rarely was it the language of members, who, coming from wealthier backgrounds, had greater familiarity with the non-Jewish languages of Western Europe. Revealing the depth of ignorance within the NCJW regarding Yiddish, one notice in the *Jewish Woman* printed in 1929 suggested that it might be helpful if new section presidents ensured "at least one of the active members" on their Immigrant Aid and Education committees could speak Yiddish.[9] Given that Council had long prided itself on working with immigrant women, this suggestion demonstrates the distance separating Council members from the recipients of their care. Members of the Yiddish press, viewing Council through the lens of class, not surprisingly recognized the chasm separating Council members from the working class or poor. *Forverts,* for instance, mocked the way Council women dispensed funds to the poor "with their bediamoned hands more to show their delicate alabaster fingers with well-manicured nails than really to save the unfortunates."[10] Council leaders were not unaware that such ideas circulated among less Americanized Jews. A brief note in the *Jewish Woman* observed that many journalists writing for the Yiddish press had misunderstood Council and its projects; indeed, many even challenged Council's very "Jewishness."[11] But such expressions of concern regarding Council's image in the Yiddish community were rare. Other than the few instances mentioned above, Yiddish and Yiddish-speakers rarely entered into the public consciousness of the organization. The conflict over Yiddish in Hadassah and the NCJW would be solved more by the Americanization of immigrants than by any significant effort of the two groups to appeal to non-English speakers.

The organizations shared even more serious problems related to interactions between the national office and certain regional sections. This was a particular difficulty for Hadassah, since the national office was located in New York City and most leaders hailed from the surrounding areas. At the 1921 convention a delegate from Ohio, arguing that the national leadership did not reflect the regional scope of Hadassah's membership, suggested that the Central Committee include more women from outside New York. While some delegates supported her, others feared that her proposal would increase expenses, as Hadassah might be obliged to cover travel costs for those who lived a great distance from the organization's headquarters.[12]

During the debate one leader held up the NCJW as a model for an effective, large, national organization. She did not detail the methods by which Council avoided the conflicts that plagued Hadassah; indeed, she would have had difficulty had she tried, given that Council faced similar problems. At the 1923 triennial, rural and western sections expressed great dissatisfaction with their eastern, more powerful, cohorts. Upon leaving office Second Vice President Seraphine Pisko of Denver commented that "any woman who is big enough to be a vice-president of the Council is big enough to be taken into the inner courts of the temple and not be left hanging on the ragged edge outside, wondering what may be going on and why she is so much an outsider."[13] Pisko believed that her tenure as a national leader had not afforded her, a westerner, the same opportunities enjoyed by her eastern colleagues. Her comments reveal that she felt slighted by the way she was treated, uninvolved and unnoticed.

This was not the first time that Council leaders from areas other than the major northern cities with substantial Jewish populations complained that their concerns went unheeded at national gatherings. As early as the World War I years, southern members had raised these issues in the relatively private arena of the national board meeting. Even more so than Pisko's brief comments, these women's complaints show how regional differences could significantly influence women's political outlook. As Council sought to redefine itself in the postwar period, moving further afield of its nonpartisan origins as a religious and philanthropic organization, the issues raised by the conflict between northern and southern women earlier in the century grew more pronounced.

In 1915 a member from Savannah, Georgia, protested the small number of southerners on national committees, arguing that southern sections were inadequately represented and that the southern viewpoint on certain issues was thus ignored. Evelyn Aronson Margolis disagreed and, in Council's defense, recalled an instance where a particular southern leader's grievance had been settled by northern members acceding to her position. The dispute centered around the fact that Council had been giving money to the NAACP, an organization "for the uplift of the colored race." Southern members felt the NAACP was a political organization and that, as such, Council should not donate funds to this group. Painting a rather rosy picture of those board deliberations, Margolis remembered that since the NAACP was a group "of which the Southern people disapproved, . . . we immediately withdrew our subscription when that was explained to us."[14]

In reality, the incident proved to be more contentious than Margolis's recollection. At the 1914 board meeting a woman from Mobile, Alabama, asked her colleagues why Council contributed to the NAACP, which she considered a political, not philanthropic, organization. Executive Secretary Sadie American brushed aside her concerns, telling her that the board had too many important issues to deal with and could not allow itself to get sidetracked into sectional debates. However, her ire raised, American challenged the woman to prove that the major intent of the NAACP was political. The southern member requested permission to read a letter she had in her possession from Booker T. Washington, which, she believed, established her claim. Inez Lopez Cohen of Charleston, South Carolina, supported her southern sister, urging the board to let the woman have her say. After reading from Washington's letter, which stated that the NAACP's "main business, so far as I understand it, is to agitate in favor of equal rights for colored people," the Alabama member proceeded to outline the dangers that would befall her own "little town" should blacks be granted equal rights. Since African Americans outnumbered whites by three to one in the South, in her (incorrect) estimation their being given the same rights as blacks had in New York would guarantee "every official in town would be a nigger." She concluded that "if we are helping to give them political rights, we are doing an infamous thing." This comment raised a tumult of objections, forcing President Janet Harris to call for order. Harris then moved that a recommendation be sent to the incoming board to stop the donation to the NAACP. One member rejected this, stating firmly that "it would be a backward step in our history, in the history of our times, history of the decade, if we did not hold out a helping hand to everybody." Regardless of her impassioned defense of the NAACP, the national did withdraw its financial support, although individual sections continued to work for civil rights on the local level.[15]

This interchange reveals the different worldviews of a minority of southern Jews and their more numerous and liberal northern counterparts. More importantly, it is an early example of what would become a frequent debate in the organization over what constituted "philanthropic" work and what shaded off into the realm of the "political." By using such terms, the women generally meant to distinguish what they considered to be neutral issues from controversial ones. Where northern women saw contributions to the NAACP to be in concert with the NCJW's commitment to furthering social justice, and thus in line with their "philanthropic" goals, southern members felt that the group had overstepped its boundaries by supporting an organization committed to achieving black political equality. Although the issue of race did not reassert itself so prominently in future Council deliberations, similar altercations would occur in the future regarding what did or did not constitute a "political" issue.

As the two organizations became more prominent in the 1920s they faced not only new opportunities but also potentially serious challenges. No longer a small coterie of women with similar ideals, by the 1920s Hadassah and the NCJW included women from every region of the United States, both rural and urban, young and old. Appealing to these members and holding them in the organization when so many other opportunities existed for voluntary activism presented substantial obstacles. As Hadassah and the NCJW struggled to attract and keep members, their leaders engaged in an ever growing number of new projects while at the same time refining a distinct organizational identity. Accordingly,

both organizations began to (re)establish contacts with other organizations in their respective activist realms.

NCJW Involvement in American Politics

The NCJW had long considered itself the representative of Jewish
women to the rest of the United States. Especially during World
War I, Council, unlike Hadassah, forged relations with many other
American women's groups. Moreover, leading figures in the
NCJW held membership in gentile women's groups and counted
leading activists such as Jane Addams among their close friends.
The group's postwar involvement in European Jewish affairs did
not diminish its commitment to American social reform. During
the 1920s Council moved ever closer to those involved in a wide
range of reform efforts. Most notably, in 1920 the NCJW helped
found the Women's Joint Congressional Committee, a lobbying
organization composed of the major women's associations; well
into midcentury it remained the sole Jewish organization on that
committee.[16]

Like countless other women's organizations, in the inter-war
era the NCJW increasingly sought to effect change through lobbying and legislative action. Not surprisingly, many of its initial forays
into politics centered on immigration issues. In 1921 the NCJW
campaigned against restrictive measures; when this endeavor failed,
a Bureau of International Service was created as part of the Department of Immigrant Aid (DIA). The bureau aided women and children overseas who were separated from male family members. Its
major goal was to reunite these families, but the bureau also helped
ensure that the women would at least receive their husbands' workers' compensation and veterans' benefits. From 1923 to 1926 the
bureau transmitted nearly $50,000 from U.S. citizens to their rela-
tives abroad, and by 1928 it commanded one-third of the entire
DIA budget.[17]

When the U.S. Congress moved to restrict immigration even
further, the NCJW stepped up its lobbying, arguing that such measures had particularly horrible repercussions for Jews. According to
DIA chair Florina Lasker, some 6,000 European Jews held visas
issued to them by American consuls in the years immediately following the war, yet only a few of these people would be eligible to

enter the United States under the new quota system. Most would have to return to their devastated homelands or eke out an existence as refugees in Western European cities. Many of these people, fearing antisemitic violence in the East, refused to return to their nations of origin; many others literally had no home to which to return. Lasker testified before Congress that it "would be an act of human mercy to end their distress and anxiety" by allowing them entry into the United States. Insisting that many of these refugees had relatives in the United States who would ensure they did not become public charges, she implored Congress to make the necessary legal changes to facilitate the reunification of families.[18]

Activism on behalf of immigrants led Council women to strengthen their ties with other organizations similarly concerned with the plight of refugees, including such European groups as the Jüdischer Frauenbund. Many of these groups also dedicated themselves to promoting international peace, and Council joined them in this pursuit as well.[19] Just as with its activism on behalf of Jewish immigrants, Council's position on peace reflected a longstanding commitment that developed more fully during the postwar era. As early as 1898 the NCJW had gone on record in support of peace, urging President McKinley to avoid the war against Spain, and in 1908 it established a permanent Peace and Arbitration Committee. As we have seen, prior to the U.S. declaration of war in April 1917, Council women worked for Belgium relief and a peaceful conclusion to hostilities. When the war ended, these women joined with their "sisters of other faiths" in calling for disarmament. Through the Peace and Arbitration Committee, Council became the only Jewish organization affiliated formally with such groups as the National Council for Limitation of Armament, the Women's Committee for World Disarmament, and the American Union against Militarism.[20] In 1923 Carrie Chapman Catt, addressing the NCJW convention, proclaimed that she had always believed Jews had a central role to play in bringing about world peace. A year later Council helped put her words into action by assisting Catt with the planning of the Conference on the Cause and Cure of War. At this January 1925 conference one hundred delegates from the NCJW took their seats beside those of eight other organizations, including the General Federation of Women's Clubs, the National Women's Trade Union League, and the League of Women Voters.[21] Council maintained its interest in peace throughout the decade, lobbying for American inclusion in the World Court, recommending U.S. support of the Kellogg-Briand pact, and attending sessions of the League of Nations and other international gatherings.[22]

As Council leaders moved forward vigorously on agenda items their organization shared with other women's groups, they maintained a determined silence regarding Zionism. A Jewish journalist covering the 1923 triennial noted with displeasure that while delegates debated at length numerous questions regarding religion and peace, "the cradle of religion and peace was not even mentioned." Zionism and Palestine were topics kept off the table even if some members wished them to be brought out into the open. Phoebe Ruslander, a Council member as well as Hadassah leader, attempted to put forward a resolution supporting Palestine and its Jewish inhabitants. The chair of the resolution committee assured her that her proposal would be considered if time allowed. When no resolution on Palestine emerged from the triennial, the disgruntled journalist angrily concluded that "apparently there was no time."[23] As Council affiliated ever more closely with other American women's organizations, it seemed to some Zionist observers that the NCJW had abandoned its commitment to the Jewish people.

Yet Council leaders challenged whether Zionism constituted the most authentic means by which to express one's Jewish identity. Although pledged to aid Jews around the world, these women, like many other Reform Jews, rejected notions of a Jewish national identity. Moreover, because they embraced the cause of internationalism and attempted to speak for American Jewish women, the majority of Council leaders spurned Jewish nationalism, particularly as espoused by Zionists. They believed they had a better method for promoting Jewish and women's interests, one that simultaneously advanced the American identity of their membership. Women in the upper echelons of the NCJW prided themselves on being American Jews working in concert with Americans of other faiths. Peace initiatives or changes to immigration law did not set Council apart from the other groups with which it was allied; indeed, work on such issues brought Council into ever closer contact with prominent female reformers.

Given Council's alliance with these women's groups, it is not surprising that the organization opposed the Equal Rights Amendment (ERA) put forward by the National Woman's Party (NWP). After the ratification of the Nineteenth Amendment, feminists split into two broadly defined camps. As the National American Woman's Suffrage Association (NAWSA) transformed itself into the nonpartisan League of Women Voters, the more radical women in the NWP continued their battle for women's rights by supporting the ERA. The ERA divided the movement between women whose energies were focused primarily on achieving equality for women and those whose activism encompassed a broader array of reform initiatives. Social reformers, Council included, feared that the success of such an amendment would lead to the demise of protective labor legislation for women. The NCJW's participation in this debate has been overlooked by scholars of American women's history as well by recent chroniclers of Council itself. This neglect has contributed to the impression that the NCJW was a much more conservative, less feminist organization than its own leaders considered it to be.[24]

Council's anti-ERA stance sheds light on how the leadership struggled to maintain a position on women's rights that recognized gender difference while still affirming female equality. In 1924 Therese M. Loeb wrote a lengthy article explaining the organization's position as articulated at the previous year's national meeting. Although the resolution Loeb discussed in her article proved not to be the version approved by the triennial, its wording clearly shows the organization's embrace of both women's equality and the idea of inherent gender difference. Stating that women "now have freedom and power to strive effectively for life more ideal in every aspect, social, legal, industrial, political and educational," the resolution nevertheless concluded that "women are by nature essentially different from men." Council, Loeb argued, opposed the ERA because it sought to establish "compulsory equality," overlooking the physical differences between the sexes and the "divergence of powers and duties which inevitably arise therefrom." Yet Loeb asserted that while the NCJW hoped the amendment would not be ratified, it still wanted to find a way to "gain for us all of its unchallenged benefits."[25] Like some other feminists of the era who opposed the NWP stance, including the National Council of Negro Women, Council leaders struggled to find a way to recognize women's individuality and equal capacity to men while recognizing that gender difference affected work and private lives.[26]

But Council's opposition to the ERA did not entirely mimic that of other women's groups. An added layer of opposition emerged in Council's fear of the potentially negative consequences the measure might have on immigrant women, a point not strenuously raised by other groups. In 1925 a Council representative testified before the House Judiciary Committee on the harm the ERA could bring to immigrant women, most notably through changes to laws affecting parental guardianship and support payments to women. Believing that the ERA would bring more confusion to the lives of people who already faced great turmoil and dislocation, Council's representative argued that "we feel that the passage of an amendment so revolutionary as the one under consideration would make for insecurity and chaotic conditions, not only in the home and family, but also in the courts of justice."[27]

Council's commitment to protecting the interests of immigrant women and their children was one of the primary ways it expressed its devotion to Jews and promoted its version of American Jewish identity. Involved in aiding immigrants for some thirty years, Council stepped up its programs for these women in the wake of the dramatic changes affecting American women in the postwar period. Revisions to citizenship legislation, the granting of female suffrage, and restrictive immigration laws aimed, in part, at keeping Eastern European Jews from entering the United States, all intensified Council's interest in Americanization efforts. Americanization had long been an implicit element of Council's program, but, during World War I and in the era of "100 percent Americanism" the group, like similar gentile organizations, became even more dedicated to this work. Following the 1922 passage of the Cable Act, which made a woman's citizenship status independent of her husband's and thereby required naturalization for the wives of immigrants, Council instituted citizenship courses for this population. Yet unlike gentile Americanizers, Council diligently persuaded naturalized women that their duty to their new nation extended beyond the attainment of citizenship to active participation in public life through voting and club work.[28]

Council believed that its cooperation with non-Jewish

women's organizations helped in its efforts to integrate immigrants into American life. Rose Brenner, president from 1920 to 1926, had a great interest in this integrative function of her organization; she was not coincidentally one of the leaders most firmly opposed to the NCJW formally embracing Zionism. During her tenure she wrote several articles outlining Council's crucial mission not only to Americanize Jewish immigrants but also to provide gentile women with a more realistic image of Jews and Judaism, advocating organizational work as a means to accomplishing both these goals. Even such seemingly mundane tasks as writing memos or arranging small meetings, she argued, taught women the skills necessary for them to join other, even non-Jewish, groups. In doing so Council, she believed, facilitated the acceptance of Jews, especially the foreign-born, into American life more broadly: "For the responsibility resting on the Council is not only the training of its own members, but the preparation for American life of the great body of foreign-born women, of the town and the farm, whose psychology is best understood and whose hearts are most tenderly sounded by their sister Jewesses."[29]

Brenner later elaborated on these concepts in an article titled, "The Great Interpreter." Fearing that the majority of gentile Americans still considered their Jewish neighbors as foreigners with only a weak grasp of the English language and American culture, she insisted that the Council needed to "interpret" Jews to the rest of America. Lately, she stated, Jews had been popularly depicted in such a way that "the Jew as we know him, and Judaism as we love and follow it, seem altogether unfamiliar to the mass of American people." She recalled how a New York City public school teacher had recently complimented her for speaking English "without an accent." Far from taking offense, Brenner excused the woman's comment, noting that "she might very well have received [her impression of Jews] from a perusal of stories and sketches of our own Montague Glasses and Fannie Hursts"—writers who presented immigrant Jews in a less than favorable light. Referring to Glass's characters in particular, Brenner proudly noted that the Council ensured that his "Potashes and Perlmutters have not usurped all the interpretive functions."[30] Jewish leaders such as Rose Brenner wanted to present an acculturated and, to their minds, fully American image to the non-Jewish world with which they interacted. For Brenner and others in the NCJW, the major goal of the organization was to serve as cultural interpreters—intermediaries between the gentile majority and the immigrant Jewish minority.

But interest in civic and political life had its limitations. The group continued to studiously avoid discussion of "controversial" issues, even as it opposed the ERA, advocated for peace, favored U.S. entry into the League of Nations, and opposed immigration restrictions. To the Council leaders of the 1920s, "controversial" topics equated most frequently with Zionism or antisemitism—subjects that might highlight Jewish nationalism or distinctiveness. One member, Rebecca Long, erupted in sarcasm at the 1923 Triennial after being told she could not discuss the KKK at the meeting:

> Perhaps I'm sometimes sorry that my name is not Rebecca Levy. . . . Then, to the Ku Klux [sic], it would at once square off the limitations of my usefulness and end cordiality before it had begun. It would spare me the temptation to take him unaware and when close quartered in his affections and approved in his service, to save him from almost believing that one can be well-bred and honest and still be a Jew.
>
> Sometimes I'm sorry that I am not a Russian or a Polish Jew—a newcomer with the still clear experience of the practice of pogrom. But—thank God for the Ku Klux if he makes swift work of our softness and soullessness. Oh, Ku Klux! You have taken me and bumped my head until, thank God, I can again see stars!

Her comments were enthusiastically cheered.[31] Long's and the audience's reaction to the ban on "controversy" reveals the ambivalence some NCJW members felt about their leaders' insistence on acculturation at all costs. Here, Rebecca Long acerbically laments the fact that she lacks the distinctiveness of the more recent arrivals, the very distinctiveness Brenner and others aimed to eradicate. Moreover, she chides her leaders for trying to deny the presence of antisemitism in America. Other voices of discontent joined Long's to complain about the national leadership's stance. An editorial in a Pittsburgh Jewish paper questioned whether the group had gone too far in seeking to be like other non-Jewish, American women's organizations. The editorial argued that the NCJW's program was so broad "that those questions which are essentially Jewish do not receive the maximum consideration." Although the editors congratulated Council for having promoted greater unity among American Jews, they concluded that "we are inclined to believe that the NCJW is undertaking to do too much and it is adventuring into fields that do not require JEWISH attention so much as [do] JEWISH PROBLEMS" [capitals in the original].[32]

During the 1920s, Council leadership moved their organization into the mainstream of American women's political activism. While some members and Jewish observers feared that the NCJW had begun to drift from its Jewish roots, most Council leaders disagreed, arguing that the organization's involvement in political work helped "interpret" Jewish culture to the non-Jewish majority while at the same time aiding Jewish women in the United States and overseas. The NCJW leadership did not see a contradiction in advancing Jewish, American, and women's causes, but rather promoted all three simultaneously. Hadassah leaders took a decidedly different path in the 1920s. Where the NCJW fostered connections to other American women's organizations, Hadassah turned its attention to Zionist women at home and abroad as it had begun to do during the war years. Fully committed to their American identity, Hadassah leaders opted to turn their attention overseas, exploring how American Jewish women could advance the cause of their counterparts in Palestine and in the Zionist movement more broadly.

Hadassah and Zionist Women's Issues

Unlike the NCJW, Hadassah infrequently mentioned U.S. politics following the conclusion of World War I. In one rare case, the *Newsletter* drew attention to the proposed immigration restrictions of 1924, but other than that the paper scarcely noted the world outside Palestine and Zionism. More frequently, published accounts focused readers' attention on life in Palestine and Hadassah's own growing list of accomplishments. At the same time they highlighted success, leaders also underscored the need for continued struggle. Despite Hadassah's and other Zionists' work, Henrietta Szold told her members in 1923, life in Palestine remained "primitive." Many homes had no modern appliances, and Jewish women remained legally unequal to men. Szold laid the greatest blame for women's legal status on the rabbinical establishment, whose ideas, she believed, lagged behind even "Mohammedan law."[33]

By the mid-1920s one of the major issues facing Jewish women in Palestine was whether they would be allowed to vote and hold office in the Mandate government established by the British authorities. Under the British Mandate, the religious communities in Palestine were organized into elected, administrative bodies. Immigrant Jews, who had tended to retain their native citizenship under Ottoman rule, instantly grew more involved in politics. With this newly awakened engagement came growing division as Orthodox elements vociferously spoke out against allowing women to vote and hold office. From 1918 to 1920 the various secular and religious factions deliberated over the question of women's suffrage. In response to this unsettled situation, Rosa Welt-Straus, mother of Hadassah's Nellie Straus Mochenson, joined other women in forming the Palestine Jewish Women's Equal Rights Association (PJW-ERA) in 1918. The association battled against anti-suffrage forces and eventually secured women's right to vote and hold office in the national assembly elected in April 1920.[34]

But these rights were far from assured. Conservative elements in Palestine continued to agitate for women's disenfranchisement even after the 1920 election, going so far as to walk out of the assembly's first session after other delegates denied their request to hold a second election without women. Polish Zionist Puah Rakovsky recalled that the Orthodox "demanded categorically the 'liquidation' of the women."[35] Late in 1923 the moderate Orthodox faction *Mizrachi* began to lobby for a male-only referendum on whether women should be allowed to vote. Women in the Equal Rights Association were incensed that such a referendum was even considered, and Rosa Welt-Straus contacted Hadassah, among other women's organizations, urging these groups to publicly oppose the measures.[36] Haddasah women immediately joined the battle, sending telegrams to influential people and printing their organizational position in Palestine newspapers. At the July 1925 convention, Hadassah unanimously adopted a resolution urging the Fourteenth Zionist Congress to uphold women's suffrage in the National Assembly. In August of that year the *Newsletter* reported that the Equal Rights Association had again called on the women of the world to press the Jewish government to oppose continuing

Orthodox attempts to revoke women's suffrage.[37] All this work did some good given that, in Rakovsky's words, "the demand[s] by Hadassah in North America carried serious weight."[38]

As negative publicity surrounding the referendum mounted, groups supporting the measure began to disagree on technicalities—whether women should be allowed to participate in the referendum, for instance. Some Orthodox men started to back away from the issue, stating that the only referendum they would support was one in which all rabbis took part. Yet many Orthodox rabbis refused to vote, asserting that any referendum on women's suffrage was meaningless because Jewish law clearly stood opposed to women's equal rights with men, and therefore no secular referendum could comment further on the issue.[39] Eventually the Mizrachi and others agreed to hold a referendum in which the women could take part, although the ultra-Orthodox *Haredi* party remained firmly opposed. Despite the partial compromise worked out by Mizrachi, the referendum was never held. Puah Rakovsky attributes the defeat in large part to female assembly delegates who pointed out how Mizrachi had first "appealed to Orthodox women to participate in the [1920] election on behalf of the Torah, and then the same Mizrachi spokesmen supported a strict ban against the participation of women in our national institution, once again on the basis of our holy Torah."[40] After the Haredi party fell apart due to internal disputes, women increased their representation in the government and eventually secured their legal equality. In April 1926 Hadassah announced triumphantly, "Jewish National Assembly Proclaims Equal Rights," citing the government's declaration in January that women had obtained civil, political and economic equality. The policy was ratified a year later by the Mandate authorities in the constitution of *Knesset Israel* (community of Israel).[41]

The activism on behalf of women's suffrage amounted to only a fraction of Hadassah's involvement with a growing network of women's groups in Palestine. Shortly after World War I many of these organizations joined together in the *Histadrut Nashim Ivriot* or Jewish Women's Organization (JWO). Formalized in 1924 as a federation of various women's associations, the group worked in a variety of areas, including social welfare, maternal and infant health, and job training. From the outset it had difficulty raising funds and so turned to the major Diaspora women's groups, Hadassah and the Women's International Zionist Organization (WIZO), for assistance. Hadassah paid particular attention to the JWO's health care projects and helped in this arena.[42] Yet in a short time confusion arose over funding and jurisdictional issues. As the JWO requested ever greater financial input from Hadassah, the American women demanded that their organization's contribution to the JWO infant centers be more explicitly acknowledged, particularly since Hadassah women considered this work that they had originated.[43] Because it was continuing its battles with the Zionist Organization of America (ZOA), Hadassah guarded its organizational autonomy closely, insisting on public recognition for work it developed and underwrote. Despite growing frustration, leaders nevertheless resisted overwhelming the JWO with an American presence. While not entirely opposed to Diaspora women assisting initially with the new organization's work, some leaders maintained that the JWO should be an "organic product of the land," not a Palestine chapter of Hadassah, financed and led by American women.[44] Others, however, urged affiliation between the two groups, particularly after it became apparent that WIZO itself was pursuing this goal.

Founded in Great Britain in 1920, WIZO was composed of many smaller women's Zionist groups throughout Europe. From the outset WIZO was not as strongly or effectively organized as the American women's group, despite its close connection to the World Zionist Organization (WZO), whose leader Chaim Weizmann was married to the head of the women's group. Although originally it seemed that WIZO and Hadassah might unite, most Hadassah leaders had little desire to attach their organization to the weaker European association. Underlying this sentiment was their commitment not to subordinate Hadassah to the ZOA, Keren Hayesod, or the WZO, with which these women felt WIZO was already too closely aligned. Furthermore, in their minds, WIZO did not allow Palestine women to run their own projects. In 1923 Henrietta Szold opined that WIZO had not been very successful because the most productive women working in Palestine still had to send their plans to London for first approval. Szold's implication was that the central office maintained too much control over the Palestine work; ironically, this was a charge often leveled against Hadassah itself. Still, noting WIZO's intent to formalize its connection to the JWO, Szold warned that Hadassah could ill afford not to create "some sort of relation with the W.I.Z.O." Szold wanted to avoid Hadassah's marginalization both in Palestine and the inner circles of Zionist politics, recognizing as she did WIZO's close ties to the international male leadership.[45] Her political acumen led her to advocate separation, but one that would incorporate a great deal of cooperation between the rival organizations.

Aside from personal connections to the male leadership of the World Zionist Organization, WIZO also gained leverage in the international movement by engaging in agricultural projects, work more in line with the movement's conception of appropriate Zionist activities. Programs like these supported the pioneers and underscored the idea that WIZO was helping to create a "New Jewish Woman" who would take her place alongside the "New Jewish Man," both strong farmers who turned their wills to building the nation. Hadassah's work in the urban areas and with the poor appeared bourgeois and philanthropic alongside these physical and nominally more Zionist initiatives.[46] Hadassah leaders in Palestine bridled at suggestions that, compared to WIZO, their group was insufficiently Zionist. Nellie Straus Mochenson complained about a visit from a man who declared himself to be the organizer of "our friends in Yanish[i]k," that Lithuanian town where local women had opted to affiliate, at least initially, with Hadassah. This organizer confidently informed her that WIZO had Zionist credibility while Hadassah most decidedly did not. Although Mochenson vigorously disagreed with him "he smiled the . . . omniscient smile of a Yiddish speaking propagandist and said that for the purposes of propaganda Hadassah was not a Zionist Organization." In defending Hadassah, Mochenson openly challenged the European perspective on what constituted legitimate Zionist work.[47]

This conversation emphasizes another problem between the two groups: organizational territory. Mochenson's visitor had wanted her to help him break the attachment the Yanishik women felt to Hadassah. Although Hadassah itself had urged these women to support their own Palestine work directly and requested that they no longer forward money to the New York offices, Mochenson hesitated to turn the fledgling group entirely over to WIZO. She wrote Alice Seligsberg that she was reluctant to help this man establish contacts with any other women's groups in Lithuania until Hadassah's relationship with WIZO was clearly defined, stating that "I consider it extremely bad policy to give them a handle of this sort."[48] Mochenson did not want to forsake the idea that Hadassah might recruit chapters in Europe, at least until Hadassah and WIZO had officially clarified the exact nature of the "cooperation" advocated by Szold. Indeed, Nellie Straus Mochenson believed that Hadassah should not cooperate with WIZO at all. Even before her exchange with the Yiddish "propagandist" she told Alice Seligsberg that she had written Szold twice to convey her objections: "She surely thinks I have an obsession on the subject—to tell her how much I disapprove of Hadassah's allying itself in any way with the W.I.Z.O." Believing that Hadassah, the more effective of the two organizations, could forge productive bonds with non-American women, Mochenson argued that it should resist succumbing to the Zionist movement's devaluation of its work or its place in the world movement.[49]

Other Hadassah members, opposing Mochenson, advocated closer relations with WIZO than even Szold herself proposed. These women contended that Szold, far from being too welcoming of WIZO, was needlessly worrying about its potential to dominate Hadassah. One delegate to the 1923 convention declared that WIZO had accomplished little of import and, thus, she believed its leadership would welcome any assistance Hadassah offered with "open arms." "We are the rich 'Mrs. Hadassah,'" she said, implying that WIZO would find it hard to turn down Hadassah's financial assistance and that such contributions would give Hadassah some clout in the group. Szold disagreed, and the proposal was not carried forward. The issue, however, did not die. Two years later delegates introduced a similar resolution, one that surely ignited the worst fears of women like Nellie Straus Mochenson. Henrietta Szold opposed this second measure just as she fought any move that threatened to resubmerge Hadassah within another Zionist organization. Having just achieved a modicum of autonomy from the ZOA, the major leaders were unlikely to relinquish their independence again so willingly, even to another women's organization.[50] In the end, the two women's groups agreed that Hadassah would maintain responsibility for Zionist work among American women, leaving Zionist organizing in the rest of the world to WIZO. Ever one to cut to the chase, Rose Jacobs sarcastically described this arrangement as a Zionist version of the "Monroe Doctrine."[51]

Other issues beyond alliances with the male movement, perceptions of appropriate Zionist work, and recruitment of new members complicated interactions between Hadassah and WIZO. The American women's success in Palestine contributed to the often tense relations, since Hadassah's effectiveness in Palestine could not help but draw the attention of European women interested in supporting practical Zionist work. In 1923 Nellie Straus Mochenson reported from the World Congress of Jewish Women in Vienna how startled she was that "women from all over complained about the W.I.Z.O." They told her that, to their minds, all WIZO did was meddle and interfere with their ability to establish direct contact with Palestine. Some women pleaded with Mochenson to send them a monthly newsletter that would inform them of "what was really going on" in Palestine and how they might be of use. While she wanted to help them she could not envision a way to do so without being insubordinate to WIZO—"(a thing I should dearly love to do, but am withheld from by thoughts of Miss Szold's organisation principle)."[52] Szold's desire to maintain cordial relations, along with the Hadassah's later assent to the Zionist "Monroe Doctrine," prevented women like Mochenson from moving Hadassah onto the international plane of organizing.

Without a clear articulation of its connection to WIZO or even consensus among the leadership regarding what Hadassah's relationship to it should be, the two groups were destined to run into trouble in Palestine. Confusion regarding their respective connections to the JWO only inflamed the problems. When the three groups decided to produce a journal, *Ha-Ishah* (The woman), these troubles came to a head. *Ha-Ishah* was envisioned as a monthly publication to acquaint women around the world with female activism in Palestine. The articles were to be primarily in Hebrew, with occasional material written in English or German. Initially WIZO vetoed the plan for Diaspora women to finance the journal, but in August 1925 it consented to fund part of the project. By November of that year, however, the WIZO leadership reneged on its support and withheld the promised funding for six months.[53] Possibly in light of this frustrating turn of events, Szold, in her capacity as Hadassah president, requested that the JWO list Hadassah as an equal publisher since, according to her, the very idea for the journal had originated "with us."[54] Regardless of billing apportionment, after much delay the journal eventually appeared as a joint venture. Relations between the three sets of women, however, grew more strained.

Given WIZO's lukewarm support, the journal quickly encountered serious financial difficulties. The Palestine women could not garner enough advertising or subscribers to keep *Ha-Ishah* solvent, and neither WIZO nor Hadassah allowed the JWO to raise funds outside of Palestine. Soon the JWO women complained that even Hadassah had grown disinterested in subsidizing the journal. Relating to a colleague that the JWO believed Hadassah expected one-half the credit though it failed to perform one-half of the work, Szold admitted that there might be some truth to the claim. Despite her earlier advocacy of a strong Hadassah presence in producing the journal, Szold hesitated when the Palestine women wanted to find new subscribers in the United States. "Why they do not look to Poland and Galicia, which we have always been told are countries so much more Jewishly intelligent than we are in America, I do not know," she remarked, referring to the general movement's perception that Hadassah women—and by extension all American women—were insufficiently Zionist.[55] Moreover, she surely tired of WIZO attempts to coopt the JWO even as it left one of the group's major endeavors in dire financial straits. By 1929, Hadassah leaders, aggravated by the complex and problematic negotiations with both the JWO and WIZO, voted to terminate their portion of *Ha-Ishah*'s funding.[56]

At about the same time that Hadassah dropped out of *Ha-Ishah*, the JWO and WIZO moved forward with serious negotiations aimed at unifying the two groups. Some Hadassah women, jealous of WIZO and fearing that it would succeed in becoming the primary, and perhaps eventually the sole, women's Zionist organization in Palestine, felt that Hadassah should compete with WIZO for the JWO affiliation. Rose Jacobs, for instance, later commented that Hadassah should have pursued a union more aggressively in order to curtail WIZO's ambition to be the "spokesman [for female Zionists] in the total international picture." Henrietta Szold and others rejected this position, stating that they did not want to interfere in private negotiations between the two groups. In the end, Hadassah stood by and watched as the JWO formally joined the WIZO as its Palestine branch in the early 1930s.[57] Hadassah maintained its presence as an American organization responsible for medical work in Palestine but forfeited the chance to become the heart of an international movement.

Due to turf battles, internal disputes within the Zionist community, and Hadassah's fear of losing its autonomy, the American group's attempts to reach out to other Zionist women did not prove as fruitful or as seamless as did Council's interactions with gentile Americans. Following their failure to reach a workable compromise with the JWO and WIZO, Hadassah leaders focused their energies on fortifying their own organization. In order to prove itself a strong Zionist organization, able to withstand the encroachment of both the male-led ZOA and the female-led WIZO, Hadassah needed to sustain its own unique program and build its membership. For all these reasons, throughout the 1920s Hadassah vigorously pursued recruitment efforts among the non-Zionist American population, especially members of the rival American Jewish women's organization, the NCJW.

Recruiting American Women to Zionism

Both Council and Hadassah strove for large membership rolls in order to keep revenue streams constant and enhance their own power in Jewish organizational life. Throughout the 1920s the two groups sponsored numerous membership campaigns that ultimately strained relations between the leaderships, as each vied to promote most effectively its own vision of American Jewish women's identity and subsequent public role. These two visions necessarily conflicted, given the NCJW leadership's stance regarding Zionism and that ideology's centrality to the lives to Hadassah women.

Conflict also resulted because both groups bluntly asserted their intention to enroll every American Jewish women in their own organization. In 1921, for instance, the NCJW proudly announced in the inaugural edition of its journal, the *Jewish Woman*, that it would "endeavor to introduce every Jewish woman in our communities to affiliate with us."[58] Such exhortations seem not to have done the trick; later the Extension Committee blatantly linked Council's very survival to its members' capacity to recruit others. An advertisement in 1924 warned members that "The Need of the National is Urgent! Can your Section afford to jeopardize our broad program by failing to meet your quota?" These campaigns continued throughout the decade as Council sought to maintain its preeminence among American Jewish women.[59] Hadassah used similar methods to increase its membership during the 1920s when it pledged to make "every woman a Hadassah woman." Henrietta Szold candidly tied the need for new members to the organization's demands for greater sums of money. At one point, responding to sustained criticism that Hadassah was not serious or Zionist enough and focused too much attention on bourgeois women, Szold wrote a friend that "if we did not penetrate into non-Zionist circles, it would be impossible to raise the huge sums we do raise. . . . It might be advantageous for some of the ladies [in Palestine] to come over here and take a hand in the 'black work' of collecting funds."[60]

Despite Szold's frustration, Hadassah saw its membership drives as more than a means by which to augment its own coffers. Announcing a drive late in 1926 to increase membership, the *Newsletter* asserted that there were thousands of women in America who "must be changed from passive, if amiable, spectators into collaborators in the upbuilding of Palestine."[61] The desire to build membership was inextricably linked to the group's commitment to promoting Zionism. Just as fund-raising laid the foundation for life in Palestine, new membership solidified the place of Zionism in the United States. Indeed, one led to the other. Henrietta Szold believed that fund-raising helped the Zionist mission because "where money goes the heart follows."[62] Women might start out apolitical, uncommitted to Zionism per se, but through their increasing interest in helping Jews overseas, Hadassah leaders believed, they could be persuaded to support Zionism. This strategy, however successful it proved, necessarily brought them into conflict with NCJW leaders who resented Hadassah's attempts to lure away their members.

Shrewdly understanding that middle-class American women, like those in Council, might be easier to reach through methods that downplayed an overt attachment to controversial political ideologies, Hadassah leaders focused recruitment efforts around ventures that united women in both groups, such as immigrant aid, health care, and social work. The Chicago chapter's plan to solicit donations from a variety of sources, even non-Jews, illustrates the organization's attempt to place its work within the broader context of international relief. Having grown weary of ceaseless fund-raising drives and the expense they entailed, the Chicago chapter studied the methods of nonsectarian relief organizations and concluded that "if people all over the world, and so many Jewish people, contribute to the Red Cross for health work, we have a perfect right to appeal to Jews to contribute to health work in Palestine." Members set out across the city asking individuals and organizations for donations, presenting Hadassah's Palestine work in this apolitical, nonsectarian manner. With the first drive they raised $6,500, spending a mere $200, and in 1923 brought in $12,000, with an outlay of only $300. The success in Chicago led the national convention to urge Hadassah's board to "aid the Chapters in securing annual contributors to Hadassah, Zionist or non-Zionist, Jewish and non-Jewish, as the case may be."[63] The advancement of Hadassah's work as nonpartisan at heart, embracing health and welfare initiatives but not political ideology, proved an expeditious means of raising money.

Well before this national commitment to raising funds among non-Zionists and even non-Jews, the leaders had begun to advocate making contact with other middle-class Jewish women. Informal meetings, they averred, were among the best means by which to bring non-Zionist women slowly into the movement. Criticizing the large-scale efforts of the male-led Zionist movement, Hadassah leaders argued that most people did not join Zionism at "much-lauded mass meetings" but rather through routine participation in small groups. Particularly during the war years, Hadassah leaders counseled members to reach out to others through a shared interest in relief activities. Large numbers of women, they argued, might be persuaded to assist Hadassah with relief work despite their reluctance to embrace Zionism forthrightly. With time, leaders believed, such sympathetic women would "perceive that there is a greater task before them than that of providing raiment for the children of Palestine—that of providing a home for the Children of Israel."[64] By using such gendered strategies, talking to women one on one and asking them to participate in relief work for Jews in

Europe and Palestine, Zionist women could indirectly influence the newcomers.

The most effective means of promoting non-Zionist involvement in Hadassah's work was through the sewing circles, groups that provided clothing for those in Palestine. Pittsburgh and Chicago claimed the two largest and most organized of these circles, and both included Council members. Realizing the utility of these circles for recruitment, Hadassah leaders urged every chapter to start one. By attracting women with such seemingly apolitical and unideological work as preparing infants' clothes to send overseas, Hadassah activists could introduce non-Zionist Jewish women to their ideals in a relaxed and nonthreatening atmosphere. The group realized great success with such efforts. In 1926 Ruth Cohen noted that "in many Jewish women's organizations not under the auspices of Hadassah the sewing circle is the only link with Palestine. It is often the e[n]tering wedge for Hadassah in a city and the kernel about which the whole chapter is built." Hadassah reported 547 sewing circles acting in cooperation with the Palestine Supplies Department in 1924; among these were twenty-five sections of the NCJW, even though the national leadership still refused to take an official position on Zionism. By 1927 more than 700 sewing circles existed throughout the United States, and over the course of ten years they contributed some $500,000 in goods and donations to Palestine.[65] The sewing circles proved invaluable in terms of monetary and material sustenance, but also, and more importantly, they introduced potential members to Hadassah's work. Commenting on the success of the sewing circle as a recruitment tool, Hadassah leaders proudly proclaimed in January 1927 that "there is a 'Hadassah-spirit,' a spirit of harmony and unification which has attracted women from all ranks, even anti-Zionist women, and has made of them first, Hadassahites, and then convinced Zionists, to whom nothing Jewish in Palestine or outside Palestine is strange."[66]

Drawing on the success of the sewing circle model, in 1923 a Hadassah committee began to devise plans aimed at encouraging collaboration on Palestine work with other national Jewish women's organizations.[67] The next year Henrietta Szold bluntly asked her members, "how can we interpenetrate the other Jewish women's organizations?" Aware that sections of the NCJW and other groups had been cooperating with Hadassah on the local level for years, she proposed that the national office keep a table listing the major Jewish women's organizations and noting the extent of collaboration taking place between Hadassah and local sections. Armed with incontrovertible evidence of rank-and-file support for Zionist projects, Hadassah's national leadership could request that these groups take an official position on Zionism. Stressing the common theme inherent in all Hadassah's recruitment campaigns, Szold asserted that "we must work from below upwards." Singling out the NCJW in describing her proposal, Szold argued that if it could be shown that ninety of the 120 Council sections supported Zionism, the NCJW national leadership would be hard pressed to continue its reticence on the subject.[68]

They soon realized they had a difficult task before them. At the 1924 convention a Boston delegate reported that Council had recently passed a resolution limiting the sums it dispensed to outside groups. Arguing that Hadassah's work was apolitical and nonsectarian, and thus not dissimilar from Council's own program, she appealed to the NCJW for funding. However, her efforts did not result in success. Her account touched off a round of grumbling at the convention with some delegates referring to Council women as having "stone hearts," which prompted a woman with ties to both organizations to demand the floor. Stating that such opinions forced her, a Council member for twenty-four years, to "analyze my heart," she concluded that "it was beating and I was certain it wasn't stone." She further asserted that some ninety-five percent of the delegates to this Hadassah convention also held membership in the NCJW. Although this was surely an inflated figure, her perception nevertheless reflected the high level of cooperation taking place between the two groups. The delegate concluded by asserting that although Council as an organization failed to support Zionism, its members joined in Hadassah's Zionist work on an individual basis.[69] Throughout the 1920s Hadassah's *Newsletter* reveals an observable growth in local chapters reporting cooperation with Council sections, testifying to the success of Hadassah's efforts to "interpenetrate" other Jewish women's groups, especially the "stone-hearted" NCJW.

One city where cooperation between the groups proceeded apace was Pittsburgh; indeed support for Zionism was strong throughout western Pennsylvania. In 1924 NCJW sections from this region passed a resolution urging the national office to meet with Hadassah national leaders, affirming the similarity between the work of both groups. This resolution led to a meeting between Henrietta Szold, Rose Jacobs, Council President Rose Brenner, and Executive Secretary Estelle Sternberger early the next year. Although the Hadassah board reported that the meeting was "amicable," they concluded that "no hope of immediate participation in Palestine work was held out." Their official spin on the event, later presented in the *Newsletter*, nevertheless assured readers that "such occurrences herald a time when it will be recognized that Palestine, the center of Jewish life, is the concern of all Jews."[70]

Rose Brenner presented a much cooler version of the meeting to her own board in November 1925. Indeed, the text of her presentation makes it clear that she felt the meeting should never have taken place at all. She privately noted that it had occurred only because the Pennsylvania sections had "most unwisely" passed a resolution requesting it. "A long and amicable conversation was held," she concluded publicly, "and clearly demonstrated that Hadassah's work has no place in the program of the National Council." She further insisted that these organizations could maintain friendly relations only when each confined itself to its own sphere of activity. Surely aiming to remind the upstart sections of Council's purview, Brenner asked the board to endorse a policy reiterating the group's dedication to "the Jewish woman, in America, AND ON HER WAY TO AMERICA; . . ." [capital letters in the original], emphasizing the fact that Council was an organization concerned with American Jews.[71] While World War I heightened the group's interest in international affairs, the official program was to remain limited to projects connected to the United States, not Palestine. Brenner condoned political work that formed a part of the social reform agenda of similar American women's groups, but she abjured all appeals for Council to consider involvement in Zionist work. Her position suffered when Hadassah did its best to present its own work as "philanthropic" or noncontroversial, rather than "political." Brenner could not ignore the Pennsylvania sections, which in 1925 claimed the largest number of sections per state in the nation. And by 1925 the Council leadership could no longer ignore Hadassah or Zionism either.[72]

Throughout the 1920s, Hadassah continued recruiting locally, bringing Council women into cooperative projects and thereby encouraging them to join the organization directly. To reduce conflict with the NCJW national office, Hadassah leaders employed language, patterned after Rose Brenner's, that advanced the notion of a noncompetitive partnership between the two groups. In 1926 Hadassah President Irma Lindheim sent greetings to Council's triennial, claiming that Council and Hadassah pursued comparable work but in distinct arenas: where Council helped immigrants on their way to the United States, Hadassah brought aid to immigrants settling in Palestine. "May a strong bond unite these two great sisters organizations," she proclaimed. "In the purposes which they share in common let them cooperate, in the purposes which are specifically their own, let them complement each other."[73] Borrowing Brenner's message to undercut her ultimate intent, Lindheim argued that Council and Hadassah did not have to compete. Together they could aid Jewish women throughout the world.

In a symposium on "Cooperation Among National Women's Organizations" published in the *Jewish Woman* in 1928 NCJW President Ida W. Friend argued that Jewish women's organizations needed to develop mechanisms to avoid duplication in fulfilling their general goals. Yet the example she set forth supporting her ideas exuded not a little disdain for life in Palestine. Presenting a tale of one woman to illustrate how Jewish organizations could work together, she described a Jewish girl in Palestine who had received Hadassah's assistance but wanted to go to the United States to find her fiancé. Council provided the young woman with advice on immigration, helped her to locate her fiancé, and eventually settled them in the United States. After introducing the young woman to the local section of the National Federation of Temple Sisterhoods, Friend stated that "we thus have the completed circle of co-operation in which each organization within its sphere has contributed to the happiness of a deserving sister who without such aid might still be languishing in a distant village of Palestine."[74] While the overall goal was to reduce overlap, it seems another implicit aspiration of the NCJW was to help young women leave Palestine, not emigrate there.

President Friend's anecdote, along with Brenner's earlier

coolness to Hadassah in general, reflected a sense of distrust of Hadassah and its work common among a certain core of the NCJW leadership. While many of their rank and file were moving closer to Hadassah's ideals, some of the key leaders maintained a chilly distance, fearing both the loss of their ability to set their organization's political agenda and the loss of members to the Zionist group. Distrust arose particularly among those Council leaders who did not accept Hadassah's commitment to mutual cooperation as entirely sincere, believing that Hadassah wanted to augment its own membership rolls at any cost. At a 1927 board meeting Florina Lasker stated that "we may just as well be perfectly candid about the fact that Hadassah wants a good deal more than just moral support." Lillian Burkhart Goldsmith concurred, telling the board that for three years the southern California Council women had tried to involve Hadassah members in their work, but during that time only one Hadassah woman had offered any assistance. Most Hadassah members, Goldsmith insisted, refused to assist Council in any meaningful way.[75] Hadassah's recruitment tactics called for cooperation, but a cooperation with a definite end in mind: bringing more women to the Zionist movement. While they might pay lip service to helping the NCJW, in reality Hadassah women focused their considerable energies on building Palestine and bolstering the American Zionist movement, not helping Council.

By 1929 the Zionist women's group had achieved major success in bringing new members to the movement. At the start of the 1930s Hadassah rivaled the NCJW in size, claiming 44,000 members, an increase of 42,000 in only fourteen years. Hadassah proudly discussed instances of collaboration between the two groups in its "Chapter Notes" column. The analogous column in Council's publication, the *Jewish Woman*, remained silent about any Zionist activism in its sections. By the late 1920s, however, Council could no longer ignore Zionism as an issue of importance to American Jewish women. Even if it avoided advertising for Hadassah in its own pages, Council began to present more frequent stories on Zionist topics. Finally, late in 1929, several Council leaders attended Hadassah's convention, including Council President Ida W. Friend and Rebekah Kohut. At this convention, Kohut was elected to Hadassah's national board. The following year a Hadassah representative was invited to attend a Council triennial for the first time ever.[76]

Events on the international stage abetted these changes. In 1929 Arab riots in Palestine left 125 Jews dead, and many American Jews began to take a greater interest in preserving the safety of that community. Rebekah Kohut declared that the riots "broke down this great big fence that divided the Zionists from the anti- or non-Zionists. We rushed right in with our money to help them. It was the kind of picture that we have known, of one Father, and that we are all brothers and sisters."[77] The philanthropic activism of the war years kicked into action once again as American Jews saw their coreligionists threatened.

Where women like Brenner and her colleagues might question the political ramifications of Zionism, other women in their organization had begun to see Zionist work as a continuation of their European agenda—aid to the Jewish people throughout the world. Their thoughts were influenced not only by Hadassah's shrewd and successful recruitment strategies and the terrible events in Palestine, but also by increasing contact their organization had with leading Jewish activists in Europe, many of whom were Zionists themselves. As the NCJW laid plans to revive an International Council of Jewish Women, their leaders found the issue of Zionism nearly impossible to keep off the table. Despite their best efforts to mold an international organization in the image of its American originator, Council leaders could not arrest the growing international interest in Zionism.

World Congress of Jewish Women

In 1912, during the International Council of Women (ICW) meeting in Rome, women from Europe and the United States formed the International Council of Jewish Women; however, this group did not survive the war years. Council's continued involvement in the ICW, along with Rebekah Kohut's dedicated efforts with the Reconstruction Unit reinvigorated ties between European and American Jewish women and renewed the call for an international organization. In November 1922, when the unit finished its mission in Europe, Elinor Sachs-Barr remained behind to finalize plans for a World Congress of Jewish Women to be held in Vienna in May 1923.[78]

In a pre-congress editorial in the *Jewish Woman,* NCJW Executive Secretary Estelle M. Sternberger affirmed the belief that a congress would strengthen the bonds between Jewish women around the world. In language starkly reminiscent of that used by Hadassah leaders as well as her own colleagues, Sternberger articulated the congress' goals in language emphasizing women's natural propensity for nurturing:

> It is the wearied and broken heart of Israel's unfortunate mothers and daughters that the women at Vienna will hold in their hands. Theirs will be the tender task of healing it with the balm of counsel and united service. The Jewess of Europe and the Jewess of America are to give expression, not only to the spiritual kinship that binds them together, but also to their mutual responsibility of caring for those who turn their pleading eyes to us for a blessed release from their perplexing agonies.

Valorizing what she perceived as women's natural aptitudes, Sternberger stated that the congress would "contribute [a] new chapter to the revelation of womanhood's power." Yet in affirming women's capacity for public work, she never lost sight of the fact that the primary function of the congress was to help fellow Jews. Despite allegations in the American Jewish community that the NCJW had become assimilated, Sternberger insisted that "this conference testifies that our women, wherever they may be, will never hide themselves from their own flesh and kindred—that they will ever dedicate themselves to the task of delivering our distressed sister from the vale of tears through the door of new hopes."[79]

Although seemingly united by gender, congress founders ignored many other facets of Jewish identity, most notably class. Middle-class and affluent women had devised ways to aid less fortunate Jews throughout the world, yet the recipients of their care were never considered equals, and they were not entertained as potential delegates to the congress. From its inception, this international gathering of Jewish women constructed boundaries demarcating what constituted a Jewish woman, or a leader of Jewish women. Ignored by congress organizers, socialist women in the United States returned the favor. The women's column of the Workmen's Circle, for instance, never mentioned the congress, even though its columnists frequently reported on the activities of a wide variety of women's groups, even if only to criticize them. While it might be argued that socialists would not have wanted to attend such a bourgeois event, the absence of Circle women, and especially their counterparts in Europe—the women of the Jewish Labor Bund—meant that their Diaspora nationalism would not receive a hearing at this international gathering.

The congress convened in Vienna in May 1923 amidst loud, antisemitic protests. Ninety delegates represented some twenty nations. Distinguished Europeans such as Viennese activist Anitta Müller-Cohen, Bertha Pappenheim of the Jüdischer Frauenbund, and Rosa Pomeranz Melzer, a social welfare activist and Zionist member of the Polish Parliament, attended on behalf of their countries, the vast majority of which were located in Western and Central Europe. Despite the antisemitic protests outside the hall, Dr. Michael Hainisch, president of the Austrian Republic, and his mother Maria, an early advocate for equal rights, both addressed the assembled women.[80]

Like the organizations after which it modeled itself, the congress tried to avoid divisive topics, including all sensitive political and religious matters. Congress chair Rebekah Kohut announced at the opening: "It might well be asked why we are optimists, when we see the helplessness of parliaments and national and international bodies showing an impotence which is most depressing, and we answer, because we have no political program—we are not fighting for self-aggrandisement or for any particular group." She vigorously asserted that what the congress was fighting for was peace. Sounding a common theme, Müller-Cohen wrote before the congress that "we women have a better programme than all politicians. We come with pure hearts and with warm sympathies. We are not fighting for power; we wish to promote the welfare and stability of our people." Both these women resembled their contemporaries in other women's organizations, believing that women had a special nature and unique ability to contribute to the public world.[81] Kohut and Müller-Cohen's assertion that women were not "political" enabled them to ignore the ways in which their decisions, and omissions, ultimately had political consequences.

Clearly it would have been impossible for the presenters to avoid all references to politics or religion. Presenters discussed

Jewish immigration, involvement in prostitution, the *Ostjudenfrage* (East European Jewish question), social services, Jewish education, and women's position in the Jewish community. While touching upon political and religious subjects, these presentations did not spark controversy since they were limited to topics long associated with middle-class Jewish women's organizational work. A few delegates managed to work in discussions of Zionism, definitely a controversial topic for this assembly, but they did so without mentioning the word itself.[82] Instead, they presented Zionism as the Palestine equivalent of social welfare projects conducted in New York, Amsterdam, Vienna, and Krakow: aid to the Jewish "family," not political nation-building.

One of these women, Nellie Straus Mochenson, privately expressed ambivalence toward the congress. She conceded it gave her the opportunity to interact with non-Zionist delegates and that this had probably helped the movement. But she questioned whether the proceedings had served any concrete purpose: "If it was merely a spiritual Turkish bath, like so many other assemblages of the kind, why then it seems a great extravagance." Perhaps her frustration arose from conversations with the likes of Amsterdam's Dina van Geldern, who proposed a resolution that the international organization to be created from the congress remain neutral on all political, religious, and philanthropic questions—surely an impossible goal to achieve.[83]

Despite Mochenson's fears that the congress had not produced tangible results, the delegates resolved to support Jewish settlement in Palestine. Mochenson played an important role in drafting and lobbying for the resolution, and she made a "deep impression on all delegates present," according to Rebekah Kohut. Kohut, in turn, most likely did more than her fair share of behind the scenes work guaranteeing that the resolution was adopted without a divisive debate, ever a goal of hers.[84] The resolution, like the presentations on Palestine, studiously avoided any mention of the word "Zionism," rather endorsing Jewish settlement in Palestine, asserting its importance for Jews around the world, and urging all Jewish women to help establish the basics requirements for life in that country. By building support for Zionism's projects while tabling the discussion of Zionism itself for the time being, the Congress's resolution paralleled Hadassah's recruitment strategies with non-

Zionist women in the United States. Happy though she was about the passage of the resolution, Mochenson described it as "luke warm, but nevertheless, . . . the first to be passed unanimously."[85]

Expressing great satisfaction with Mochenson's work, Henrietta Szold reminded Hadassah members back in the United States that Mochenson had only indirectly represented them in Vienna— as a Palestine representative whose trip was funded by Hadassah. Szold strongly urged them as an organization to play a more direct role in future international gatherings. With the American NCJW virtually running the congress and WIZO claiming an official presence, Hadassah's absence formally marginalized the American Zionist group, a situation leaders did not want to see repeated. Szold's comments reveal a heightened interest in the international women's community as Hadassah embarked on its struggles with WIZO while endeavoring to recruit NCJW members to Zionism.[86]

At the second World Congress of Jewish Women, convened in June 1929 in Hamburg, Germany, Hadassah President Irma Lindheim formally attended on behalf of her organization. As in 1923, the delegates represented the most active and influential Jewish women from the United States and Europe. While much remained constant from one congress to the next, a noticeable difference occurred in the treatment of the Zionist question, reflecting the growing interest in the movement despite the continued official silence from such groups as the NCJW and the Jüdischer Frauenbund.[87] The second congress saw a significant rise in the discussion of topics relating to Jewish settlement and life in Palestine. Austrian Zionist Anitta Müller-Cohen addressed the congress on "The Influence of Cultural Work in Palestine on Women," drawing responses from Lindheim and from the Zionist and Palestine resident Helene Hannah Thon. Rosa Welt-Straus discussed women's suffrage in that country. Colorfully noting that upon achieving the vote it was "wonderful to see, how the women in Jerusalem with child in arm and a cigarette in their mouths came to the ballot box," she reminded delegates that women's right to vote was still not secure. Although women had won equal rights in 1926, she feared that various forces opposed to women's suffrage would not rest until they had repealed the measure.[88] The breadth of topics covered relating to Palestine, as well as the prominence of Zionist women in the discussions and proceedings, speaks to the changing status of Zionism within the international Jewish women's community. This was no longer a topic to be avoided or supported only obliquely with vague phrases. Zionist women took their place alongside others at an international gathering debating Jewish women's status, problems, and possible solutions.

But greater acceptance of Zionism—even allowing for the mention of the word in discussions—did not mean that disagreement evaporated. One argument flared around whether to support the newly created Jewish Agency, an entity involving non-Zionists along with Zionists that would assist Jewish settlement in Palestine, though not, technically, a Jewish state. After a presentation by Irma Lindheim supporting the agency, Rebekah Kohut confessed a "secret"; namely, that she herself supported the Jewish Agency. Trying to quell discord, she concluded with a renewed appeal for peace and unity: "if some of you are against Zionism or the Agency or against some other things in our Jewish conditions, shall we not remember for all times, that we must all love and understand and respect each other?" Grete Bial from Breslau took center stage to disagree. She stated that she spoke on behalf of German Jews who, she said, felt they were German citizens and did not think that the "Jewish nation" existed solely in Palestine. Indeed, she pushed for greater clarification from the Zionists as to what precisely a "Jewish Homeland" in Palestine meant. Another prominent German, Paula Ollendorf, supported Bial. Underscoring the anti-Zionist perspective, she contended that just as American Jews thought themselves "100 percent American" and "100 percent Jewish," so German Jews felt about their nation. "But," she concluded, "as I already said to a good friend of mine in the United States: if I were ever to become a Zionist it could only be within the framework of Hadassah; because they're the only group carrying out truly Jewish women's work." Her final statement reveals how effective Hadassah's methods and gendered discourse were among the women opposed to Zionism in principle not only in the United States but in Europe as well.[89]

Despite Bial's and Ollendorf's protestations, the 1929 congress passed a Palestine resolution similar to the 1923 version. Attesting to the heightened power of the Zionist delegates, Rebekah Kohut told her American board that "the majority of the [congress] members were very, very anxious that the Conference go on record as supporting Palestine and Zionism, and there was a threatened bolt from the Conference on the part of a large number of women" if that did not occur.[90] Kohut assured Council members that although the Zionist issue was brought up "forcibly" at the congress, the new international organization would still resist embroiling itself in controversial issues: "we have started out, not only with peace all over the world, but we are going to try to have peace within our own ranks. With peace in our own ranks we believe we can work for the peace of the world, too."[91] While it may not have been possible for everyone to agree on the Zionist issue, proponents were able to build tremendous support by emphasizing how the work in Palestine resembled the effort of other women's organizations. This strategy, though, depoliticized what was happening on the ground at the very same time that the Zionist movement itself strove toward a political solution.

The presence of avowed Zionists, and open debate about what constituted Jewish identity and community, made other women's absence from the congress all the more striking. As in 1923, there is little evidence to suggest that many, if any, working-class Jews attended. The only non-European elected to serve on the new executive committee was from Palestine. While attempting to forge alliances with Jews throughout the world, congress organizers maintained the distinctions that many of the constituent groups had long held themselves. The working-class and poor, Yiddish or Ladino speakers, and Middle Eastern Jews, even those born in Palestine, appeared as people in need of service, not potential colleagues.[92] Indeed, a debate erupted at the congress when Rosa Welt-Straus spoke out against the condition of Yemenite Jewish women in Palestine. Anitta Müller-Cohen urged her not to judge other cultures too harshly, asserting that Palestine was located in "the Orient" and that people who had lived in Palestine for centuries did not have the same values as Westerners.[93] Her words echoed Hadassah publications that supported the idea of modern, scientific methods counteracting supposedly widespread beliefs in "myths and magic" among Palestine residents. One such pamphlet described Palestinian Jews and Arabs practicing "ancient rites . . . [including] conjurings, smearings, amulet-wearing, weird incantations and the application of hot irons to affected portions of the body." While

Hadassah prided itself on treating all residents of Palestine, regardless of religion, equally it seemingly did not discriminate in also associating these people with, as Miller-Cohen labeled it, "the Orient."[94] Back at the congress, no Yemenite women weighed in on this discussion, and at no point were non-Jewish residents of Palestine discussed in a substantive way. In the United States, anti-Zionist, socialist women continued to ignore the international Jewish sisterhood. The Workmen's Circle's first convention of affiliated women's clubs, which met shortly before the congress, failed to mention the upcoming World Congress. Moreover, its delegates passed a resolution advocating closer work with the international women's peace movement, specifically the Women's International League for Peace and Freedom, and notably not the WCJW.[95]

The congress debates over Zionism show that for all their efforts women like Kohut could not maintain total peace in their ranks. Nevertheless, gendered descriptions like those used by Hadassah to describe its own work and recruit non-Zionist women proved remarkably successful at the World Congress as well. By linking their projects in Palestine to the social welfare work pioneered by women working first among immigrants and then with refugees, Zionists in both organizations highlighted the ways in which their plans for Palestine helped the Jewish family—a family threatened by war, antisemitism, and recently by increased conflict in Palestine itself. However, utilizing Hadassah's strategy, supporting a supposedly neutral, humanitarian agenda ultimately led the group to support one form of Jewish nationalism over others. But this did not happen because of gendered rhetoric alone. In seeking to break down barriers, the new organization succeeded in upholding many others that had long existed in the Jewish "family," including barriers of class, language, and national or regional origin. The makeup of the international movement mirrored that of the national middle-class groups, like the NCJW or the Jüdischer Frauenbund. This led to the continued invisibility of certain types of women, most notably the politically active women of the Workmen's Circle and the Jewish Labor Bund, in an international organization theoretically open to all Jewish women. Lacking voices which might have offered other models of Jewish international identity or Jewish nationalism, more and more non-Zionist women, emboldened by the similarities between their relief agendas and those of women like Anitta Müller-Cohen and Nellie Straus Mochenson, openly embraced Zionism by 1930. Given such women's educational and financial resources, as well as their ties to men with similar resources, this trend belied Mochenson's fear that the congress was nothing but a "spiritual Turkish bath." Participation in the congresses proved to be a substantial coup for Hadassah and for the Zionist movement as a whole. By 1930 few middle-class American Jewish women continued to openly oppose Zionism. Rhetorical strategies about aiding the Jewish family overseas through the provision of, quite literally, a "haven in a heartless world," had firmly entrenched the Zionist solution in the minds of middle-class American Jews years before the terror of the Holocaust.

Moving into the Mainstream

By 1930 middle-class Jewish women from around the world had come to support the practical goals of the Zionist movement even if they still hesitated to identify themselves or their organizations openly as Zionist. Hadassah women in the United States and Zionist women at the world congresses met their non-Zionist counterparts halfway, realizing that it was easier to recruit new adherents in a more piecemeal, nonideological fashion than to overwhelm the reluctant with political tracts, lectures, and exhortations to support the nationalist cause. Their methods, and more importantly the methods' effectiveness, reveal the important ways that seemingly apolitical acts can have profound political consequences. During the 1920s the Zionist Organization of America lost large numbers of members while Hadassah flourished. This achievement, frequently overlooked by historians, had significant results not only for the women's organization but for building the American Zionist movement during a period in which it otherwise declined.

Hadassah's recruitment strategy centered on articulating its gendered Zionism, one that valorized women's talents and interests. Rather than discuss Zionist ideology or the political ramifications of establishing a Jewish homeland in Palestine, Hadassah attracted non-Zionists by engaging their interests as women. Hadassah publications stressed its services to women and children, its devotion to medical work, and its ability to heal the breach between Arabs and

Jews. These projects, though clearly aimed at promoting Jewish life in Palestine, resembled work pursued by a wide variety of contemporary women's organizations. In the postwar era, when many women's groups, both Jewish and non-Jewish, turned their attention overseas, Hadassah promoted its own involvement in international and peace issues all the more strongly. By appealing to women in ways that highlighted those topics and undertakings common to so many middle-class women, Hadassah was able to attract a large number of new recruits to the Zionist movement during the inter-war period.

Hadassah leaders particularly recruited members of the National Council of Jewish Women, an organization resolutely non-Zionist until after World War II. Both these groups participated in similar work and used analogous rhetoric and imagery to describe their projects. These commonalities worked to Hadassah's benefit. Just as the NCJW had long before established close ties to the National and International Councils of Women and many other women's groups, so too in the 1920s could many of its members volunteer to assist the Zionist organization, Hadassah, without feeling a conflict of interest. By moving Hadassah into the mainstream of female organizational activity its leaders ultimately succeeded in making Zionism as an ideology more acceptable to middle-class American Jews. Hadassah's work, although often perceived as being apolitical, philanthropic, and feminine, in the end played no small role in helping Zionism begin its move from the fringes to the center of American Jewish life.

Council women, especially those opposed to Zionist affiliation, formulated another means by which to promote their American and Jewish identities. Unlike Hadassah, they turned their attention to the American sphere, forging bonds with non-Jewish women's organizations and striving to be the "interpreter" of Jewish culture to their middle-class, non-Jewish counterparts. Like these women, Council supported a broad political agenda that sought to preserve protective labor legislation, opposed the Equal Rights Amendment, and promoted world peace. Although they focused their energies on the American context, Council women did not abandon or ignore their Jewish identities. Council broadened its overseas agenda after the war not only by working for peace but also by expanding its involvement with immigrant aid, reconstruction work, and collaboration with European Jewish women similarly concerned with the plight of the refugees. Like Hadassah, women in the NCJW sought to create an international Jewish women's community; however, most Council leaders stressed their American nationality and strove to avoid discussion of Jewish nationalism.

But to many middle-class American Jews the Council's "Great Interpreter" approach failed to address sufficiently all their concerns or meet all their needs. Neither could the Diaspora nationalism that they all but ignored, deeming it the ideology of socialists, of the ghetto, and Yiddish the language of an inglorious past rather than a hopeful future. By studiously avoiding "controversy" the NCJW resembled other American women's groups, and it succeeded in acculturating many members to mainstream American society. Yet this policy also denied its members a space in which to express their fears about antisemitism or explore the powerful draw many felt to the gendered Zionist nationalism of Hadassah. In promoting their group as the "Great Interpreter" the leaders of the NCJW espoused a consistent message of acculturation. Hadassah, on the other hand, provided women with a practical means by which to identify as Jews, through participation in overtly gendered projects to aid the Jews of Palestine, and as Americans, by linking their organization to the "supplemental nationality" championed by such prominent American men as Louis Brandeis. In the end, however, the fact that many middle-class women in the inter-war period opted to join both groups perhaps suggests that they desired a means to be both politically active "Jewish Americans" and "American Jews" contributing to the development of a permanent national homeland in Palestine.

These two groups experimented with ways to be both American and Jewish while at the same time championing women's issues and talents. Although their leadership found much to disagree on politically, the rank and file of the two groups grew closer together because of their common interest in social welfare, education, the status of women and children, and the condition of Jews worldwide. While these shared concerns brought middle-class, English-speaking American Jewish women closer during the 1920s, they also raised barriers between these groups and women from poorer and/or more radical backgrounds, such as those in the Workmen's

Circle. As Council and Hadassah moved ever further into the broad mainstream of American social reform-oriented feminism, they did so without significant involvement or input from working-class, Yiddish-speaking women. Although such women joined Hadassah and Council, they could hope to achieve prominence only by embracing these groups' visions of what it meant to be an American Jew. Women with different understandings of their American, Jewish, and gender identities had to travel alternative paths to full involvement in public life.

The Feminization of the Workmen's Circle, 1920–1930

Like women in the NCJW and Hadassah, those in Arbeter Ring worked vigorously to raise relief funds during the war, putting aside their earlier attempts to achieve equality through the separate ladies' branches. After the war some women in the Circle returned to their interests in gender issues and attempted once again to construct a coherent way of reconciling their often conflicting positions as socialists, workers, and mothers. In the 1920s many of them formed voluntary ladies' auxiliaries and women's clubs. These groups provided women with greater flexibility than did formal branch membership, allowing them to pursue work of immediate concern to many women, including social welfare and education projects. The women who launched these groups sought ways to combine their interests in class and gender issues, and be active publicly while continuing to care for home and children.

Creating their own groups enabled women to address their problems by offering an alternative to the regular branch and membership modeled on men's work lives. The women's groups provided female companionship, sociability, and an agenda attuned to women's needs. Constrained by the socialist movement's reluctance to deal with gender difference, Circle women used their own groups to create a distinct space for themselves within the organization itself. Their actions resembled those of middle-class women's organizations, where separate female organizing also persisted even after the attainment of suffrage.[1] Yet while these women willfully separated themselves, they were far from marginalized. The women's groups in the Circle ultimately formulated a new type of involvement—one that recognized gender difference while still firmly supporting the broader socialist agenda.[2] By engaging in work traditionally associated with women, and which was receiving greater attention nationally due to the efforts of middle-class women's social reform initiatives, these socialists not only delineated a space for themselves within the Circle but ultimately succeeded in expanding the order's overall mission.

Arbeter Ring in the Postwar World

Following the war the Workmen's Circle, like other Jewish organizations, continued its interest in overseas relief. Members sent support to Jews in Poland and Russia through the People's Relief Committee, and the landsmanshaft branches gave financial aid to family members and relatives still residing in Eastern Europe. In addition to providing short-term financial and material assistance, the Circle also built children's schools and helped adults gain the skills necessary to learn a trade.[3] Just as they had during the war, the Circle's female members stayed in the trenches, raising funds and preparing clothing for shipment overseas but rarely appearing in prominent leadership positions. While the relief agenda remained substantially the same, other issues began to attract members' interests.

Zionist topics crept into the pages of the Circle's monthly paper *Der fraynd* with greater regularity after the war, particularly in the late 1920s, although the organization continued to adhere to its anti-Zionist posture. At the same time it affirmed the development of the labor movement in Palestine, the Circle continued to abjure direct support for the nationalist and political goals of the Zionist movement as a whole. In October, 1927, for instance, *Der fraynd* reported on the Fifteenth Zionist Congress as an example of the "abnormal" modern Jewish condition. The most straightforward renunciation of the Zionist cause appeared following the Arab riots in 1929, when *Der fraynd* published Bundist Yakov Pat's negative assessment of events taking place in Palestine. Pat harshly criticized Zionist interpretations of the riots, arguing that the Zionists had helped inflame tensions by ignoring the Arab nationalism inherent in the conflict. Sharply denouncing the attacks on Jewish settlers, Pat nevertheless insisted that although these Jews were innocent victims, the Zionists most definitely were not. He asserted that the only way to solve the current standoff was for Zionists to abandon their desire for a Jewish homeland and make peace with Arabs. Continuing in this vein, in 1930 the Workmen's Circle urged members to support the workers' movement in Palestine, arguing that it provided the only practical solution to the problems of that land. Leaders maintained that political Zionism had long ago proven its futility and that the time had come for workers in Palestine to reach a compromise with their Arab neighbors and the British authorities.[4]

But in the 1920s events in Palestine interested Circle members only marginally. Of far more immediate concern was the internal dispute that threatened to divide the organization. With the founding of the Communist Party and the Third International, or Comintern, intense conflict entered the ranks of the Arbeter Ring. In 1917 the Circle threw its support behind the Russian Revolution, and through the early 1920s it pursued projects aimed at relieving the plight of Jews in Ukraine and elsewhere in the Soviet Union. But over time the division between socialists and communists widened, mirroring the larger strain enveloping the entire Socialist Party in the United States. Leftists in both the party and the Circle wanted to affiliate with the Comintern, an action opposed by more mainstream members. The socialist movement voted down the leftist program in 1919, at which point the leftists formed an underground campaign that eventually took over the Jewish Socialist Federation. When that group seceded from the Socialist Party, loyal members, including many Workmen's Circle leaders, formed a new group, the Jewish Socialist *Farband* (union, association). Both the federation and the Farband included people affiliated with the Circle. In 1921 the communists founded the Workers' Party, and the Jewish Socialist Federation became the Yiddish section of that organization. The next year the Workers' Party started a Yiddish newspaper, *Frayhayt* (Freedom), to counter the more moderate *Forverts*.[5]

The discord that wracked the socialist movement also affected the Circle. Throughout the 1920s local branches and district organizations were riven by conflict between leftist and "rightist" members. The Circle initially attempted to retain members in the branches despite the growing ideological divide, but as the 1920s progressed this became an increasingly impossible goal. The vitriol in the attacks from both sides intensified, and rare was the branch that remained immune from the internal strife of these years. In 1930 some 8,000 leftists organized their own "proletarian" fraternal organization, the International Workers Order, and formally withdrew from the Workmen's Circle.[6] Women participated in these struggles alongside male members. One woman attributed the late appearance of a separate women's group in her branch to the intensity of the battles with the communists. No one in her branch had time to think about organizing women, she recalled, while the branch fought for its very existence. Another woman noted that the internal strife of the early 1920s led to the temporary demise of her women's club in Atlanta, although it was revived in 1925.[7]

The conflict took a toll on the organization not only in terms of personal relationships but also in overall membership rates. The Circle reached its peak membership of 85,000 in 1925 but consistently lost members thereafter.[8] As branch relations deteriorated some members opted to leave the organization entirely. Yet factors aside from ideological conflict also contributed to the postwar membership decline. Immediately after the war immigration restrictions significantly curtailed growth: With fewer immigrants arriving in the United States from abroad, the Circle lost one of its major sources of new recruits. The relative prosperity of the 1920s enabled some Circle members to move into the middle class. When this happened, many of them did not renew their affiliation with the socialist fraternal order. This situation occurred most frequently in small cities and towns with a modest overall Jewish population. Along with this movement out of the working class, 1920s-style welfare capitalism also contributed to rising numbers of people leaving the organization. As some businesses and unions began to meet those workers' needs that once had been covered only by the mutual aid societies, members started to withdraw from fraternal organizations. Finally, postwar conservatism did little to encourage growth in an organization affiliated with socialism, even if it was considered "rightist" by its more radical members.[9] The political context of the period, most notably the postwar Red Scare, did much to ensure a meager enrollment of new members. Particularly in small cities, the Arbeter Ring's operations were nearly paralyzed; few people wished to join a group targeted by the government as being potentially subversive. The National Executive Committee (NEC) protested local governments' actions against the branches, such as arresting leaders or meddling in Circle affairs. In some cases the committee provided trial funds for leaders facing prison sentences, and throughout the country it fought to maintain its right to provide insurance to its members. In this trying atmosphere the NEC endeavored to hold on to the group's old members while at the same time attracting new recruits. To this end it sent speakers to the branches, distributed informational materials, and initiated a variety of membership campaigns.[10]

Given these circumstances, the Circle leadership struggled to find ways to augment membership without recruiting new faces to the movement. Young people who had grown up with the Circle and members' wives became the focuses of postwar recruitment campaigns. Both were, theoretically at least, already familiar with the organization and its ideals. For the first time in the Circle's history, women became a population energetically courted by male leaders. As early as the autumn of 1918, when immigration restriction first began to threaten recruitment, a campaign to raise membership to 70,000 was initiated. Campaign activity during October and November focused exclusively on women, specifically the wives of current members.[11] These campaigns continued throughout the next decade, though without much visible success. In 1926 an article in the English-language section of *Der fraynd* praised women for their work on behalf of the Circle but pointed out that they accounted for only 9,000 of the total 84,000 enrolled members.[12] While this figure reveals the low level of female membership in the Circle, it hides the fact that significant numbers of women remained active in the organization even if they were not dues-paying members. Despite the organization's concerted efforts to attract female members, many women in these years opted to work on behalf of the Circle without formally joining the group itself.

During the 1920s women began to construct new ladies' auxiliaries, volunteer groups the form of which had existed since the Circle's earliest years and which consisted of members' female relatives. The auxiliaries did not require that a woman actually enroll in the Arbeter Ring, although some women in the auxiliaries did pay dues. Ladies' branches from the prewar era continued to function, but by the 1920s they were few in number as most women chose to join the auxiliaries, or later, the *froyen klubn* (women's clubs) instead.[13] The women's clubs were groups affiliated with a particular branch and closely resembled ladies' auxiliaries; indeed, at first only the names represented any real difference between these two types of volunteer groups. By 1927, recognizing the potential for membership growth, Circle leaders began devising ways to bring these two types of volunteer groups formally into the organization. Seeing a new means by which to increase enrollment, Circle leadership moved to institutionalize the numerous informal women's groups by integrating their members into the organization as dues-paying members. Yet unlike the prewar ladies' branches, which could include members at any class (i.e., dues) level, the formal women's clubs and branches included only those membership classes limited to women.[14]

Although the Circle leadership eventually endorsed the informal women's groups and intensified its membership campaigns among women, this did not mean that women felt secure about their status within the organization. Just as they had in the Circle's first days, women in the 1920s felt unwelcome when trying to participate in male-led meetings and conventions. Regardless of the organizational commitment to recruit more women, many men still preferred that their wives and other women abstain from involvement in the business of the regular branches. In 1925, for instance, the *Convention Bulletin* reported humorously about the recent "picture" presented by female delegates accompanying their husbands to the annual meeting:

> This "picture" is simply scandalous. Is it not enough that these delegates suffer from their wives at home that they should also suffer from them at the convention? No, this "picture" should be abolished. Conventions were not created for women. True, women do indeed have the same rights as men but women should be prohibited from receiving such rights as to make men's lives bitter during convention time. The convention must once and for all speak out against such women's rights.[15]

Even if written in a lighthearted tone, this piece indicates that many men felt threatened by women's formal participation in the Circle. Although committed to the ideal of gender equality, they preferred that equality not extend to those arenas they considered their own, including Circle meetings and conventions.

Such sarcasm did not abate even as the organization forthrightly worked to institutionalize the women's clubs by decade's end. In 1929 a humor publication teased General Secretary Joseph Baskin about trying to take all the credit for bringing women's clubs into the organization. A cartoon showed him bounding across a crowd of women, grasping the hands of two women in his own large hands and pulling reluctant new members along with him. The headline above the cartoon names him the "General of the Feminine Multitudes," while underneath a caption states that "our general secretary wants to take the whole credit for the plan to incorporate the froyen klubn into the Arbeter Ring. Give him credit, give it to him!" The cartoon appears to be poking fun not only at Baskin's willingness to take sole credit for a membership boost but also at the women themselves, who are portrayed as unwilling, dismayed, or indifferent to his attentions. Although women were becoming a greater presence in the order clearly there persisted a sense of unease about how their participation might alter the organization. A brief, satirical article beneath the cartoon noted that from the moment that women's clubs began to meet, the National Organization Committee "started to break its head" over the question of what premiums to give these women in order to draw them into the Circle. The response was that in order for the membership drive to be a success one should offer women perfume, roses, powder, and silk stockings as rewards for joining the Arbeter Ring.[16] Such humor reveals that at least some men feared the effect of heightened female participation on their socialist workers' organization.

Women's reminiscences demonstrate that these national documents were not merely the product of satirists but reflected actual views held at the local level. Women in Rochester, New York, for instance, recalled that when they planned to form a special women's group, some men and their "backward" wives opposed the idea. The men feared "that we, the organized women, would spoil their wives along with their happy homes, and thereby we would become independent with our own women's organization." The proponents found themselves having to go door to door in order to explain their plans and "the necessity of the organization" to potential members as well as to their husbands.[17] Other women described more bluntly how alienated they felt from their husbands' organization and how this led directly to their forming separate groups. A Borough Park woman, recalling the meetings she attended with her husband in 1917, noted that she listened attentively to the discussions and longed to take part in the proceedings. But she could not participate since she did not pay dues herself and so technically did not belong to the branch. Moreover, she simply did not feel comfortable. When other women in the branch announced the formation of a women's group, she reacted with joy, embracing the notion that women might have a space of their own where they could play a more active role. Another women candidly stated that at Circle meetings a woman "sat like a stranger, she did not mingle in the proceedings. When it came time to vote on something, [the men] directed the women not to vote because they were not members. Even there the woman was a stranger." When a local women's group was formed, she eagerly joined, appreciating a forum where she did not feel ashamed and where she might be able to get over her nervousness about speaking in public.[18] Throughout the nation, similar groups arose, bringing women together with others who understood their lives and their reluctance to speak in front of groups, and who shared their desire for public activism.

Creating an Activist Arena for Women

The life of Adele Kean Zametkin, the Circle's major female columnist during World War I, illuminates the struggles faced by radical women in combining motherhood and political work. Although her wartime columns in *Der fraynd* enthusiastically supported gender equality and were imbued with class consciousness, in her private life Zametkin behaved not unlike more conventional women of her era. Her daughter, the author Laura Hobson, wrote movingly of Zametkin in her memoirs, presenting a woman somewhat at odds with the political positions expressed in her "Iber der froyen velt" columns. Hobson described her mother as a Jewish immigrant socialist who refused to teach her daughters either Yiddish or Russian, a supporter of gender equality who succumbed to pressures to conform to tradition.[19] When Zametkin moved in with her husband, the socialist Michael Zametkin (they were not officially married until 1929), he already had a young son. Following the birth of her own son, Adele Zametkin entered dental school, but she felt distressed leaving her young boys with a friend while she was away at classes. After looking into other day care alternatives, which she found unsatisfactory, Zametkin quit school in order to stay at home with the two boys and later her twin daughters. Zametkin wrote to Hobson years later that she "finally had to give up the dreaming. I dropped college and became the housewife, but not the typical one." Indeed, she was far from typical in some respects. When Hobson graduated from Cornell, Zametkin arrived at the ceremony in the sidecar of her son's Harley-Davidson.[20]

Like many other women of her generation, Zametkin was forced to choose between pursuing a career and raising her children. She never explicitly blamed her husband or the socialist movement for not enabling her to do both, and by all accounts she embraced her role as stay-at-home mother. She later wrote Hobson that "I was the mother who dreamed dreams, and the cradle by my side pulled me away, and I had to give up, until the dreams for my own rosy future turned into dreams . . . for my little ones." Nevertheless she did not entirely give up her own work, her own dreams. While at home, she maintained involvement with the movement through her writing and by helping immigrant women learn English. When Zametkin died in 1931, Hobson recalled that there were many lengthy obituaries printed in the Jewish and socialist press. Reflecting on the *New York Times* obituary, Hobson stated that it showed "a lot about the kind of woman she was, way back there, long before the phrase, women's liberation, had ever been heard."[21]

Zametkin's life shows the trouble that women, particularly working-class women, had in trying to reconcile professional aspirations with their desire to stay at home with young children. Zametkin opted to drop out of college, raise her children, and pick up work writing columns for *Der fraynd* and other Yiddish newspapers at home. After the war, Zametkin stopped writing for *Der fraynd*. Her new column, titled "*Fun a froy tsu froyen*" (From a woman/wife to women/wives), turned toward more traditionally female concerns. These pieces, which were published in the Yiddish paper *Der tog* (The day), along with a second column *In der froyen velt* (In the women's world), focused on such topics as food preparation, childcare, housework techniques, sex education, and hygiene. A year before her death she published these pieces in a 600-page volume titled *Der froy's handbukh* (The wife's handbook), which she gave to her daughter despite the fact that Hobson knew no Yiddish.[22]

Other women, less prominent than Zametkin, faced the same problems when they attempted to participate in the Arbeter Ring. Like Zametkin, they sought means by which to pursue public activism while maintaining responsibility for the home. Attempting to deal with these conflicting ambitions, women created a more flexible and supportive atmosphere than that provided by the regular branches. These new groups enabled women to join in Circle work without paying a membership fee. Because many families continued to be unable, or unwilling, to pay for two memberships despite the relative prosperity of the 1920s, these groups proved popular with a growing number of women.[23]

Hannah Klein's experience demonstrates how important it was for some women to remain affiliated with the Circle without paying the same dues as men. Klein, who ultimately became a member of Women's Branch 210-B, was active in radical politics in Russia. Upon her arrival in the United States, she eagerly joined the Workmen's Circle—in fact, she was a charter member of Branch 255. In time, however, she and her "life partner" found that they could not afford to make two dues payments. When Branch 255 succumbed to internecine fighting, her partner stayed in his branch and Klein dropped out of the Circle. Still, the group "occupied the main place in my social interests and bills or no bills, it was my organization." As the couple's economic status improved, Klein rejoined as a class 3 member—the class reserved for members' wives. Yet she felt inhibited because she no longer had the right to vote on every piece of branch business, only the management of those funds to which her dues contributed. In the end she joined the women's branch. "At last I found a place where I could be active," she exclaimed, calling Branch 210-B her "spiritual home." Her experience, like that of other women, demonstrates that women felt their inequality more keenly when they attempted to participate side by side with men than they did in separate groups. Despite the greater formal inequality, in a single-sex forum women felt more involved and more fully integrated into Circle life.[24] Rokhl Vol underscored the importance of women's alternative space, arguing that the women's clubs, and later the women's branches, enabled women to develop public speaking skills, learn how to run a meeting, and create their own activist agenda. She maintained that with the appearance of these groups, women in the Workmen's Circle felt they had a "worth—[that the woman] is a useful member of society."[25] For these women, the level of monetary attachment to the Circle or formal equality in terms of dues status proved less important than believing their contributions were meaningful and their participation respected.

Creating such groups was by no means a simple process. Organizers found they had other barriers to cross in addition to economic constraints and men's reluctance to let their wives leave home at night. The dynamics that had plagued women before the war continued to hamper their public activism into the 1920s. Without a commitment from their husbands to help with household duties, many were too busy with childcare and other household concerns to attend meetings. Women in Atlanta made a direct connection between women's domestic duties and a declining interest in Circle activities. Like Circle women elsewhere in the United States and Canada, they eventually opted to bring women together in separate, voluntary groups that would allow them to pursue their own interests while working in concert with the larger Circle mission. Though they insisted that they themselves had never been "wives of the *ezrat nashim*" (women's section of a synagogue), they nevertheless chose to found a club separate from the men.[26] Such women believed that making groups more flexible and relevant to women's lives would attract greater numbers of women to the Circle cause.

Women in Branch 210-B similarly reflected on how women's reproductive lives had negatively influenced their ability to engage in public work. Although many of them had been active back in their native Pinsk, upon arrival in the United States they found their lives restricted to the domestic sphere. They became disconnected from other Pinsk transplants, absorbed in their household duties and children's lives. By the 1920s, when their children had grown older, these women had more free time. Some of them, remembering their radical European pasts, awakened to the fact that although they had traveled to "another world," many of the same problems against which they had protested in their youth still persisted. Twelve of these women decided to form a women's club and moved quickly to attract more members.[27]

While women usually conceived of the idea to start a voluntary women's club themselves, they often had to rely on their branch's male leadership to help them get the message out to members' wives and other women. Sometimes this meant speaking to individual men and assuring them that a women's club would not ruin their happy homes. Other times the men themselves helped separatist organizers explain their goals to colleagues. Women in Branch 392, for instance, had long helped men with their work, but by the 1920s they began to want more experience and more direct involvement than they were afforded in the "regular" branch. They believed the only way to attain these goals would be to form their own separate women's club, which they did in the mid-1930s. Unlike the case in other settings, the male leaders of Branch 392 played a central role in the club's formation by helping to distribute a letter to all branch members outlining the goals of the proposed group. While women usually sparked the initial interest in a separate group, the regular branches had the material resources needed to spread the word to potential recruits.[28]

At the same time women were organizing their clubs and auxiliaries, the Arbeter Ring's national leadership pursued numerous campaigns to increase female membership. As it became apparent that volunteer groups were attracting more women than formal membership drives, leaders began to take an even greater interest in the women's groups. Circle men had long provided social insurance and attempted to enhance the education of fellow members, but when women promoted similar activities, unhampered by male guidance, the leadership and its supporters began to express concern that the organization was moving too far afield of its socialist origins. As more women joined the volunteer groups, expressing a commitment to the Circle but a coolness toward actual, formal membership, *Der fraynd* began publishing a series of articles explaining to women the necessity of keeping their work focused on socialist goals.

Perspectives on Women's Work

During the 1920s the women who replaced Zametkin as authors of the women's column in *Der fraynd* kept up her political outlook while at the same time trying to draw new women into the movement, many of whose interests leaned more toward *Der froy's handbukh* than *Das Kapital*. In an article written early in 1920, Esther Lurie asked how the Circle might make itself more appealing to workers' wives. She insisted that, as the publication of a workers' organization, *Der fraynd* could not follow the example of other magazines by printing fashion features. Since women bore great responsibility for rearing the next generation, Lurie felt that the Circle could attract new readers by focusing on topics related to the home: for instance, printing more articles on child development and Yiddish schools. Lurie also urged the Circle to instruct women on political issues, to teach them that these too were "women's issues." Perhaps acknowledging that many socialist women followed in Adele Kean Zametkin's footsteps rather than trying to balance paid labor outside the home with domestic responsibilities, Lurie counseled the organization to bring politics and labor issues directly into the private sphere through their organization's newspaper. Jewish women, who usually left the workforce upon marriage, could still be active and useful members of the socialist struggle through their participation in the Arbeter Ring.[29]

Seeming to follow her advice, *Der fraynd* made a concerted effort over the next several years to acquaint its female readers with a host of political topics, especially labor issues affecting women. Its major author during this period was Rokhl Holtman. Unlike the wartime columns, Holtman's articles dropped Zametkin's comparative instruction on the global pursuit of women's suffrage and focused almost exclusively on the American political scene. Her writings continued to stress class and economic issues as the most salient factors in working-class women's lives, whether or not women worked for pay themselves. Holtman expressed particular antipathy for the pro-suffrage organizations that had promised great change once women won the right to vote. In January 1923 she went so far as to argue that women's suffrage had done little to alter the American political economy, presenting as evidence rising poverty rates and increasing numbers of women in the Ku Klux Klan.[30] In another article, Holtman faulted the Women's Bureau of the Labor Department for not having done enough to improve women's working conditions. "The capitalist world has long recognized that in its hunt for profits and earnings the best material for exploitation is the woman," she argued. To her mind, women's suffrage alone could little affect the working-class struggle, and middle-class women's involvement in government bureaucracy had failed to ameliorate the plight of their working sisters.[31] Her articles aimed to enliven in Circle women a keen appreciation for class-based politics and class solidarity. The working class, she averred, had finally awakened from the illusion that the "battles for the bourgeoisie were ostensibly battles to free all mankind. . . . The fate of the working woman is closely tied to the fate of the whole working class. She should fight its battle and its victory will bring her worthy liberation."[32]

Holtman often disparaged nonsocialist women's clubs in the United States and continually urged Circle women to remain true to their socialist ideals and worker origins. In a brief, and biased, history of the women's club movement, Holtman repeatedly criticized the apolitical nature of such groups. One would think, she remarked, that given the size of the General Federation of Women's Clubs it would be a major player in the nation's political life. Yet the group was heard from so rarely that Holtman felt it would not be amiss to question its very existence. Holtman ridiculed such groups, arguing that they had arisen only due to middle-class material comfort and its resultant ennui:

> The American woman of the middle class has in the last 25 years achieved the highest that she can imagine. America has become simply the garden of Eden for the petit bourgeois. That, about which the woman of this class dreams—a beautiful home, a player piano, a Victrola, an automobile and beautiful clothes as well—has been attained. And what does one do with so much free time! They come to the assistance of the clubs, where one spends time with a little glass of tea, a little packet of playing cards and occasionally reads a "paper" about a literary or political question.

Further mocking club women's aspirations to intellectualism, Holtman asserted that "the distinguished ladies do not just deal with theory. They also do practical work." Such practical work, she joked, amounted to little more then discerning which streets in the "shtetl" lacked beauty and then strenuously endeavoring to decorate them. Working-class women must stop mimicking these "ladies," she argued, encouraging them to form their own clubs affiliated with the Workmen's Circle.[33] Holtman clearly wanted women to participate in public work, but she also cautioned socialist and working-class women against adhering too closely to what she considered a middle-class model of activism. Seemingly, radical women, the editors of *Der fraynd*, and the leaders of the Workmen's Circle were beginning to relent in their opposition to separate women's groups so long as such groups benefited the movement at large.

Prominent member Rose Asch, who belonged to a regular branch, also weighed in on the discussion regarding the nature of women's participation. Like others writing on gender issues, Asch began by giving her readers a bit of historical background and a crash course in socialist theory as it applied to gender relations. Capitalism, she believed, had driven women into the workforce without providing adequate support in the home. Therefore, women lacked the opportunities afforded to men, both young and old, to develop their intellects. Inequality between the sexes, she argued, was not inherent but rather had developed over time due to women's sole responsibility for the monotonous work of the home. Asch claimed that the same inequality that had ruled gender relations for centuries also held sway in the Arbeter Ring. Only in its first years, she pointed out, did a woman serve on the National Executive Committee. Recently a woman had attained a national post, but this, Asch argued, had more to do with the fact that the woman's husband was a renowned member of the group than with the woman's own accomplishments. In looking for the cause of women's plight, at least in the Arbeter Ring, Asch concluded that the guilt lay squarely with the women themselves. In order to attain national positions, she argued, women needed first to be active on the local level and to join the organization independently of their husbands. She did not mention who would look after the home.[34] Recognizing the heightened activity of women in the public sphere brought on by war relief efforts, the attainment of suffrage, and the popularity of women's clubs and organizations, Asch and other columnists urged Workmen's Circle members not to abandon their socialist principles. Assuring women that they could continue to do the work that they enjoyed, the columnists nevertheless underscored that such endeavors should resist mimicking the supposedly apolitical, leisurely pursuits of middle-class clubs.

Circle women heeded these messages, at least in part. During the 1920s, while the Arbeter Ring tried to hold on to its socialist politics as more of its membership moved out of the working class, female members became an ever more vibrant presence in organizational life. Like *Der fraynd*'s female columnists, many Circle women believed that in the past Jewish women in the United States lacked an organizational life outside the realm of charity provision. Women in New Brunswick's Branch 208 argued that charity groups had managed to help the poor but had limited women's public activism to a narrow sphere. Yet opposing Rose Asch, these women felt that their own club, not "regular" membership, would expand women's horizons, bring them "out of their kitchens," instruct them in current social problems, and put them on the same level as men. Many other women similarly began to look for a way to engage in public work. In the end they opted not to engage in paid labor, as many die-hard socialists urged, or work their way through the Circle's ranks as a "regular" member as Asch insisted they should. Like middle-class women before them and their sisters in other socialist women's clubs, they took their traditional duties and interests out of the private sphere and brought them into the public realm. In the process these women broadened the notion of what was considered appropriate work for a Jewish socialist.

Women's groups engaged in a variety of activities to benefit the Circle and its causes. Much of their work centered around holding fund-raisers for various cultural and educational initiatives they hoped to institute in their branchs. Just as the war had expanded the scope of Council's and Hadassah's agendas, so too did many Circle women's groups initially concentrate on providing relief for Jews overseas. Anna Kronshtadt remembered that the first project of her women's group was to collect relief money for Pruzhene, the home of her landsmanshaft branch. The women collected food for the European town and hoped one day to raise enough money to set up a Jewish school there. Similarly, the first project for women in Branch 392 was to try to open a school in Lublin, the native city of many branch members. Other women's groups raised money to aid Jews in Poland and the rest of Europe.[35]

Fund-raising for domestic endeavors was also a priority for these groups, which raised money for hospitals and sanatoriums in the United States and provided assistance to unions and striking workers. The first activity of the Rochester women's branch was selling "bricks" (penny stamps) for the branch to build its meeting house. Later they held herring and potato dinners to raise money to build a "Lyceum." The women recalled that members would give their last bit of money to attend these dinners, even if it meant going hungry the next day. Other groups held lectures, formed drama clubs and choruses, gave dance lessons, and created a host of cultural programs aimed at raising women's awareness about political, economic, and social issues, while providing a sociable outlet for group members.[36]

Mini Shneyder of Branch 200 felt that women were the best guardians of the growing "tree" that was the Workmen's Circle. She argued that it had taken women so long to get involved in the organization because in Eastern Europe they had been responsible for maintaining the family while their husbands aspired to full-time study. Upon emigrating to the United States, these men found that their industrial jobs made it impossible for them to continue any sort of cultural work, and therefore they left it to the women. Shneyder argued that as men began to engage in activities associated with work, women bore greater responsibility for cultural, educational, and domestic concerns. She advised women not to downplay their contributions to the Circle: "even baking and cooking for banquets and washing the dishes is important work, it is the clay and bricks with which [women] help build the institutions of Jewish survival, of our continued existence." Writing in 1939, she asserted that the vast majority of Circle funds came through lectures, theater, concerts, and school organizations—all women's projects. These funds helped sustain the organization but also assured the survival of Yiddish language and culture.[37]

While men did not always give women credit for the work they did on behalf of the Circle, one area of life where women's contributions were acknowledged as critical was in the maintenance of the Yiddish school movement. Women's clubs were widely considered its "financial mainstay." These schools, along with their after-school elementary programs and weekend classes for teenagers, had a secular curricula consisting of instruction in Yiddish language, literature, and culture.[38] One prominent Circle leader, Nathan Chanin, was struck by the high level of female activity associated with these institutions. He found that in areas where the national administration's contribution was small, women often raised the bulk of the funds. Especially in the small towns of the South, where men tended to be only marginally interested in the schools, women shouldered the financial burden.[39]

Many women claimed the schools were a prominent catalyst for their group's formation; indeed, numerous clubs came into being to raise funds to open a school or keep an existing one in operation. Rochester women recalled how the Circle had opened a school with other local, progressive organizations. But too many "landlords" ultimately led to its demise. The Rochester women believed they should open their own institution; by 1926 they achieved success, and the mothers' club associated with the school later evolved into the local branch's ladies' auxiliary. Women in New Brunswick's Branch 208 also wanted a school, believing that it would do much to keep younger people involved in the Workmen's Circle. Realizing that children were growing up divorced from the movement and that some were embarrassed by their parents' involvement in the Circle, women organized a youth club in 1924 that succeeded in attracting young people to the group. Soon thereafter the branch began to debate whether to open a full-fledged Yiddish school.[40]

By the late 1920s, the Circle's national leadership, observing the widespread growth of the women's groups and the influential projects these groups pursued, resolved to incorporate the auxiliaries and informal clubs directly into the Circle. This action served a dual purpose: to increase membership in a period of decline and to ensure a level of direct, official regulation of the development of this burgeoning socialist women's movement. With greater frequency throughout the 1920s and into the 1930s, women presented the Circle as a family, arguing that women contributed to it just as they cared for their own families at home. And the leadership came to agree with them. In 1929, as the leaders prepared to draw the women's groups into regular, formal membership, the English portion of *Der fraynd* stressed this new, familial image of the Circle:

The significance of this declaration [to form women's clubs] is obvious. In a society where women are taking an equal part with men in world's work, it is an inestimable boom to our organization to be thus assured of the full support and co-operation of our womenfolk. It means that The Workmen's Circle family will hereafter be a replica, on a larger scale, of the modern family, in which husband and wife participate fully and equally in promoting the welfare of the family.[41]

By the end of the decade even the national leaders became accustomed to viewing their organization as a cooperative partnership between men and women. While each might contribute to the organization in different ways, and hold different formal levels of power, they both remained dedicated to the organization and its socialist program.

Formal Establishment of the Froyen Klubn

Announcing the convention of the ladies' auxiliaries to be held in New York City on March 1, 1929, *Der fraynd* pointed out that in recent years women had begun to question whether their groups should become more than an "appendix" to the regular branches. Misinterpreting the history of Circle women's activism, the editors insisted that although women's groups had existed in the past, they had only served the general branches and never aspired to any sort of independence. Now, however, the women's groups would become "independent" by formalizing their existence as women's club branches of the national. Where the Yiddish portion of *Der fraynd* focused on formalizing women's participation in Circle activities, equating the clubs' "independence" with a greater dedication to the Circle itself, an article in the English section stressed American women's general importance to the philanthropic and cultural life of the nation. The article affirmed the leaders' hope that women's groups would grow until "our women members play the same, vital, civilizing part in the life of the Workmen's Circle that the American woman does in the cultural and philanthropic life of the country."[42] This open embrace of purely "cultural and philanthropic" work represents a shift from the Circle's stance in the early 1920s, when Rokhl Holtman chided women for being insufficiently political in their activism. The change reflects the Circle's contin-ued need for greater enrollment as well as a growing realization of the importance of the work performed by the separate women's groups to the organization as a whole. Moreover, it reveals the dif-ferent tone of the Yiddish, and more traditionally socialist, side of *Der fraynd* and the more acculturated, English portion.

At the convention participants debated at great length the final status of the women's clubs and their official ties, duties, and responsibilities to the Workmen's Circle. Delegates addressed other issues, too, providing a rare glimpse into the world of Circle women's political interests, so often obscured by women's absence in the leadership ranks and thus the historical record. They passed resolutions favoring providing tools for Russian Jews to learn a trade, and instructed their leaders to encourage Circle women to join the Women's International League for Peace and Freedom and establish formal connections with the Women's Trade Union League. They encouraged Circle leaders to reach out to housewives with propaganda regarding the labor movement in order to raise the level of nonworking women's involvement. Moreover, they resolved that the women's clubs should each have a representative on local Yiddish school administration boards. The convention also approved new means by which women could join the organization by creating a special class 5 for club members and allowing class 3 members to join the women's groups.[43]

Anticipating resistance from the general membership to the proposed changes in membership and women's club status, *Der fraynd* published a glowing endorsement of the women's conven-tion, one which, at the same time, managed to downplay the women's organizing efforts in the early 1920s. The author of the editorial acknowledged that there were Circle men who would doggedly resist the women's club movement, but nevertheless insisted that reactionary elements were a small minority of the overall membership. The editorial praised the female delegates' demeanor and actions at the conference, expressing pride that despite their inexperience women ably ran a large convention, han-dled tough questions, and chose effective leaders. The author failed to note that many of these women most likely learned the skills he praised so highly in the volunteer and, to his mind, unsystematically organized women's clubs created both before and after the war.[44]

Feminization of the Workmen's Circle

At the Circle's general convention in May the women's clubs were inducted into the Circle as independent branches with the same responsibilities as the regular ones. Women's club branches would be indicated by a "b" following the branch number, or the women's club could apply to have its own branch number separate from the regular branch in their area. As noted, women in the clubs could only enroll in the organization at the class 3 or 5 membership rate. They could send delegates to Circle conventions and vote on all matters except those relating to benefits for which they did not pay. In essence, other than to ensure that all women's clubs members were now also dues-paying members, these changes did little to alter what had already been occurring on the local level for several years. Nevertheless several men expressed concern about the new membership class 5. A female delegate from Chicago reassured the detractors that they "should not be afraid of the women." She insisted that women had as much to offer the Circle as men; they were willing to carry equal burdens and wanted to have equal rights.[45] Despite her wishes, these new women's clubs did not have equal rights in membership or voting privileges; the male detractors had little to fear. Furthermore, not all of the women's groups embraced this new separate-and-unequal status. Rather than battle for full equality as the prewar "ladies' branches" had, many postwar women chose to remain separate-and-unequal on their own terms, retaining their informal clubs and not applying to become women's branches.

In October 1929, there were some 113 clubs and auxiliaries representing about 5,000 women. By April 1930 only fifty-seven of these had completed the process of becoming full-fledged women's club branches. As late as 1936 there were only seventy-six women's club branches claiming 3,038 members—still a far cry from the convention's initial goals.[46] Anna Yifah, writing about why her club rejected the branch option, commented on the fact that for years the leadership had prohibited female delegates from voting on an assortment of issues, and queried why they now vigorously encouraged women to enter the Circle as dues-paying members. Given their suspicions over the national leaders' motives, her group refused to become a women's branch, arguing that they already formed an "organic part" of the regular branch and saw no need to separate themselves further into a distinct, female-only, dues-paying branch.[47] As dues payers such women perceived their inequality keenly. Devising alternative means to aid the Circle enabled them to feel more involved; being formally dependent, they felt in actuality more independent. They believed that their informal status as auxiliaries provided them greater autonomy to pursue their own agendas. Their formal inequality enabled them to be more integrated in branch life than they felt they ever would be as formal, but still less than equal, members.

By accepting a certain amount of inequality in exchange for greater autonomy, the women's clubs opened the doors to a greater level of female public activity than was the case prior to the war. While some of the rise in female participation can be attributed to women's greater amount of free time as their children grew up, this cannot entirely explain the shift in women's priorities, especially for the younger women who first entered the group during the 1920s. Circle women found that they could exert influence outside the traditional avenues of power by subtly shifting the focus of the organization into areas of their expertise and interest. While women lacked formal authority in the organization, their simultaneous attention to gender and class issues provided the Circle with an entirely new slate of activities. One of the most significant changes resulting from these women's initiatives was the formation of a Social Service Department, which was supported by members of both sexes but spearheaded by a woman, Rose Asch-Simpson (more commonly known as Rose Asch), one of the few women to gain national prominence in the organization. The department institutionalized women's concerns, exemplifying the fact that women's work did not remain solely in the realm of the voluntary, on the periphery of the organization's central agenda. While both men and women played crucial roles in founding the new department, the primary instigator for the move into this area was Rose Asch. Yet, as with the women's clubs, within less than two decades of its founding, male leaders began to claim a preeminent role in its creation, in the process downplaying Asch's centrality.[48]

Social Service and the Workmen's Circle

Rose Asch was never associated with the ladies' branches or women's clubs, having been a lifelong member of regular Branch 367. Before coming to the United States she was an active revolutionary in her native Vilna. Her sister Esther recalled that the two girls were raised in a household that, while patriarchal and traditional in many respects, also instilled in them a fervent desire to help others. Esther believed she grew up, like her father, to pursue these goals in an idealistic fashion, whereas Rose, following in their mother's footsteps, proved to be more practical. Asch's career demonstrates that commitment to practical endeavors. After emigrating to the United States at the turn of the century she attended a normal school in Pennsylvania. A year following her 1907 marriage to Herman Simpson, an editor for the socialist paper the *Call*, Asch began to work for the Arbeter Ring, helping the main office handle the dramatic rise in paperwork. Within a year she took over the management of the group's Cemetery Department, and a short time thereafter convinced the National Executive Committee to let her department handle funerals as well as burials.[49]

In her capacity as head of the Cemetery Department, Asch soon realized that workers' mutual aid needs often extended beyond sickness or funeral benefits. She was particularly concerned about the family members of a spouse who was ill or died. Through her work with the Cemetery and Sanatorium Departments, she discovered that the Circle was not doing all it could to address the members' many concerns. For instance, what became of a member's family when he lay bedridden in the Circle's sanatorium for a year or more? Despite the benefits provided to the ill spouse, his family was forced to turn to nonsocialist providers of charity. Unfortunately, Asch contended, these family members, most often women and children, had to deal with red tape and unsympathetic bureaucracies. Asch believed the Circle could do more to help in such circumstances, by lending a hand to a member's widow as she struggled to maneuver through the system to obtain her pension check, or aiding immigrant workers who lacked the knowledge and language skills to find the services they needed. She praised existing Circle services, especially the sanatorium, the Cemetery Department, schools, and cultural initiatives, but asserted that even when the branches did their best to help the needy, the absence of a central, organizing body meant that too many people fell through the cracks.[50]

In 1925 she wrote an article for the English section of *Der fraynd* outlining her thoughts regarding the need for the Circle to move into social service provision. She argued against the contention that social work necessarily equated with more traditional forms of charity, urging those radicals opposed to charity to acknowledge the fact that they could not ignore the numbers of workers relying on such provisions:

> We generally speak of social work with . . . disdain, for no other reason than the fact that it smacks of charity. And this is just the point I want to attack. We are ashamed of charity and yet thousands of our members, the poor and the sick, are recipients of alms from charity organizations. Why not control this social work for our members by our organization? Why not organize a department that should function in a manner conducive to the benefit of our needy members and at the same time save them from degradation and shame?[51]

Asch firmly believed that workers had a great variety of needs, needs that could be met ably by the socialists affiliated with the Arbeter Ring. Arguing that sometimes even socialists required social welfare services, she maintained that socialist provision of this assistance could offset that middle-class charity so despised by the leadership: "We knew that as a department supported by the members, it becomes actually a paid socialized service which may be expected and which is easy to request." Or, as she put it in Yiddish, a member might "fihlt zikh . . . heymish" (feel at home).[52]

Her own branch supported her proposal, as did allies in other branches in the New York area. In December 1926 these branches held a conference to discuss the proposed department. Some 154 delegates from eighty-four branches attended the event, to which Rose Asch invited a number of social work professionals. A Committee of Twenty and an advisory board of six prominent members, including two representatives from the NEC, were established to study the question further. A second conference in January 1927 attracted even more branch support and approved the Committee of Twenty's proposal that the New York branches tax themselves to fund a new social work department. At the same time Rose Asch and Boris Fingerhut began to lobby the NEC for its support.[53]

As successful as the proposal might have been among the New York branches, it met considerable resistance from the national leadership, many of whom believed that the new department's broad purview would serve only to raise taxes.[54] A meeting between Social Service advocates and the NEC was held in April 1927. Since the detractors tended to voice their opposition to the department on the grounds of added cost, proponents explained how the new department could actually save the Circle money in the long run. This argument did not appease the opponents. Only after much lobbying on the part of Asch and her male allies did the NEC resolve to endorse a Social Service Department "in principle" and set up a joint committee of NEC and department supporters to work on building further NEC support for the plan.[55] Yet by June of that year the NEC had already begun to move away from its tentative support for the new department. General Secretary Joseph Baskin, reporting to the NEC that month, stated that the number of expelled "leftist" members had reached nearly 8,000 and that new memberships amounted to only 5,000. The losses, he maintained, were most keenly felt in Canada and "country-towns" outside New York City. Believing that the inability to attract a sufficient number of new members was due to excessive local taxation, Baskin urged the NEC to curb new expenditures.[56]

But additional expense was not all that troubled the Social Service Department's opponents. Like Asch, Circle historian Maximilian Hurwitz believed that the radicals hated "anything that savored of charity" and that this sentiment, along with "Coolidge prosperity," contributed significantly fierce opposition to the department.[57] Jurisdictional and turf battles also factored into the argument. In 1926 Nathan Rothman, chief clerk of the Sanatorium Department, wrote an article for the English portion of *Der fraynd* asking "Is a Social Service Department Necessary?" He opened the article by recalling an Aesop's fable, stating that "at last the mountain has given birth to a mouse." Having waited two months for "Miss Rose Asch Simpson" to present her plans for the Social Service Department, Rothman "discovered that the whole system of Social Work consisted in extending help to our tubercular patients." Although Asch's vision of the new department included much more than this, Rothman dismissed her plans, asserting that the general office had been handling, and could continue to take care of, the needs of the membership without the institution of a new department. Rejecting the idea that a social service department could provide services not currently handled by the Circle, he maintained that "the G[eneral]O[ffice] . . . should also be a clearing house for all ideas of human helpfulness, advice, counsel, assistance, and everything else that goes with fraternity. The Workmen's Circle is strong enough, powerful enough, financially, and morally sound enough to undertake real human enterprises which will place it in the foremost ranks of the advanced fraternal organizations."[58] Rothman was loath to see changes in administration, particularly changes that might decrease his own department's authority.

The joint meeting between department advocates and the NEC did not mollify the opposition, who continued to worry that a new tax would not be sufficient to cover all costs incurred by the department. The compromise reached by these groups provided for official NEC participation in the department's work but also stipulated that the Social Service Department could not begin operations for another year.[59] Early in 1928 the NEC authorized the department to begin collecting tax funds from the branches, and in April Rose Asch and Henry Fruchter alerted the Committee for a Social Service Department that they had collected two quarters' tax from about one hundred branches, a total of over $1,000. They ran into problems, however, as many branches withheld their payments until after they were assured that the Social Service Department would be efficiently run and of use to members. Asch and Fruchter asked the NEC for a temporary office and also requested that a subcommittee be formed to help the Social Service Committee get the department up and running. The intransigence of the NEC held firm; leaders decided not to allow the department to begin functioning until they had first collected a full four quarters' taxes in advance taxation.[60]

Dealing with the conundrum of an NEC that required the bulk of the money to be collected prior to opening operations and a membership that wanted to see the operations before providing the funding called for a strong-willed leader. Rose Asch proved to be just such a person, and she refused to be dissuaded from her project. A cartoon published in 1927 illustrates her forceful determination in the pursuit of her dream. The cartoon depicts her with a baby, labeled "social service," to which she is singing a lullaby about how she will drive away the baby's enemies and banish them to the cemetery.[61] Led by such single-minded dedication, social service proponents finally prevailed in July 1929, when the department officially opened its doors. Rose Asch served as supervisor and ran the department with a social worker and a secretary. It quickly became a highlighted feature of the order, offering a wide range of services, such as employment referrals, psychological services, legal aid, advice on childcare and domestic problems, and more. During the Great Depression the department handled approximately 2,000 cases a year; from 1934 to 1935 alone the department interviewed some 6,837 people and provided assistance to 2,369 of them.[62]

Having tried to make her way up the traditional ladder of power, Asch found herself drawn to issues that many in the male-dominated leadership deemed unimportant. Her espousal of working-class social service provision implicitly critiqued her colleagues' lack of attention to the diverse problems of the private sphere. By advocating a socialist Social Service Department Asch not only aided a great number of needy individuals and families, she also expanded her own power within the organization and brought attention to what had previously been considered "women's issues," those not directly related to paid labor and men's public life. Where many women had tried to redefine membership to give themselves more autonomy, Asch successfully brought these new concerns into the central structure of the organization itself.

Arbeter Ring women found work for themselves in those areas of life commonly associated with women: social welfare, education, and cultural work. Even such radical women as Rose Asch, who had never been involved in the ladies' branch or women's club and was one of the few women to claim a major role in the leadership, found that by focusing on certain types of work they could facilitate their movement, and other women's interests, into the public sphere. By the late 1920s women were well on their way to forging a prominent space for themselves in the Workmen's Circle. They were recognized as the primary supporters of the Yiddish school movement, as founders of such cultural ventures as the Workmen's Circle's choruses, and as leaders of the Social Service Department. Still, despite women's success in increasing female activism and changing the tenor of the organization, their actual work at home remained solely their responsibility and an underappreciated one at that. In 1935 a youth group, praising the contributions of women to their branch, commented that, "Five years ago you realized the great importance of women, finding some interest outside of their everlasting duties to their homes and families. Upon your removal of the chains of your everyday life, you have enriched your lives and those of your families."[63] While housework and childcare remained uncelebrated, many male members had come to consider women's educational, cultural, and social contributions vital to the Circle's continued existence.

Feminizing the Socialist Brotherhood

After World War I, socialist women in the Arbeter Ring joined other American women in creating cultural groups, raising money for children's education, and pioneering in social welfare provision. By the start of the Great Depression the Workmen's Circle no longer resembled, and no longer depicted itself as, a socialist brotherhood. Rather, members of the group considered themselves individuals in a larger family. Gone were the images of strong men, standing alone or with other men against capitalist oppression. Replacing such pictures were drawings of entire families: fathers and mothers surrounded by their children.

Women and their ideas about gender equality played a central role in this transformation. Over the years they created spaces for themselves in an organization that had originally given them a cold reception. The unwillingness of the Circle or the socialist movement in general to reenvision gender relations in a substantive way initially limited the ability of women, especially those who were married, to engage in Circle activities. Rather than forego membership in an organization they admired, women devised new means by which to be a socialist and a mother, to be active in public while maintaining responsibility for the private sphere. Women did not turn away from political activity; indeed, they embraced wholeheartedly the Circle's recommendation that they be active outside the home. In the end, they expanded the parameters of what "political" action meant. Like women in the NCJW and Hadassah, Arbeter Ring women created a way to engage in public action on behalf of Jews while simultaneously furthering the interests of women. Refusing to adhere to the notion that only men belonged in "politics," women in all three groups created their own activist spaces and, in the process, shaped the contours of modern American Jewish life.

Feminization of the Workmen's Circle

The strategies employed by Circle women illuminate the struggles faced by all activist women, especially radicals, early in the twentieth century. While on the surface it might appear that separatist organizing meant women's surrender to the constraints placed upon them by men, closer examination demonstrates the profound impact these strategies had on Jewish American organizations. Denied traditional political power but wishing to remain within the socialist movement, Circle women, like those in Hadassah and the NCJW, devised alternative ways to engage in public work. By organizing on their own and promoting women's issues and interests, Circle women managed to achieve prominence in the organization. Although they ultimately conceded the battle regarding equality in membership benefits and national leadership posts, these women succeeded in broadening the organization's purview and sustaining it during a period of great change and challenges to its very existence. By 1930 the Workmen's Circle was a major player not only in the realms of Jewish politics and relief work but also in the fields of Yiddish education and culture. As witnessed in the Circle women's struggle to define a female place in a socialist brotherhood, gender politics played a crucial role in this transformation. Workmen's Circle women's struggles, their available options, and final decisions reveal the gender politics inherent in leftist movements where equality is an insufficiently theorized goal, one which all too often demands that women ignore their differences with men. Yet unlike other organizations, Circle women found that they could not merely overlook the divergence between their lives and the services offered to them by their organization. Denied equal benefits on the basis of physical difference, yet unwilling (and unable) to ignore that difference, Circle women forged alternative means by which to meet some of their needs. In the process of separating, they managed to exert significant influence over the development of the organization, sustaining it through a period of tremendous change and serious challenges to its very existence.

Conclusion

Whether we will or no, the consciousness of our Jewishness is forced upon us. We may glory in it, we may try to evade it, but it is inescapable. We are forced to consider ourselves as one tribe . . . even when [some Jews] have renounced Judaism and have become Christianized or turned atheists, they are still recognized as Jews. They remain members of the family.

Rebekah Kohut, *As I Know Them: Some Jews and a Few Gentiles* (New York: Doubleday, Doran, 1929)

Rebekah Kohut, like countless other American Jews in 1929, envisioned the world's Jews as one large family. Just as in a personal family, where relationships might not always be easy, Kohut argued that all members, no matter how troublesome, remained part of the whole. For centuries American Jews had cared for one another, aiding the poor and others in need. American antisemitism, while not as virulent as the European, especially Russian form, required that Jews not abandon their coreligionists. American Jewish women joined in these endeavors, maintaining a strong adherence to group identity. As large numbers of Eastern European immigrants arrived on the shores of the United States in the late nineteenth century, American Jews found their duty to their "family" increased. Jewish women, such as those in the National Council of Jewish Women, organized to provide relief, aid, and other services to this poorer population.

With the arrival of the new immigrants came more numerous ways to identify as a Jew. While the older immigrants, the German Jews, tended to forswear identifications that did not rest on a religious foundation, many newer immigrants expressed their Jewishness in ways more closely resembling an ethnicity rather than a religious confession. This was particularly the case for people, such as Workmen's Circle members, who adhered to socialism and Bundism, denouncing religion outright. In these years the American Jewish community experienced widening fissures based on class, ideological conviction, religious observance, and language usage. While still committed to promoting Jewish life in the United States and protecting Jews abroad, American Jews found themselves with an increasing variety of ways to identify as Jews.

Despite these growing differences, the outbreak of World War I in Europe led to a new-found unity within the diverse American community. The war deepened profoundly the connection American Jews felt for those overseas, bringing them together to aid refugees fleeing war and pogroms. During the war various relief groups exhorted American Jews to care for their "family" abroad, to look out for their unfortunate "brothers and sisters." Yet while the war initially brought solidarity to the American Jewish community, it ultimately could not conceal the substantial rifts dividing them. These rifts became all the more obvious as the war drew to a close and various subgroups advanced their own solutions to the postwar Jewish "problem."

Along with class and political division, tensions that had existed between men and women before the war resurfaced with greater intensity after it. Women's participation in war relief work brought them actively into the public sphere and, in the case of NCJW and Hadassah, led to the expansion of their prewar programs, even though for the duration of the war these projects were put to the service of the American Jewish Joint Distribution Committee (JDC) and the larger Zionist movement. Particularly in the case of the NCJW, greater interaction with gentile women's organizations further raised women's feeling of competence. By the end of the war growing numbers of women, most notably the female leadership of the NCJW and Hadassah, resented their unequal partnerships with men. Having suppressed a great deal of their autonomy during the war, women quickly grew disenchanted with the silencing that seemed to accompany collaboration with men's groups. As wartime unity gave way to heightened division in the Jewish community, so too did wartime cooperation between men's and women's organizations lead to a renewal of separatist strategies by women at war's end.

Women in the NCJW, Hadassah, and the Workmen's Circle all employed separatism to a greater or lesser degree before the war, finding that it allowed female members an area away from men to hone the skills needed to assume leadership positions—posts they failed to attain in integrated groups. The women who began the NCJW and Hadassah long acknowledged the importance of maintaining distinct spaces for women. In 1893 Hannah Solomon, angered by the dismissive attitude of male leaders, concluded that women should organize on their own. A decade later Henrietta Szold and her cohorts recognized that the Zionist movement was not attracting female adherents and went on to form a separate organization, at the same time formulating a distinct "women's interpretation of Zionism" that they felt better spoke to women's needs, interests, and capabilities. Workmen's Circle women initially took a different path from those in the female-only groups, struggling to attain total equality with men. In the space of a few years some of their number began to argue that absolute equality with men, premised on a male model, neglected areas of life unique to women. Soon they too endeavored to find a means by which women could organize on their own, even as they continued to advance the cause of gender equality. Hadassah and the NCJW felt that men's groups overlooked certain constituencies, notably women and children, and believed that women were better suited to work with these populations. Circle women in the ladies' branches found men inattentive to women's needs and struggled to show reluctant fellow members that an insurance benefit and membership model based on the male breadwinner did not adequately address their concerns. Each in their own way, the women in these three organizations perceived the importance of gender difference and denied the principle that difference resulted in inequality.

During the 1920s women in all three organizations, following different paths, returned to structures based on separatist organizing. The Circle women remained the most closely attached to male-run entities but nevertheless proceeded to form voluntary ladies' auxiliaries and women's clubs that provided them with an organizational space free of male ambivalence or obstructionism. The NCJW continued to aid the JDC but also inaugurated an overseas program of its own, in the process establishing ever closer ties with middle-class European Jewish women. Back home Council leaders built on wartime alliances forged with gentile women's groups, and during the 1920s they became integrally involved in the female reform movement associated with such women as Jane Addams and Lillian Wald. Hadassah fought bitter battles with the male-led Zionist Organization of America to regain its independence. Like their counterparts in the NCJW, Hadassah leaders reached out to Jewish women overseas, in Europe and Palestine. Regardless of their ultimate goals, women in each of these three organizations expressed a firm commitment to separatism, arguing that women needed some degree of autonomy from men, even as, together in concert with men, they worked to ameliorate the conditions of Jews at home and abroad.

This renewed commitment did not result solely from tense interactions with Jewish men. Advances in women's rights and the proliferation of gentile women's organizations also served as powerful catalysts for Jewish women's activism. Far from eliminating a sense of gender difference in the Jewish community, suffrage encouraged women's desire for groups of their own devising. Participating in war relief and entering electoral politics moved all American women, Jewish and gentile, into the public sphere. However, this movement into the public arena failed to dampen Jewish women's preference for separatism. Conversely, even some socialist women persisted in advancing an ideal of complementarity, holding that Jewish men and women could work together on behalf of fellow Jews from around the world, each within their own activist sphere.

Joining other American women, Jewish women stepped up their public activism and explored ways to promote women's issues. At the same time they maintained their involvement in Jewish politics. Working in different areas, women in all three groups made significant contributions to American Jewish life. The NCJW increased its involvement with women's issues both in the United States and in Europe. It helped to form the Women's Joint Congressional Committee (WJCC), the World Congress of Jewish Women, and numerous national Councils of Jewish Women overseas. In concert with its work in the WJCC, Council became active in a range of legislative issues, joining social reformers in opposing the Equal Rights Amendment and promoting peace and disarmament. During the same years Hadassah established itself as a central presence in the daily life of Jewish Palestine by inaugurating countless medical and social services. It supported women's right to vote in Palestine and vigorously recruited American women to Zionism. Through their ladies' branches, auxiliaries, and women's clubs, Circle women initiated a host of new projects. They sponsored Yiddish education and other cultural endeavors, such as summer camps and choruses.

In all these efforts women argued that they were bringing uniquely female characteristics to the public sphere, acting differently than men and initiating work long neglected by them. Jewish women, like their gentile predecessors in the Progressive era, argued that they were taking their special interests and capabilities out of the home and putting them to the service of the wider community. This Jewish "social housekeeping" led to the introduction of new community-provided services and, more importantly, to a redefinition among Jews of what constituted "women's work" and "politics" more broadly. Lillian Wald once commented that "when I went to New York, and was stirred to participate in community work. . . . I believed that politics concerned itself with matters outside [women's] realm and experience. It was an awakening to me to realize that when I was working in the interests of those babies . . . I was really in politics."[1] Like Wald, it took more Jewishly identified women some time to realize the full import of their actions. Perhaps less active than non-Jewish American women in the days before World War I, Jewish women blossomed in the 1920s. As other American women experimented with public life in the first days of their full participation in electoral politics, so too did Jewish women engage in activities that questioned the dividing line between male and female spheres, between self-interested political concerns and selfless communal work. Far from being disinterested outsiders looking in, Jewish women were at the center of the fray, initiating a variety of social welfare, educational, and cultural projects, bringing issues previously considered domestic or feminine directly into the political realm.

Women found, however, that using gendered and maternalist justifications for their participation in the public sphere was not without complication; they discovered that this line of reasoning could be used against them. While gendered arguments and separatist strategies provided women with the confidence and organizational base from which to work effectively alongside men, these also could be utilized by opponents, both male and female, to curtail women's bid for gender equality. Men in the Zionist movement argued that Hadassah leaders' attempts to take a more active role in the administration of the movement at large amounted to "playing politics," a self-interested gambit for power. While men involved in the Zionist wrangling of the 1920s clearly sought power for themselves, the notion that women might engage in the same battle for administrative control proved deeply disturbing. Even some Hadassah members believed that, as women, their leaders should leave the supposedly more complicated, ideological aspects of movement administration to the men. Women, they argued, had their own activist sphere and were quite capable within it, but they were unqualified for central roles in the national leadership.

Proponents of women's equality sought to revalue their work as meaningful, as "political," and to make the case that they were as qualified as men, even if they believed men and women had different leadership styles. They encountered opposition from men and women who disagreed with the premise that women's work was equal to men's, that women, though different, were as capable as men of leading the national movements. This is evident in the case of the Workmen's Circle, where men had long engaged in activities that in other contexts were designated part of the female sphere—namely, social service provision. Yet men in the group valued their work as "political" and deemed women's involvement in similar activities less serious, more bourgeois. Both socialist and Zionist men expressed anxiety over women's increased participation in those movements. As women in the 1920s claimed a more prominent place in the two movements, they changed the general climate, transforming these once predominantly male bastions of activism into groups involved with a wide array of issues. Not only did they make the groups more amenable to women, they changed the very format and structure of movement organizations.

Women in all three groups had a profound impact on American Jewish life. They initiated new services to the Jewish community, provided Jewish women with a rich activist life, and promoted Jewish concerns both nationally and internationally. Although during this period women failed to attain prominent leadership posts in the major organs of American Jewish politics such as the JDC, the

American Jewish Committee, the American Jewish Congress or the Zionist and socialist movements, this does not mean that their influence was minimal. Gender issues stimulated crucial changes in the Workmen's Circle, while commonly held ideas about gender enabled NCJW women to find affinity with gentile women from similar backgrounds in the WJCC. Most significantly, Hadassah's promulgation of a gendered Zionism enabled it to recruit large numbers of non-Zionist women to the cause by 1930. By employing maternalism and other gendered perspectives, Hadassah was able to fit its own political work into a paradigm familiar to many American women. By 1930, not only Jane Addams praised Hadassah projects; so too did numerous non-Zionist Jewish women. In time women concerned about preserving Jewish life in the modern world, but less comfortable with the geopolitical implications of Zionism, loosely allied themselves with the movement through cooperation with Hadassah. Following World War II most American Jews, including Workmen's Circle members, supported the idea of Palestine as a haven for persecuted Jews, even as many continued to hesitate endorsing the establishment of a Jewish nation-state. The Holocaust did much to change the minds of the most recalcitrant anti-Zionists, but, as this book has shown, American Jewish women were already on their way to supporting the idea of Palestine as a refuge ten years before the start of the Second World War.

During the 1930s all three organizations once again mobilized to provide relief to the Jews of Europe and pursued work similar to that rendered in the earlier conflagration. The NCJW helped refugees and would-be immigrants while assisting with the founding of the National Coordinating Committee, a centralized organization of groups working with these populations. Berliner Recha Freier recruited Hadassah to guide the Youth *Aliyah*, a large-scale project to transport German Jewish children to Palestine. From 1933 to 1950 some 50,000 children arrived in Palestine, later Israel, from Germany. Workmen's Circle members, horrified by the Nazi-Soviet Pact, denounced Stalin's sacrifice of Poland and its Jews. The group pledged to support the Polish resistance and keep Jewish culture alive in the United States. In 1941 the Workmen's Circle abandoned its earlier pacifism and supported the U.S. bolstering of the Allied war effort. The organization declared that "the

Workmen's Circle is opposed to war and to the shedding of blood. . . . The present critical times force us to regard the present war as different from all previous wars. This war is a struggle by free countries against tyranny." Once the United States entered the war, Workmen's Circle members struggled assiduously to advance the war effort, buying war bonds, volunteering with the Red Cross, and providing aid to the armed forces. Hadassah and NCJW members pursued similar work during the 1940s.[2]

After the war all three organizations, horrified by revelations of the Holocaust, resolved to aid the survivors in any way they could. Each group raised money for the central fund-raising entity, the United Jewish Appeal, and for the Joint Distribution Committee. The Holocaust brought Council and the Workmen's Circle closer to supporting the Zionist cause officially; in 1946 the NCJW declared its support for the proposed state of Israel as a refuge for Jews from around the world, and two years later, upon the formation of that state, the Workmen's Circle joined the NCJW in accepting Israel as a haven for persecuted Jews and a center of Jewish culture. In the ensuing years Council took a more active role in supporting the developing state by instituting educational and children's projects, including the Center for Research in the Education of the Disadvantaged in 1968. Although some Workmen's Circle members refused to support Israel, and many others expressed regret that Hebrew, not Yiddish, was to be the language of the new Jewish state, over time the majority of Circle members involved themselves with Israeli issues and projects.[3] Hadassah continued its work in Israel and became a powerful presence in the medical life of that land as well as in the organizational life of the United States. Current membership statistics reveal the extent of Hadassah's success: at the turn of the twenty-first century the Zionist Organization of America claimed 50,000 members, while Hadassah, the largest American Jewish women's organization, counted 300,000. In addition to Hadassah's regular membership some 25,000 men joined the group as "associate" members. Having resisted so strenuously becoming a women's auxiliary to the ZOA earlier in the century, Hadassah has ultimately created its own men's auxiliary, even if it resists naming it as such.[4]

The horrors of World War II and the Holocaust prompted the turn toward Zionism by many American Jews, and Hadassah undoubtedly reaped the benefits of this change in attitude. Yet by emphasizing the centrality of gender, by investigating the ways in which Hadassah conceptualized its work and recruited new members, we can better understand how fundamental gender was to Hadassah's program and ultimate success. Moreover, highlighting gender politics underscores Hadassah's substantial accomplishments at home, in Palestine/Israel, and in the world Zionist movement. Gender also played an essential role in the development of the NCJW and the Workmen's Circle, although with less far-reaching political consequences. By the early twenty-first century the NCJW had maintained its position as the voice of American Jewish women in mainstream organizational feminism, lobbying the United States government on such issues as gun control, domestic violence, and reproductive choice while continuing its Israeli and Jewish communal work.[5] Women in Workmen's Circle, no longer separated into their own groups, managed to enter the ranks of the national leadership in large numbers. In 2002 seventeen of the thirty-three National Executive Board members were women, and women held about half of the national staff positions.[6] Separatism, far from stifling women's voices, facilitated American Jewish women's entrance into the public realm in a manner that did not necessitate their sacrificing commitment to either Jewish or women's issues. Gendered and separatist strategies, although dividing women from men for a time, ultimately enabled women to bring their concerns into the public sphere, affecting the course of American Jewish history and shaping the contours of modern American Jewish identity.

NOTES

Introduction

1. This was not the first foray of American women onto the international sphere. They had been active in the abolitionist and peace movements during the antebellum period, and through these movements, especially abolitionism, they established contacts with like-minded British women. See Lois W. Banner, *Elizabeth Cady Stanton: A Radical for Woman's Rights* (Boston: Little, Brown, 1980); Kathryn Kish Sklar, "'Women Who Speak for an Entire Nation': American and British Women Compared at the World Anti-Slavery Convention, London, 1840," in *The Abolitionist Sisterhood: Women's Political Culture in Antebellum America*, ed. Jean Fagan Yellin and John C. Van Horne (Ithaca, NY: Cornell University Press, 1994), 301–34; and Harriet Hyman Alonso, *Peace as a Women's Issue: A History of the U.S. Movement for World Peace and Women's Rights* (Syracuse, NY: Syracuse University Press, 1993). Recent scholarship is uncovering a first-wave international sisterhood. See Bonnie S. Anderson, *Joyous Greetings: The First International Women's Movement, 1830–1860* (New York: Oxford University Press, 2000); and Nancy A. Hewitt, "Re-Rooting American Women's Activism: Global Perspectives on 1848," in *Women's Rights and Human Rights: International Historical Perspectives*, ed. Patricia Grimshaw, Katie Holmes, and Marilyn Lake (New York: Palgrave, 2001), 123–37.

2. See, for example, Nancy Cott, *The Grounding of Modern Feminism* (New Haven, CT: Yale University Press, 1987); and Leila J. Rupp, *Worlds of Women: The Making of an International Women's Movement* (Princeton, NJ: Princeton University Press, 1997).

3. Rebekah Kohut quoted in *World Congress of Jewish Women, Vienna, May 6–11, 1923* (Vienna: Druckerei-U. Verlags-A.G. Ignaz Steinmann, 1923), 10.

4. For settlement house work see, for example, Robyn Muncy, *Creating a Female Dominion in American Reform, 1890–1930* (New York: Oxford University Press, 1991); and Doris Groshen Daniels, *Always a Sister: The Feminism of Lillian D. Wald* (New York: Feminist Press, 1989). On temperance see Ruth Bordin, *Frances Willard: A Biography* (Chapel Hill: University of North Carolina Press, 1986); and Ian R. Tyrrell, *Woman's World/Woman's Empire: The Woman's Christian Temperance Union in International Perspective, 1800–1930* (Chapel Hill: University of North Carolina Press, 1991). On reforming delinquent girls, see Mary E. Odem, *Delinquent Daughters: Protect-*

ing and Policing Adolescent Female Sexuality in the United States, 1885–1920 (Chapel Hill: University of North Carolina Press, 1995). For women and urban activism, see, for example, Maureen A. Flanagan, *Seeing With Their Hearts: Chicago Women and the Vision of the Good City, 1871–1933* (Princeton, NJ: Princeton University Press, 2002).

     5. American women's involvement in World War I and the relief initiatives of those years have not been studied extensively by historians of the period. For American women in World War I, see Maurine Weiner Greenwald, *Women, War and Work: The Impact of World War I on Women Workers in the United States* (Westport, CT: Greenwood, 1980); Barbara J. Steinson, *American Women's Activism in World War I* (New York: Garland, 1982); and Steinson, "'The Mother Half of Humanity': American Women in the Peace and Preparedness Movements in World War I," in *Women, War, and Revolution,* ed. Carol R. Berkin and Clara M. Lovett (New York: Holmes and Meier, 1980), 259–84. More recently European historians have begun to examine gender dynamics during the war, looking at the structural, economic, and occupational changes that transformed women's lives, and analyzing shifts in the gender system. These works, together with those investigating racial dynamics as colonial subjects arrived in Great Britain and France to serve as soldiers and laborers are adding greater complexity to the study of the female experience during World War I. See Philippa Levine, "Battle Colors: Race, Sex, and Colonial Soldiery in World War I," *Journal Of Women's History* 9 (Winter 1998): 104–30; Tylar Stovall, "The Color Line behind the Lines: Racial Violence in France during the Great War," *American Historical Review* 103 (June 1998): 737–69; Angela Woollacott, "'Khaki Fever' and Its Control: Gender, Class, Age and Sexual Morality on the British Homefront in the First World War," *Journal of Contemporary History* 29, no. 2 (1994): 325–47; Woollacott, *On Her Their Lives Depend: Munitions Workers in the Great War* (Berkeley: University of California Press, 1994); and Woollacott, "From Moral to Professional Authority: Secularism, Social Work, and Middle-Class Women's Self-Construction in World War I Britain," *Journal of Women's History* 10 (Summer 1998): 85–111. These works move beyond documenting women's participation in war work or evaluating the changing position of women as a result of the war by revealing the impact of the war years on constructions of gender and race. Similarly, historians have turned their attention to the construction, or attempted reconstruction, of gender systems following the war. Once again, scholars of the European experience have led the way in this endeavor. See, for example, Mary Louise Roberts, *Civilization without Sexes: Reconstructing Gender in Postwar France, 1917–1927* (Chicago: University of Chicago Press, 1994); and Birgitte Soland, *Becoming Modern: Young Women and the Reconstruction of Womanhood in the 1920s* (Princeton, NJ: Princeton University Press, 2000). For American women's activism after the war, see, for example, Cott, *The Grounding of Modern Feminism;* Molly Ladd-Taylor, *Mother-Work: Women, Child Welfare, and the State, 1890–1930* (Urbana: University of Illinois Press, 1994); and Muncy, *Creating a Female Dominion.*

6. Kohut quoted in *World Congress*, 10.

7. Scholars have begun to question the efficacy of the "German-Jewish" versus "East European Jewish" split in American Jewish historiography. Traditionally, historians have separated Jewish migration to the United States into two major waves. The first, beginning in the 1840s, was associated with Jews from Central Europe, the German-speaking lands in particular. By the time the second wave, the Eastern Europeans, arrived from the Russian Empire starting in 1881, "German" Jews as a group were quite well established. They tended to be middle- or upper-class, spoke English, and were fairly assimilated. Eastern Europeans, on the other hand, spoke Yiddish (although their children would speak English), tended to be working class or poor, and were often Orthodox or atheistic socialists. For an example of recent work questioning the stark division set up by this paradigm, see Hasia R. Diner, "Before the Promised City: Eastern European Jews in America before 1880," in *An Inventory of Promises: Essays on American Jewish History in Honor of Moses Rischin*, ed. Jeffrey S. Gurock and Marc Lee Raphael (Brooklyn: Carlson, 1995), 43–62. Moses Rischin first commented on this possibility; see Moses Rischin, *An Inventory of American Jewish History* (Cambridge, MA: Harvard University Press, 1954).

8. For the history of Jews in the United States, see Eli Faber, *A Time for Planting: The First Migration, 1654–1820*, vol. 1, *The Jewish People in America*, ed. Henry L. Feingold (Baltimore: Johns Hopkins University Press, 1992); Hasia R. Diner, *A Time for Gathering: The Second Migration, 1820–1880*, vol. 2, *The Jewish People in America*, ed. Henry L. Feingold (Baltimore: Johns Hopkins University Press, 1992); Gerald Sorin, *A Time For Building: The Third Migration, 1880–1920*, vol. 3, *The Jewish People in America*, ed. Henry L. Feingold (Baltimore: Johns Hopkins University Press, 1992); and, Henry L. Feingold, *A Time for Searching: Entering the Mainstream, 1920–1945*, vol. 4, *The Jewish People in America*, ed. Henry L. Feingold (Baltimore: Johns Hopkins University Press, 1992). On pre-war Jewish women's activism, see, for example, Karla Goldman, *Beyond the Synagogue Gallery: Finding a Place for Women in American Judaism* (Cambridge, MA: Harvard University Press, 2001); and Pamela S. Nadell and Rita J. Simon, "Ladies of the Sisterhood: Women in the American Reform Synagogue, 1900–1930," in *Active Voices: Women in Jewish Culture*, ed. Maurie Sacks (Urbana: University of Illinois Press, 1995), 63-75.

9. These organizations have not received the attention they deserve. For the major works on the NCJW, see Ellen Sue Levi Elwell, "The Founding and Early Programs of the National Council of Jewish Women: Study and Practice as Jewish Women's Religious Expression" (PhD diss., Indiana University, 1982); and Faith Rogow, *Gone to Another Meeting: The National Council of Jewish Women, 1893–1993* (Tuscaloosa: University of Alabama Press, 1993). For Hadassah, see Joan Dash, *Summoned to Jerusalem: The Life of Henrietta Szold* (New York: Harper and Row, 1979); Carol Kutscher, "The Early Years of Hadassah, 1912–1921" (PhD diss., Brandeis University, 1976); Carol Bosworth Kutscher, "From Merger to Autonomy:

Hadassah and the ZOA, 1918–1921," in *The Herzl Yearbook*, vol. 8, *Essays in American Zionism, 1917–1948*, ed. Melvin I. Urofsky (New York: Herzl Press, 1978), 61–76; Marlin Levin, *Balm in Gilead: The Story of Hadassah* (New York: Schocken, 1973); and Donald H. Miller, "A History of Hadassah, 1912–1935" (PhD diss., New York University, 1969). The major English-language sources on the Workmen's Circle are Melech Epstein, *Jewish Labor in the U.S.A.: An Industrial, Political, and Cultural History of the Jewish Labor Movement*, vol. 1, *1882–1914* (New York: KTAV, 1969); Maximilian Hurwitz, *The Workmen's Circle: Its History, Ideals, Organizations and Institutions* (New York: Workmen's Circle, 1936); Arthur Liebman, *Jews and the Left* (New York: John Wiley, 1979); and Judah J. Shapiro, *The Friendly Society: A History of the Workmen's Circle* (New York: Media Judaica, 1970). See also A. S. Zaks, *Di geshikhte fun arbeter ring, 1892–1925, ershter teyl* [The history of the Workmen's Circle, 1892–1925, vol. 1] (n.p.: National Executive Committee, Arbeter Ring, 1925).

10. Until the mid-1930s, Workmen's Circle members were more interested in promoting socialism and Yiddish culture than in "reclaiming *Eretz Israel*" (The Land of Israel). In response to the Nazi persecutions of the Jews beginning in the 1930s, Workmen's Circle supported individual decisions to move to Palestine and, eventually, the state of Israel, yet never officially endorsed the Zionist program. See J. Shapiro, *Friendly Society*, 184–85, 195.

11. The World War I years have also been neglected by scholars of American Jewry. For various aspects of the war and major relief efforts, see Salo W. Baron, *The Russian Jew under Tsars and Soviets*, 2nd ed (New York: Schocken, 1987); Yehuda Bauer, *My Brother's Keeper: A History of the American Jewish Joint Distribution Committee, 1929–1939* (Philadelphia: Jewish Publication Society of America, 1974); Jonathan Frankel, *Prophecy and Politics: Socialism, Nationalism and the Russian Jews, 1882–1917* (London: Cambridge University Press, 1981); Jonathan Frankel, ed., *Studies in Contemporary Jewry: An Annual*, vol. 4, *The Jews and the European Crisis, 1914–1921* (New York: Oxford University Press, 1988); and Marsha L. Rozenblit, *Reconstructing a National Jewish Identity: The Jews of Habsburg Austria during World War I* (New York: Oxford University Press, 2001). On redefining the "political," see Kristi Andersen, *After Suffrage: Women in Partisan and Electoral Politics before the New Deal* (Chicago: University of Chicago Press, 1996).

12. Although the focus of much new research, Jewish women have traditionally been overlooked in historical works on Jewish philanthropy. For example, a considerable amount of work has been done on such male-led initiatives as the Joint Distribution Committee (JDC) and the American Jewish Committee (AJC), but very little scholarly attention has been paid to Jewish women's involvement in such activities. General works on Jewish philanthropy in the United States also tend to underplay the important role of women's groups. Studies specifically on Jewish women, however, detail women's critical involvement in the development of relief and social welfare work within the Jewish community. For works on Jewish charity and philan-

thropy, see, for example, Barry A. Kosmin and Paul Ritterbad, eds., *Contemporary Jewish Philanthropy in America* (Savage, MD: Rowman and Littlefield, 1991), v–ix; Alfred Jacob Kutzik, "The Social Basis of American Jewish Philanthropy" (PhD diss., Brandeis University, 1962), 315–62, 673–76. For international relief, see Bauer, *My Brother's Keeper;* Naomi Cohen, *Not Free to Desist: The American Jewish Committee, 1906–1966* (Philadelphia: Jewish Publication Society of America, 1972); Merle Curti, *American Philanthropy Abroad: A History* (New Brunswick, NJ: Rutgers University Press, 1963); and Oscar Handlin, *A Continuing Task: The American Jewish Joint Distribution Committee, 1914–1964* (New York: Random House, 1964). For Jewish women and charity, see Dianne Ashton, *Rebecca Gratz: Women and Judaism in Antebellum America* (Detroit: Wayne State University Press, 1997); Evelyn Bodek, "'Making Do': Jewish Women and Philanthropy," in *Jewish Life in Philadelphia, 1830–1940*, ed. Murray Friedman (Philadelphia: ISHI, 1983), 143–62, 327–30; Rudolf Glanz, *The Jewish Woman in America: Two Female Immigrant Generations, 1820–1929*, vol. 2, *The German Jewish Woman* (New York: KTAV, 1976), 125–36; Diner, *A Time for Gathering;* Goldman; William Toll, "A Quiet Revolution: Jewish Women's Clubs and the Widening Female Sphere, 1870–1920," *American Jewish Archives* 41 (Spring/Summer 1989): 7–26; Beth S. Wenger, "Jewish Women of the Club: The Changing Public Role of Atlanta's Jewish Women, 1870–1930," *American Jewish History* 76 (March 1987): 311–33; and Wenger, "Jewish Women and Voluntarism: Beyond the Myth of Enablers," *American Jewish History* 79 (Autumn 1989): 16–36.

13. Jonathan Woocher discusses American Judaism as a "civil religion," by which he means that American Jews "began to create an American Jewish polity, a matrix of voluntary organizations and associations which carry out functions of communitywide concern. . . . This faith expressed and sustained the unity American Jews felt among themselves, legitimated the endeavors of the community to maintain Jewish group life while promoting maximal involvement in American society, and inspired Jews to contribute to the support of other Jews and the pursuit of social justice." Woocher discusses the philanthropic endeavors of Jewish men both in the United States and internationally, but he fails to address the important role played by women in such work. Jonathan S. Woocher, *Sacred Survival: The Civil Religion of American Jews* (Bloomington: Indiana University Press, 1986), 20. Woocher applied concepts first developed by Robert N. Bellah to the Jewish context. See, for instance, Robert N. Bellah, "Civil Religion in America," *Daedalus* (Winter 1967): 1–21. On the history of Zionism, see Samuel Halperin, *The Political World of American Zionism* (Detroit: Wayne State University Press, 1961); Ben Halpern, *A Clash of Heroes: Brandeis, Weizmann, and American Zionism* (New York: Oxford University Press, 1987); Walter Laqueur, *A History of Zionism* (New York: Holt, Rinehart and Winston, 1972); Mark A. Raider, *The Emergence of American Zionism* (New York: New York University Press, 1998); Yonathan Shapiro, *Leadership of the American Zionist Organization 1897–1930* (Urbana: University of Illinois Press, 1971);

Melvin I. Urofsky, *American Zionism from Herzl to the Holocaust* (New York: Doubleday, 1975); David Vital, *The Origins of Zionism* (Oxford: Clarendon Press, 1975); and Vital, *Zionism: The Crucial Phase* (Oxford: Clarendon Press, 1987).

14. These analytical categories are from Nancy F. Cott, "What's in a Name? The Limits of 'Social Feminism,' or, Expanding the Vocabulary of Women's History," *Journal of American History* 6 (December 1989): 809–28. Cott defines "female consciousness" as an understanding women have regarding their abilities and activities, which are seen as unique to women. Cott employs "communal consciousness" to describe those endeavors in which women participate along with the men of their group, however "group" may be defined. A "feminist consciousness" is one that challenges male claims to superiority.

15. See Cott, *Grounding;* Muncy, *Creating a Female Dominion;* Rupp, *Worlds of Women;* Estelle B. Freedman, "Separatism as Strategy: Female Institution Building and American Feminism, 1870–1930," *Feminist Studies* 5 (Fall 1979): 512–29; and Freedman, "Separatism Revisited: Women's Institutions, Social Reform, and the Career of Miriam Van Waters," in *U.S. History as Women's History: New Feminist Essays,* ed. Linda K. Kerber, Alice Kessler-Harris and Kathryn Kish Sklar (Chapel Hill: University of North Carolina Press, 1995), 170–88.

16. In those instances where U.S. women's historians have turned their attention to Jews, all too often their gaze has lingered only on the fiery immigrant, labor activists of the late nineteenth century. That exciting period of American Jewish history has also been the subject of many Jewish women's historians, who have used such studies to document the female immigrant experience and examine the "world of our mothers." For Jewish immigrants, labor activism, and American socialism, see Mari Jo Buhle, *Women and American Socialism, 1870–1920* (Urbana: University of Illinois Press, 1981); Susan Glenn, *Daughters of the Shtetl: Life and Labor in the Immigrant Generation* (Ithaca, NY: Cornell University Press, 1990); Alice Kessler-Harris, "Organizing the Unorganizable: Three Jewish Women and Their Union," *Labor History* 17 (Winter 1976): 5–23; Kessler-Harris, "Rose Schneiderman and the Limits of Women's Trade Unionism," in *Labor Leaders in America,* ed. Melvyn Dubofsky and Warren Van Tine (Urbana: University of Illinois Press, 1987), 160–84; Harriet Davis-Kram, "No More a Stranger Alone, Trade Union, Socialist and Feminist Activism: A Route to Becoming American (Rose Schneiderman, Pauline Newman)" (PhD diss., City University of New York, 1997); Sally M. Miller, "From Sweatshop Worker to Labor Leader: Theresa Malkiel, A Case Study," *American Jewish History* 68 (December 1978): 189–205; Annelise Orleck, *Common Sense and a Little Fire: Women and Working-Class Politics in the United States, 1900–1965* (Chapel Hill: University of North Carolina Press, 1995); Sydney Stahl Weinberg, *World of Our Mothers: The Lives of Jewish Immigrant Women* (Chapel Hill: University of North Carolina Press, 1988). See also studies of immigrant women's literature; for example, Norma Fain Pratt, "Culture and Radical Politics: Yiddish Women Writ-

ers, 1890–1940," in *Decades of Discontent: The Women's Movement, 1920–1940*, ed. Lois Scharf and Joan M. Jensen (Westport, CT: Greenwood, 1983), 131–52.

17. Studies that look at Jewish women outside the labor movement and place them in the broader context of American life include Joyce Antler, *The Journey Home: Jewish Women and the American Century* (New York: Free Press, 1997); and Linda Gordon Kuzmack, *Woman's Cause: The Jewish Woman's Movement in England and the United States, 1881–1933* (Columbus: Ohio State University Press, 1990).

18. For instance, the NCJW is mentioned several times in Nancy Cott's examination of 1920s activism; Hadassah is not. See Cott, *Grounding*.

19. See, for instance, Bauer, *My Brother's Keeper*; Judah J. Shapiro, *Friendly Society*; Urofsky, *American Zionism*; and Y. Shapiro, *Leadership*. Recent works on American Zionism tend to take Hadassah more seriously, although they still do not address gender dynamics within the Zionist movement. See, for example, David H. Shpiro, *From Philanthropy to Activism: The Political Transformation of American Zionism in the Holocaust Years, 1933–1945* (Oxford: Pergamon Press, 1994). Recent works on gender and Zionism, which focus mostly on Europe and Palestine, include Michael Berkowitz, "Transcending 'Tzimmes and Sweetness': Recovering the History of Zionist Women in Central and Western Europe, 1897–1933," in *Active Voices: Women in Jewish Culture*, ed. Maurie Sacks (Urbana: University of Illinois Press,1995), 41–62; and *Western Jewry and the Zionist Project, 1914–1933* (Cambridge: Cambridge University Press, 1997), 175–93; David Biale, "Zionism as an Erotic Revolution," in *People of the Body: Jews and Judaism from an Embodied Perspective*, ed. Howard Eilberg-Schwartz (Albany: State University of New York Press, 1992), 283–307; Paula Hyman, *Gender and Assimilation in Modern Jewish History: The Roles and Representations of Women* (Seattle: University of Washington Press, 1995), 146–50; Claudia Prestel, "Zionist Rhetoric and Women's Equality (1897–1933): Myth and Reality," *San Jose Studies* 20 (Fall 1994): 4–28; and Margalit Shilo, "The Double or Multiple Image of the New Hebrew Woman," *Nashim: A Journal of Jewish Women's Studies and Gender Issues* 1 (Winter 1998): 73–94. For a recent work on gender and Bundism, see Daniel Blatman, "Women in the Jewish Labor Bund in Interwar Poland," in *Women in the Holocaust*, ed. Dalia Ofer and Lenore J. Weitzman (New Haven: Yale University Press, 1998), 68–84. A recent study of the *landsmanshaftn* by Daniel Soyer nicely integrates women into the larger historical discussion of Jewish immigrant aid associations. See Daniel Soyer, *Jewish Immigrant Associations and American Identity in New York, 1880–1939* (Cambridge, MA: Harvard University Press, 1997). For a work that analyzes non-Jewish mutual aid organizations from a gender perspective see Mary Ann Clawson, *Constructing Brotherhood: Class, Gender, and Fraternalism* (Princeton, NJ: Princeton University Press, 1989).

Chapter 1

1. Quoted in T. J. Boisseau, "White Queens at the Chicago World's

Fair, 1893: New Womanhood in the Service of Class, Race, and Nation," *Gender and History* 12 (April 2000): 58.

2. Israel Kugler, "A Life in the Workmen's Circle: Reminiscence and Reflection," *Labor's Heritage* 3 (October 1991): 40; Y. Veintroyb, "Der arbayter ring (a kurtser historisher iberblik)," [The Workmen's Circle: A short historical overview] in *Der arbayter ring zamel bukh* [The Workmen's Circle collection book] (New York: Arbayter Ring, 1910): 150–52. For membership figures for dues-paying members only, see I. Sh. Herts, *50 Yohr arbeter ring in yidishn lebn* [Fifty years of Workmen's Circle in Jewish life] (New York: National Executive Committee, Arbeter Ring, 1950), 184. See also Daniel Soyer, *Jewish Immigrant Associations and American Identity in New York, 1880–1939* (Cambridge, MA: Harvard University Press, 1997); and Mary Ann Clawson, *Constructing Brotherhood: Class, Gender, and Fraternalism* (Princeton, NJ: Princeton University Press, 1989).

3. David T. Beito, "Mutual Aid, State Welfare, and Organized Charity: Fraternal Societies and the 'Deserving' and 'Undeserving' Poor, 1900–1930," *Journal of Policy History* 5, no. 4 (1993): 426.

4. Y. Kaminski, *Fertsik yor arbeter-ring: a geshikhte in bilder* [Forty years of the Workmen's Circle: A history in pictures] (New York: National Executive Committee of Workmen's Circle, 1940), 17. Circle members also affiliated with the anarchist and later Communist movements.

5. While the Bund and the Workmen's Circle abjured political nationalism, both were committed to personal as well as communal Jewish identity, a commitment that is inadequately conveyed by such terms as "ethnic identification." See Paul Buhle, "Jews and American Communism: The Cultural Question," *Radical History Review* 23 (Spring 1980): 12–17. On the Bund in Europe see Ezra Mendelsohn, *Class Struggle in the Pale: The Formative Years of the Jewish Workers' Movement in Tsarist Russia* (Cambridge: Cambridge University Press, 1970); and Henry J. Tobias, *The Jewish Bund in Russia: From Its Origins to 1905* (Stanford: Stanford University Press, 1972). For the development of Bund ideology see Jonathan Frankel, *Prophecy and Politics: Socialism, Nationalism and the Russian Jews, 1882–1917* (London: Cambridge University Press, 1981), 171–257; and Oscar I. Janowsky, *The Jews and Minority Rights (1898–1919)* (New York: Columbia University Press, 1933), 72–85. Until 1907 the Bund had a fraternal order of its own in the United States, after which time its members joined Circle branches. See Arthur Liebman, *Jews and the Left* (New York: John Wiley, 1979), 286.

6. Herts, 189.

7. Z. Speyer, "35 yor dvinsker bund brentsh 75" [Thirty-five years of Dvinsker Bund Branch 75], in *Dvinsker bundisher brentsh 75 arbeter ring, 1904–1939* [Dvinsker Bund Branch 75 Workmen's Circle, 1904–1939] (New York, n.p., 1939), p. 6, Box 17, Folder 101, YIVO; Becky Cohen, . . . "Ikh dermon zikh. . ." [I reminisce] in *Tsen yoriger yubiley zhurnal pinsker froyen brentsh 210-B arbeter ring* [Ten year anniversary journal Pinsk Women's Branch 210-B Workmen's Circle] (New York: n.p., 1939), Box 20, Folder

121, YIVO.

8. Yeta Golding in *Der vilner (1909–1939)* (New York: published by Vilna Branch 367, 1939), p. 29, Box 30, Folder 167, YIVO.

9. For example, see *47 yor brentsh 3 arbeter ring* [Forty years of Branch 3 of the Workmen's Circle] (New York: Arbeter Ring, 1946), Box 15, Folder 90, YIVO; Isidor Kohn quoted in *Der vilner (1905–1940)* (New York: published by Vilna Branch 367, 1940), pp. 35–36, Box 16, Folder 96, YIVO. Similar dynamics were recorded in the Canadian branches of Workmen's Circle. See Ruth A. Frager, *Sweatshop Strife: Class, Ethnicity, and Gender in the Jewish Labour Movement of Toronto, 1900–1939* (Toronto: University of Toronto Press, 1992), 105–10.

10. Golde Shibka, "Di arbeter froy un der arbeter ring" [The working woman and the Workmen's Circle], in *Lodzer almanak* [Lodz almanac] (New York: n.p., 1934), pp. 17–18, Box 22, Folder 140, YIVO.

11. Maximilian Hurwitz, *The Workmen's Circle: Its History, Ideals, Organizations and Institutions* (New York: Workmen's Circle, 1936), 207–8.

12. Judah J. Shapiro, *The Friendly Society: A History of the Workmen's Circle* (New York: Media Judaica, 1970), 30; Yent Smit, "Mayn Loyn" [My wages] in *47 yor brentsh 3 arbeter ring;* Tillie Olsen, "Tell Me a Riddle," in *Tell Me a Riddle* (New York: Dell, 1976), 72–125; "Bagrisung fun froyen brentsh 244-B" [Greetings from Women's Branch 244-B], in *Suvenir zhurnal pruzhiner brentsh 244 arbeter ring* [Souvenir journal of Pruzhine Branch 244 of the Workmen's Circle] (New York: n.p., 1938), Box 21, Folder 127, YIVO.

13. Yent Smit, "Mayn Loyn"; and "Bagrisung fun froyen brentsh 244-B."

14. On servants freeing middle-class women to engage in pursuits outside the home during a later period, see Phyllis Palmer, *Domesticity and Dirt: Housewives and Domestic Servants in the United States, 1920–1945* (Philadelphia: Temple University Press, 1989).

15. Anne Firor Scott, *Natural Allies: Women's Associations in American History* (Chicago: University of Illinois Press, 1991), 128. See also Boisseau, "White Queens," 33–81.

16. Hannah G. Solomon, *Fabric of My Life: The Autobiography of Hannah G. Solomon* (New York: Bloch, 1946), 41–43; see also "American Jewish Women in 1890 and 1920: An Interview with Mrs. Hannah G. Solomon," *American Hebrew* 106 (23 April 1920): 748; Deborah Grand Golomb, "The 1893 Congress of Jewish Women: Evolution or Revolution in American Jewish History?" *American Jewish History* 70 (September 1980): 58; and Beth Wenger, "Hannah Greenebaum Solomon (1858–1942)," in vol. 2 of *Jewish Women in America: An Historical Encyclopedia*, ed. Paula E. Hyman and Deborah Dash Moore (New York: Routledge, 1997), 1283–86.

17. Solomon, *Fabric of My Life*, 99–100. See also *The Sentinel's History of Chicago Jewry, 1911–1961*, 180, Nearprint Box, Hannah G. Solomon, American Jewish Archives (hereafter, AJA).

18. Hannah G. Solomon, "Growth of Work through Organization," speech delivered at World's Fair, Chicago, 1933, pp. 1-9, Box 6, Folder 9,

Solomon collection, Library of Congress (hereafter LC); Ellen Sue Levi Elwell, "The Founding and Early Programs of the National Council of Jewish Women: Study and Practice as Jewish Women's Religious Expression" (PhD diss., Indiana University, 1982), 50–54; Golomb, "The 1893 Congress," 59–63; Faith Rogow, *Gone to Another Meeting: The National Council of Jewish Women, 1893–1993* (Tuscaloosa: University of Alabama Press, 1993), 9–10; Wenger, "Hannah Solomon," 1283–84.

19. "American Jewish Women in 1890 and 1920," 749; Rogow, *Gone to Another Meeting*, 16.

20. Elwell, "Founding and Early Programs," 58; Golomb, "The 1893 Congress," 66.

21. Rogow, *Gone to Another Meeting*, 10–11; Scott, *Natural Allies*, 130. Nevertheless, Hannah Solomon thought highly of women's activists and spoke in glowing terms of her trip with Susan B. Anthony to the 1904 International Council of Women held in Berlin. Solomon served on the convention's nominating committee because she alone of the Americans understood both French and German. Years later she wrote that "it was inspiring to deliberate with women of many countries, consecrated to efforts for improving social conditions. But, alas! It was a man's world in which little could be accomplished as long as the lust for power remained an unchecked human passion! Would woman's suffrage act as a check? We worked—we hoped!" Solomon, *Fabric of My Life*, 120.

22. Solomon, *Fabric of My Life*, 82–83.

23. Mrs. Philip Angel of Charlestown, West Virginia, interview by Gerald Kane, 20 April 1970, p. 2, Nearprint Box, Hannah G. Solomon, AJA. Two Jewish women, Henrietta Szold and Josephine Lazarus, did eventually present papers to the general parliament. See Rogow, *Gone to Another Meeting*, 15–16. Other women involved in the planning expressed awareness of patronizing male attitudes. Annie Nathan Meyer wrote to Solomon in 1892 stating her belief that rabbis should lead the Jewish Congress and that there should not be a separate women's group. She felt, however, that women should try to convince the men to allow female representatives to the Jewish Congress. Like Solomon, Meyer recognized that this might be difficult, given prevailing ideas about women common among such men: "I quite agree with you that under ordinary circumstances our rabbis are painfully narrow and old-fashioned as regards women's positions. . . . To me it seems very absurd to have a special Com. for Jewish women." Annie Nathan Meyer to Hannah G. Solomon, 16 May 1892, Box 3, Folder 2, Solomon Collection in LC. Meyer became a vocal opponent of women's suffrage, in direct contrast to her sister, the well-known suffragist Maud Nathan. See Joyce Antler, *The Journey Home: Jewish Women and the American Century* (New York: Free Press, 1997), 54–72.

24. Rebekah Kohut in *More Yesterdays: An Autobiography (1925–1949)* (New York: Bloch, 1950), 120.

25. Scott, *Natural Allies*, 130–34; Boisseau, "White Queens," 56–58.

26. Historians who see the NCJW as less than feminist have taken

issue with Solomon's characterization of events leading up to the Jewish Women's Congress. Deborah Grand Golomb contends that Solomon's retelling represents an attempt in her later years to justify steps the women had already taken in 1893 independently of their male cohorts. She asserts that because it would have been quite unusual at that time for women of their backgrounds to initiate a national organization on their own, "Solomon naturally ascribed a role to the men, albeit a negative one." However, women's experiences in charitable organizations, in Workmen's Circle, and, as will be shown later, in the Zionist movement attest to the complications faced by women who sought major roles in male-led organizations. While Solomon and others may have called a national Jewish women's gathering and later created the NCJW for reasons other than their disagreements with male colleagues, it is certainly possible that such conflicts did, at the very least, contribute to their aspiration for an organization free of male involvement. See Golomb, "The 1893 Congress," 61–62. While the NCJW claims a central place among Jewish women's organizations in the United States, scholars are divided as to whether its activism can be considered feminist. Paula Hyman asserts that groups like the Council can be deemed feminist (although not "hot beds of feminism") because they participated in social housekeeping and sought a place for women in the public sphere. She believes groups like the NCJW were "feminist in a larger sense, in that they enhanced the self-worth of women and worked on their behalf." Other historians, particularly Deborah Grand Golomb, reject this view. Golomb states that if feminism is taken to mean "women identifying primarily as women and working toward programs specifically related to women's concerns, then Jewish women's organizations should not be classified as feminist whether in a broad or narrow sense" because such groups worked for the entire Jewish community rather than for women alone. Golomb asserts that Council founders identified themselves "first as Jews and only second as females when they chose to place their conference in the ranks of the religious rather than the women's assemblies." She contends that the founding congress in 1893, and thus implicitly the Council, was "neither revolutionary nor radical" and consequently should not be considered feminist. See Golomb, "The 1893 Congress," 61–67; and Paula Hyman, "The Voluntary Organizations: Vanguard or Rearguard?" *Lilith* 5 (1978): 17, 22. Faith Rogow also considers the Council a conservative group espousing a brand of "domestic feminism" that never effectively challenged male power or sought to change women's status in society. She contends that Council members justified their forays into the public sphere by relying on arguments affirming their important roles as mothers. She believes that Council's ideology of motherhood and community service maintained the distribution of gender power within the Jewish community, which attempted to keep all women in a traditionally subordinate condition. See Rogow, *Gone to Another Meeting*, 1–7.

For a different interpretation examining how women's groups that seem conservative by today's standards promoted women's rights, access to the public sphere and increasing women's public activism, see Boisseau,

"White Queens," and Scott, *Natural Allies.*

27. Philip P. Bregstone, *Chicago and Its Jews: A Cultural History* (privately published, 1933), p. 45, Nearprint Box, Hannah G. Solomon, AJA. Angel, interview, p. 6.

28. Quoted in R. E. Knowles, "States Outside Activities Keep Women 'Sane, Sweet,'" *Toronto Daily Sta[r]*, n.d., n.p., clipping located in microfilm reel no. 1966: "Solomon, Hannah G. Scrapbook pertaining to her numerous activities, 1894–1953," AJA.

29. Boisseau, "White Queens"; Scott *Natural Allies;* Karen J. Blair, *The Clubwoman as Feminist: True Womanhood Redefined, 1868–1914* (New York: Holmes and Meier, 1980); Molly Ladd-Taylor, *Mother-Work: Women, Child Welfare, and the State, 1890–1930* (Urbana: University of Illinois Press, 1994). For examples outside the United States, see Leila J. Rupp, *Worlds of Women: The Making of an International Women's Movement* (Princeton, NJ: Princeton University Press, 1997); and Nancy R. Reagin, *A German Women's Movement: Class and Gender in Hanover, 1880–1933* (Chapel Hill: University of North Carolina Press, 1995). For a discussion of the NCJW in relation to other women's clubs of the era, see Anne Ruggles Gere, *Intimate Practices: Literacy and Cultural Works in U.S. Women's Clubs, 1880–1920* (Urbana: University of Illinois Press, 1997).

30. "Editorial" in *Reform Advocate* vol. 74 no. 24 (14 January 1928), clipping in Box 1, Folder 3, Solomon Collection, LC.

31. Solomon quoted in Hope Ridings Miller, "Coolness to Feminism in Early Days Recalled," *Washington* [torn off] (24 October 1935), clipping fragment located in Box 1, Folder 3, Solomon collection, LC.

32. "Mrs. Solomon's marriage has been a happy one, her husband being entirely in accord with her views and willing that she should give a good deal of time to social and religious work." Herma Clark column "When Chicago was Young," n.d., n.p., fragment located in Box 1, Folder 3, Solomon collection, LC. Clark created imaginary characters, Martha Freeman Esmond and Julia Boyd, whose "letters" describing life in Chicago were published in her column. In this column, Solomon told Martha Freeman Esmond that she couldn't have accomplished so much without her husband's personal and financial support. On Clark and her characters, see Solomon, *Fabric of My Life*, 43.

33. Rogow, *Gone to Another Meeting*, 23–24; and Seth Korelitz, "'A Magnificent Piece of Work': The Americanization Work of the National Council of Jewish Women," *American Jewish History* 83 (June 1995): 178.

34. Henrietta Szold to Sadie American, 27 March 1900, Record Group 7, Box 19, Folder 231, Hadassah Archives (hereafter, HA) This and subsequent quotations are reprinted here courtesy of Hadassah, the Women's Zionist Organization of America, Inc. See also Elwell, "Founding and Early Programs," 145.

35. Henrietta Szold to Minnie Isaacs, 22 February 1900, RG 7, Box 19, Folder 231, HA. On the similarity in Council leaders' backgrounds, see Rogow, *Gone to Another Meeting*, "Appendix A: The Women," 203–23; and

"Appendix B: Biographical Sketches," 224–40.

36. "Hadassah" is Hebrew for "myrtle"; it is also the Hebrew name of the biblical Queen Esther. The New York chapter of the Daughters of Zion first met on Purim, the holiday associated with Esther, and therefore decided to call itself the Hadassah Chapter of the Daughters of Zion. Other chapters took on names of other Jewish heroines. See Marlin Levin, *Balm in Gilead: The Story of Hadassah* (New York: Schocken, 1973), 16–17.

37. FAZ circular #2, 1911, quoted in Carol Bosworth Kutscher, "From Merger to Autonomy: Hadassah and the ZOA, 1918–1921," in *The Herzl Yearbook*, vol. 8, *Essays in American Zionism, 1917–1948*, ed. Melvin I. Urofsky (New York, 1978), 61.

38. Mrs. A. H. Fromenson to Hortense Levy, 10 May 1932, RG 4, Box 2, Folder 19, HA.

39. Kutscher, "From Merger to Autonomy," 61–63.

40. "Practical Zionism," as opposed to more ideological, political, or cultural manifestations of the movement, emphasized concrete tasks through which Western Zionists could facilitate the growth of the nation. It is most commonly associated with Louis Brandeis. Indeed, standard interpretations make much of the connection between Brandeis and Hadassah leaders. In contrast to the impression conveyed by standard histories, Carol Kutscher argues that there is no evidence in Brandeis's papers that he ever directly led Hadassah. See Carol Kutscher, "The Early Years of Hadassah, 1912–1921" (Ph.D. diss., Brandeis University, 1976), 158–59. For more on practical Zionism see Ben Halpern, *Clash of Heroes: Brandeis, Weizmann, and American Zionism* (New York: Oxford University Press, 1987), 94, 218–19, 256–59; Walter Laqueur, *A History of Zionism* (New York: Holt, Rinehart and Winston, 1972), 158–61; and Melvin I. Urofsky, *American Zionism from Herzl to the Holocaust* (New York: Doubleday, 1975), 123–26, 250–60.

41. Joan Dash, *Summoned to Jerusalem: The Life of Henrietta Szold* (New York: Harper and Row, 1979), 9–34. See also Jonathan D. Sarna, *JPS: The Americanization of Jewish Culture, 1888–1988* (Philadelphia: Jewish Publication Society, 1989); and Baila Round Shargel, *Lost Love: The Untold Story of Henrietta Szold* (Philadelphia: Jewish Publication Society, 1997).

42. Dash, *Summoned to Jerusalem*, 35, 22–23; Urofsky, *American Zionism*, 141; and Eric L. Goldstein, "The Practical as Spiritual: Henrietta Szold's American Zionist Ideology, 1878–1920," in *Daughter of Zion: Henrietta Szold and American Jewish Womanhood*, ed. Barry Kessler (Baltimore: Jewish Historical Society of Maryland, 1995), 22–29.

43. Herzl is considered the founder of "political Zionism," namely the movement to found a Jewish nation-state in Palestine. Herzl was open to the idea of creating a Jewish state somewhere other than Palestine, for instance Uganda; however, Russian Zionists, among others, rejected these plans outright.

44. Lotta Levensohn, "Recollections," Jerusalem, 1967, pp. 1–2, RG 4, Box 2, Folder 17, HA.

45. Alice L. Seligsberg, "Chronicle of Hadassah, 1912–1914," p. 1,

in RG 4, Box 2, Folder 19, HA; Dash, *Summoned to Jerusalem*, 87–91.

46. Rose G. Jacobs, "Chapter II" of her unpublished history, pp. 3–5, RG 7, Reel 4, HA; and Jacobs, "Beginnings of Hadassah," in *Early History of Zionism in America*, ed. Isidore S. Meyer (New York: Arno Press, 1977), 233–36. See also "Extracts from the Diaries of Mrs. Bernard A. Rosenblatt (Gertrude Goldsmith) of the Years 1911, 1912, 1913, 1914," pp. 1–2, RG 4, Box 2, Folder 17, HA; Dash, *Summoned to Jerusalem*, 67, 105–6. At about the same time, Senior Abel of the FAZ executive committee, who had contact with Szold through her work with Russian immigrants in Baltimore, proposed forming a national FAZ women's auxiliary. The actual task of organizing women fell to Bernard Rosenblatt who, early in 1912, consulted with Szold and the Hadassah chapter about putting together such a group.

47. Kutscher, "Early Years of Hadassah," 126–28. Indeed, Brandeis and others sometimes referred to Szold as "'the Jane Adamms [*sic*] of our Jewish world.'" Quoted in Michael Brown, "Henrietta Szold's Progressive American Vision of the Yishuv," in *Envisioning Israel: The Changing Ideals and Images of North American Jews*, ed. Allon Gal (Detroit: Wayne State University Press, 1996), 76.

48. Dash, *Summoned to Jerusalem*, 110; Goldstein, "Practical as Spiritual," 22.

49. Dash, *Summoned to Jerusalem*, 97, 104–5, 149; Urofsky, *American Zionism*, 107.

50. Lotta Levensohn, "Miss Szold as a Leader of Women," 17 November 1930, p. 2, RG 4, Box 2, Folder 17, HA. Much has been made of the close interaction between Brandeis and Hadassah. Writing about Brandeis in 1941, Rose Jacobs suggested that the affinity between the judge and the women's organization arose from his general respect for women and specifically for the work they did. She pointed out that Hadassah's founding occurred in 1912, the same year as Brandeis's public profession of Zionism, and that from then on he always took a special interest in that organization. While Zionism theoretically advocated women's equality with men, in actuality, Jacobs recalled, women "were not taken sufficiently seriously to be given responsibilities and privileges on the same plane as the men." Judge Brandeis, however, diverged from this stance by considering women equal to men in "intellect, ability and judgement." Jacobs wrote that when she first met Brandeis he left her with the impression that he was "a listener instead of a speaker, one who had respect for punctuality, regard for time and precision, a dislike for personal publicity." She observed that if other speakers at Zionist meetings used more than their allotted time, Brandeis shortened his own presentation, promising to give the rest of it at a later date. These were qualities not generally associated with the (stereo)typical male Zionist. They were, however, qualities that Hadassah leaders fostered in their own organization. They often presented such characteristics as more "womanly" than the assertive, spotlight-seeking demeanor of the most prominent Zionist leaders. See Rose G. Jacobs, "Justice Brandeis and Hadassah," *New Palestine* (14 November 1941): 17–18, clipping in Rose Jacobs Papers, RG 7, Reel 4,

HA.

51. Statistics reported in a 1917 pamphlet titled, "Hadassah," p. 11, RG 4, Box 21, HA. This pamphlet reports the following growth in membership: March 1913, 1 chapter/190 members; June 1914, 8 chapters/519 members; June 1915, 16 chapters/1,150 members; December 1916, 32 chapters/2,117 members.

52. "Report of the Proceedings of the Fourth Convention," p. 2, RG 3, Box 1, Folder 4, HA. Prior to 1914 the FAZ consisted of just over 12,000 members. Urofsky, *American Zionism*, 145.

53. "The Healing of the Daughter of My People," in the *Maccabaean* 23 (May 1913): 3–8. Reprint located in RG 4, Box 2, Folder 20, HA.

54. Rosenblatt diary extracts, 19 March 1914, p. 23, RG 4, Box 2, Folder 17, HA.

55. Rose Jacobs, handwritten notes for history of Hadassah, RG 7, Reel 4, HA.

56. Unsigned, handwritten comments on letter to Mrs. H. Kaplan of Cleveland from Ruth Cohen, executive secretary of Hadassah, 11 February 1925, Hadassah, the Women's Zionist Organization, Cleveland Chapter, Ms. 3956, Box 1, Folder 2, Western Reserve Historical Society, Cleveland, Ohio (hereafter, WRHS).

57. Only one Yiddish-language article appeared in either Hadassah monthly publication from 1914 to 1929. See "Liebe shvester fun hadassah!" [Dear sisters of Hadassah!], Hadassah *Newsletter* 3 (November 1922): 4. Carol Kutscher believes that many members were from the working class; however, very few, if any, women of Eastern European origin held prominent posts in Hadassah during this period. See Kutscher, "Early Years of Hadassah," 110–21. Henrietta Szold stated in 1915 that "for the present at least" Hadassah was not made up of women from the leisure class but of working women such as teachers, shop girls, trade workers, and stenographers. See "Report of the Proceedings of the Second Annual Convention" in Hadassah *Bulletin* no. 12 (July 1915): 7, located in RG 3, Box 1, Folder 2, HA.

58. Fani Soloviov in *50 yoriker yubileum kiever brentsh 25 arbeter ring, 1906–1956* [Fifty year jubilee of Kiever Branch 25 of the Workmen's Circle] (New York: n.p., 1956), Box 16, Folder 93, YIVO. On Jewish women avoiding domestic service as well as on economic conditions in the Pale of Settlement generally, see Susan Glenn, *Daughters of the Shtetl: Life and Labor in the Immigrant Generation* (Ithaca, NY: Cornell University Press, 1990), 8–49.

59. "Froyen" [Women], in *Di geshikhte fun 60 yor arbeter ring brentsh 207/40 yor arbeter ring brentsh 207-b* [The history of sixty years of Workmen's Circle Branch 207/Forty years of Workmen's Circle Branch 207-b] (Atlanta: n.p., 1968), p. 6, Box 19, Folder 119, YIVO. See also Khane Klein, "Yorn loyfn" [Years run], in *Tsen yoriger yubiley zshurnal pinsker froyen brentsh 210-B arbeter ring.*

60. Daniel E. Bender, "From Sweatshop to Model Shop: Anti-Sweatshop Campaigns and Languages of Labor and Organizing, 1880–1934" (PhD diss., New York University, 2001), 193–210.

61. Zaks, *Geshikhte*, 213–16 (quotation from 215). Also in A. S. Zaks, "Der arbeter ring: zayn antshteyung un antviklung" [The Workmen's Circle: Its rise and development], 1926, p. 149 [fragment torn from a larger publication], Box 1, Folder 1, YIVO.

62. Hurwitz, *The Workmen's Circle*, 208. In commenting upon the initial lack of success in recruiting women to the ladies' branches around 1904–5, Zaks maintains that "instead of going it alone/remaining separate, the radical women joined the regular branches." Zaks, *Geshikhte*, 255. For similar debates in the Socialist Party see Mari Jo Buhle, *Women and American Socialism, 1870–1920* (Urbana: University of Illinois Press, 1981), 121–35. For a different arena showing female union members joining auxiliaries, see Melinda Chateauvert, *Marching Together: Women of the Brotherhood of Sleeping Car Porters* (Urbana: University of Illinois Press, 1998), 3–16.

63. Hurwitz, *The Workmen's Circle*, 209; Zaks, *Geshikhte*, 215, 253. On the patriarchal nature of insurance benefit provision, see Soyer, *Jewish Immigrant Associations*, 7, 79–80, 86. On the German Socialist Women's Auxiliaries, Socialist women's clubs, and Socialist Party's Women's National Committee, see M. Buhle, *Women and American Socialism*, 14–20, 110–12, 145–75. In Ybor City some leftist mutual aid groups provided maternity insurance. See Nancy A. Hewitt, *Southern Discomfort: Women's Activism in Tampa, Florida, 1880s–1920s* (Urbana: University of Illinois Press, 2001), 270–71.

64. The fact that men discussed "women's illness" in general yet only ruled on the ladies' branches seems to indicate that women who joined the regular branches at class 1 status accepted insurance equal to that of men, meaning insurance that did not recognize differences in needs and conditions. Zaks, *Geshikhte*, 229, 253; Hurwitz, *The Workmen's Circle*, 209–10.

65. Zaks, *Geshikhte*, 229, 253–57; Hurwitz, *The Workmen's Circle*, 209–11. Unfortunately membership statistics do not distinguish between married and unmarried members, and they rarely distinguish between male and female members.

66. Bender, "From Sweatshop to Model Shop," 277–78.

67. *Arbeter ring: akhter yorlikher konvenshon* [The Workmen's Circle: eighth yearly convention], 1908, p. 34, Box 3, Folder 13, YIVO. At some point class 2 lost its gendered characterization. For instance, at the 1908 convention the National Executive Committee urged that wives of men in class 2 should be allowed to join the organization at class 3 membership. Class 3 membership was for wives of class 1 members and only provided death benefits. See *Arbeter ring yorlikher report* [The Workmen's Circle yearly report], printed report, 1908, p. 57, Box 3, Folder 14, YIVO.

68. Hurwitz, *The Workmen's Circle*, 210.

69. *Report fun arbeter ring tsu der elfter konvenshon* [Report of the Workmen's Circle to the eleventh convention], printed report, 1911, pp. 37–38, Box 3, Folder 16, YIVO. *Der fraynd. Konvenshon numer* [The friend. Convention number], May 1919, p. 31, Box 4, Folder 19, YIVO.

70. *Report fun arbeter ring* [Report of the Workmen's Circle], printed

report, 1908, p. 57, Box 3, Folder 14, YIVO; and *Tsehnte yehrlikhe konvenshon fun dem arbeter ring* [Tenth yearly convention of the Workmen's Circle], convention publication, 1910, Box 3, Folder 15, YIVO. *Konvenshon buletin* [Convention bulletin], vol. 7, no. 7 (20 May 1925): 26, Box 4, Folder 21, YIVO. On the Social Security Administration, see Alice Kessler-Harris, "Designing Women and Old Fools: The Construction of the Social Security Amendments of 1939," in *U.S. History as Women's History*, ed. Linda K. Kerber, Alice Kessler-Harris, and Kathryn Kish Sklar (Chapel Hill: University of North Carolina Press, 1995), 87–106.

71. Elwell, "Founding and Early Programs," 97–125. On the NFTS, see Pamela S. Nadell and Rita J. Simon, "Ladies of the Sisterhood: Women in the American Reform Synagogue, 1900–1930," in *Active Voices: Women in Jewish Culture*, ed. Maurie Sacks (Urbana: University of Illinois Press, 1995), 63–75.

72. *1897 Program of Council of Jewish Women*, Convention publication, p. 25, Box 4, Folder 1, Solomon Collection, LC.

73. Korelitz, "'Magnificent Piece of Work,'" 179–81; Rogow, *Gone to Another Meeting*, 138–52. On Jewish involvement in prostitution, especially the criminal underworld in New York, see Edward Bristow, *Prostitution and Prejudice: The Jewish Fight against White Slavery* (New York: Clarendon Press, 1982).

74. Sadie American, "Report of the Department of Immigrant Aid," *Official Report of the Council of Jewish Women Seventh Triennial*, New Orleans, 1914, pp. 175–78, Box 4, Folder 5, Solomon collection, LC.

75. Ibid., 179–80.

76. Rogow, *Gone to Another Meeting*, 140–43, 150–52.

77. Korelitz, "Magnificent Piece of Work," 188–95; Rogow, *Gone to Another Meeting*, 133–54.

78. Elwell, "Founding and Early Programs," 75–76. On settlement women forging professional careers, see Robyn Muncy, *Creating a Female Dominion in American Reform, 1890–1930* (New York: Oxford University Press, 1991).

79. Hannah G. Solomon, section of a speech, "C—Welfare Work Forty Years Ago and Today" [handwritten on top of page, "for Council"], pp. 2–4, Box 6, Folder 10, Solomon Collection, LC.

80. Scott, *Natural Allies*, 156; Muncy, *Creating a Female Dominion*, 44–53.

81. Sadie American, "Report of Executive Secretary," *Official Report of the Council of Jewish Women Seventh Triennial*, New Orleans, 1914, p. 125, Box 4, Folder 5, Solomon collection, LC.

82. Quoted in Donald H. Miller, "A History of Hadassah, 1912–1935" (PhD diss., New York University, 1969), 52.

83. "Address by Mr. Lipsky at Hadassah Convention," 1921, p. 1, RG 3, Box 2, Folder 4, HA.

84. The concept of "Muscular Jewry" was developed by Max Nordau. He believed that Jews, men most notably, should contest antisemitic

conceptions of Jews as physically inferior by engaging in organized athletics and other physical activity. See Anita Shapira, *Land and Power: The Zionist Resort to Force, 1881–1948* (New York: Oxford University Press, 1992), 13. Michael Berkowitz and Paula Hyman discuss the gendered construction of the concept in its focus on masculinity, not the physical health of all Jews. See Michael Berkowitz, *Zionist Culture and West European Jewry before the First World War* (London: Cambridge University Press, 1993); and Paula Hyman, *Gender and Assimilation in Modern Jewish History: The Roles and Representations of Women* (Seattle: University of Washington Press, 1995), 144–45. See also Claudia Prestel, "Zionist Rhetoric and Women's Equality (1897–1933): Myth and Reality," *San Jose Studies* 20 (Fall 1994): 4–28.

85. "Letter from Henrietta Szold," 26 October 1921, p. 5, RG 3, Box 2, Folder 4, HA.

86. Dash, *Summoned to Jerusalem*, 105. For an overview of attitudes toward halukah in the United States and Palestine, see Peter Grose, *Israel in the Mind of America* (New York: Alfred A. Knopf, 1983); and Hanna Herzog, "The Fringes of the Margin: Women's Organizations in the Civic Sector of the *Yishuv*," in *Pioneers and Homemakers: Jewish Women in Pre-State Israel*, ed. Deborah Bernstein (Albany: State University of New York Press, 1992), 283–304.

87. Boris D. Bogen, *Jewish Philanthropy: An Exposition of Principles and Methods of Social Science in the United States* (New York: Macmillan, 1917), 318–25; Herman D. Stein, "Jewish Social Work in the United States, 1654–1954," *American Jewish Yearbook* 57 (1956): 55–56. See also Daniel J. Walkowitz, "The Making of a Feminine Professional Identity: Social Workers in the 1920s," *American Historical Review* 95 (October 1990): 1051–75. Robyn Muncy argues that male and female professionals had different motives and ultimately developed different "professional creeds." Muncy, *Creating a Female Dominion*, 160–61.

88. Joan Dash describes Szold's frustration with FAZ meetings, asserting that she soon grew tired of the "endless, pointless wrangling" of the men. Dash, *Summoned to Jerusalem*, 104–5.

89. Proceedings and Speeches at 14th Convention, p. 4, RG 3, Box 6, Folder 2, HA.

90. Carol Kur, "Hadassah, The Women's Zionist Organization of America, Part I," in *Jewish American Voluntary Organizations*, ed. Michael N. Dobkowski (Westport, CT: Greenwood, 1985), 152; On the Addams and Wise trips, see Gertrude Goldsmith diary extracts, p. 13, RG 4, Box 2, Folder 17, HA.

91. "A Brief History of Hadassah's Activities," pamphlet published in June 1932, RG 4, Box 21, HA. While working at Hull House Julia Lathrop chided a Jewish woman who had complained that the soup being served was "trayf" [non-kosher]. "Of course you['d] rather starve!'" she said to the woman, with exasperation. Quoted in Ladd-Taylor, *Mother-Work*, 79.

92. See Hadassah *Bulletin* no. 9 (April 1915): 3–4; *Bulletin* no. 10 (May 1915): 3–4; and Jessie Sampter's review of Herzl's *The Jewish State* in

Bulletin no. 10 (May 1915): 4–5.

93. Goldstein, "Practical as Spiritual," 23. Alice Seligsberg recalled that "We were not permitted to have more than one chapter in a city and that chapter had to include rich and poor, Americanized socially elite and foreign born." Quoted in Joyce Antler, "Zion in Our Hearts: Henrietta Szold and the American Jewish Women's Movement," in Kessler, ed., *Daughters of Zion*, 43.

Chapter 2

1. Barbara J. Steinson, "'The Mother Half of Humanity': American Women in the Peace and Preparedness Movements in World War I," in *Women, War, and Revolution*, ed. Carol R. Berkin and Clara M. Lovett (New York: Holmes and Meier, 1980), 259.

2. Yehuda Bauer, *My Brother's Keeper: A History of the American Jewish Joint Distribution Committee, 1929–1939* (Philadelphia: Jewish Publication Society of America, 1974), 6.

3. Salo W. Baron, *The Russian Jew under Tsars and Soviets*, 2d ed. (New York: Schocken, 1987), 156–63; Steven J. Zipperstein, "The Politics of Relief: The Transformation of Russian Jewish Communal Life during the First World War," in *Studies in Contemporary Jewry: An Annual*, vol. 4, *The Jews and the European Crisis, 1914–1921*, ed. Jonathan Frankel (New York: Oxford University Press, 1988), 24–25; and Martin Gilbert, *The First World War: A Complete History* (New York: Henry Holt, 1994), 103, 108, 139.

4. William O. McCagg, Jr., "On Hapsburg Jewry and Its Disappearance," in Frankel, ed., *Studies in Contemporary Jewry*, 89–91; Marsha L. Rozenblit, *Reconstructing a National Jewish Identity: The Jews of Habsburg Austria during World War I* (New York: Oxford University Press, 2001), 65–66.

5. Jonathan Frankel, "The Paradoxical Politics of Marginality: Thoughts on the Jewish Situation during the Years 1914–1921," in Frankel, ed., *Studies in Contemporary Jewry*, 6; Joan Dash, *Summoned to Jerusalem: The Life of Henrietta Szold* (New York: Harper and Row, 1979), 111. Some Jews stayed, claimed Ottoman citizenship, and fought for the Ottoman army, usually in labor battalions. Such people, men mostly, hoped that this would advance the cause of obtaining a Jewish homeland in Palestine. See Billie Melman, "Re-Generation: Nation and the Construction of Gender in Peace and War—Palestine Jews, 1900–1918," in *Borderlines: Genders and Identities in War and Peace, 1870–1930*, ed. Billie Melman (New York: Routledge, 1998), 131.

6. Bauer, *My Brother's Keeper*, 3–7.

7. Mrs. Nathan Glauber, "Conference of National Jewish Organizations," *Official Report of the Council of Jewish Women's Seventh Triennial*, New Orleans, 1914, pp. 171–73, Box 4, Folder 5, Solomon Collection, LC.

8. Inez Lopez (Mrs. Octavus) Cohen of Charleston, S.C., quoted in *Full Proceedings of the Board of Managers of the Council of Jewish Women Session of December 6, 1914*, pp. 16–18, Box 1, Folder 1, NCJW Collection, LC.

9. Ibid., pp. 14–15. Similar questions over targeting funds concerned Austrian Jews early in the war. See Rozenblit, *Reconstructing*, 62–63.

For Council's participation level see "President's Report," *Proceedings of the Board of Managers of the Council of Jewish Women*, 26 April 1916, pp. 25–26, Box 2, Folder 1, NCJW Collection, LC.

10. Nora Levin, *While the Messiah Tarried: Jewish Socialist Movements, 1871–1917* (New York: Schocken, 1977), 207–8; Judah J. Shapiro, *The Friendly Society: A History of the Workmen's Circle* (New York: Media Judaica, 1970), 63.

11. "Di belgishe un yidishe opfer fun krieg" [The Belgian and Jewish victims of the war], *Der fraynd* 6 (February 1915): 3–4. See also "Di rusishe regierung un di pogromen" [The Russian government and the pogroms], and "Di shoyderlikhe noyt in poylen in galitsien" [The horrible hardship in Poland and Galicia], *Der fraynd* 6 (March 1915): 3–4. The first editorial reported on an extra-session held by the Russian Duma at which the minister of foreign affairs asserted that reports of pogroms initiated by Russian soldiers were just German inventions. The editors of *Der fraynd* were reluctant to believe the words of the Russian government. As they wrote in the second editorial, they felt that although the war affected all Europeans, the Jews in the East were by far the worst off because they were "encircled by enemies." The editors questioned whether the foreign minister and others thought that pogroms were merely an unfortunate consequence of war and there was nothing distinctive about the Jews' situation.

12. I. Sh. Herts, *50 Yohr arbeter ring in yidishn lebn* [Fifty years of Workmen's Circle in Jewish life] (New York: National Executive Committee, Arbeter Ring, 1950), 128.

13. Ibid, 129; National Workmen's Committee on Jewish Rights, *The War and the Jews in Russia* (New York: National Workmen's Committee on Jewish Rights, n.d.), 5–6. See also Jonathan Frankel, *Prophecy and Politics: Socialism, Nationalism and the Russian Jews, 1882–1917* (London: Cambridge University Press, 1981), 512–13.

14. Walter Laqueur, *A History of Zionism* (New York: Holt, Rinehart and Winston, 1972), 171–72; Yonathan Shapiro, *Leadership of the American Zionist Organization 1897–1930* (Urbana: University of Illinois Press, 1971), 86, 129; and David Vital, *Zionism: The Crucial Phase* (Oxford: Clarendon Press, 1987), 129–32.

15. Y. Shapiro, *Leadership*, 78–79; Melvin I. Urofsky, *American Zionism from Herzl to the Holocaust* (New York: Doubleday, 1975), 120, 152–55, 168–71. See also Bauer, *My Brother's Keeper*, 6–8.

16. Hadassah *Bulletin* no. 34 (August 1917): 4.

17. Convention report in Hadassah *Bulletin* no. 12 (July 1915): 1, 4, issue located in RG 3, Box 1, Folder 2, HA.

18. Henrietta Szold to Dr. I. J. Biskind, 9 September 1914, Ms. 3956, Box 1, Folder 3, WRHS.

19. Henrietta Szold to Augusta (Mrs. Julius) Rosenwald, 17 January 1915, RG 7, Box 2, Folder 234, HA.

20. Carol Kutscher, "The Early Years of Hadassah, 1912–1921" (PhD diss., Brandeis University, 1976), 162–63. On the American Confer-

ence for Democracy and Terms of Peace and People's Council, see Barbara J. Steinson, *American Women's Activism in World War I* (New York: Garland, 1982), 265–73; and, Frank L. Grubbs, Jr. *The Struggle for Labor Loyalty: the A. F. of L., and the Pacifists, 1917–1920* (Durham: Duke University Press, 1968).

21. Quoted in Dash, *Summoned to Jerusalem*, 120; Kutscher, "The Early Years of Hadassah," 162–63. Besides Szold the other Central Committee members to join were Alice L. Seligsberg, Nellie Straus Mochenson, Lotta Levensohn, Jessie Sampter and Gertrude Rosenblatt. Dash, *Summoned to Jerusalem*, 118–20. Incidentally, Rebekah Kohut of the NCJW was opposed to Magnes' pacifism because she believed that Germany was a militaristic menace. See Kohut, *More Yesterdays: An Autobiography (1925–1949)* (New York: Bloch, 1950), 107.

22. Dash, *Summoned to Jerusalem*, 120. Szold remained opposed to U.S. involvement in the war even after the Germans invaded Bolshevik Russia in March 1918. She also disagreed with using Liberty Loans as a means by which to raise money for the war, believing them to be an improper method of taxation. See Kutscher, *The Early Years of Hadassah*, 164–65.

23. The column first appeared in March 1915 although individual articles on women's suffrage and other women's issues had appeared (infrequently) in earlier issues. The two most frequent authors of the column during the war years were Adele Kean Zametkin and Esther Lurie. Adele (sometimes Adela or Adella) Kean Zametkin wrote most of the columns from 1914 until 1917. Esther Lurie covered women's issues for *Der fraynd* beginning in late 1918 and continuing through 1919. Born in Warsaw in 1877, she became a socialist when she was a student in Bern, Switzerland. She returned to Russia and became an active Bundist. In 1906 she was arrested and exiled to Siberia. She made her way to New York City in 1912 and began to write for the socialist paper *Zukunft* [Future]. Little is known about her life after the 1920s, when she disappeared. See Norma Fain Pratt, "Culture and Radical Politics: Yiddish Women Writers in America, 1890–1940," in *Decades of Discontent: The Women's Movement, 1920–1940*, ed. Lois Scharf and Joan M. Jensen (Westport, CT: Greenwood, 1983), 137–38. On Zametkin see Steven Cassedy, *To the Other Shore: The Russian Jewish Intellectuals Who Came to America* (Princeton, NJ: Princeton University Press, 1997), 101–3; the memoirs of her daughter, Laura Z. Hobson, *Laura Z.: A Life* (New York: Arbor House, 1983); and the entry on Michael Zametkin in *Arbeter Ring: Boyer un tuer* (New York: Marstin, 1962). See also the entries on each woman in the *Biographical Dictionary of Modern Yiddish Literature* (in Yiddish) (New York: Congress for Jewish Culture, 1963). Strangely, neither woman appears in *Boyer un tuer,* a biographical encyclopedia of the Circle's most active members.

24. Steinson, "The Mother Half of Humanity," 269.

25. Steinson, *American Women's Activism*, 12–218, 299–349; and "Mother Half," 259–60.

26. Marion M. Miller, "Nearing Fifty: Council Celebrates Its Birthday," *Jewish Tribune*, 21 January 1938, p. 3, clipping in microfilm number

1966, AJA; *The First Fifty Years: A History of the National Council of Jewish Women, 1893–1943* (n.p.: NCJW, 1943), 41.

27. Cora (Mrs T. J.) Feibleman, chair of the Committee of Peace and Arbitration, in "Proceedings of the Board of Managers of the Council of Jewish Women," April 1916, p. 289, Box 2, Folder 1, NCJW collection, LC; and President's Report in the same minutes, p. 27. On the prewar "preparedness" movement, see William J. Breen, *Uncle Sam at Home: Civilian Mobilization, Wartime Federalism, and the Council of National Defense, 1917–1919* (Westport, CT: Greenwood, 1984), 3–14; and Steinson, *American Women's Activism*, 114–62.

28. Rebekah Kohut, *My Portion* (New York: Albert and Charles Boni, 1927), 263–64. On Dorothy Straight (later, Elmhirst), see Joseph P. Lash, *Eleanor and Franklin* (New York: Smithmark, 1995), 280, 281, 395–96; and Eric Rauchway, "A Gentleman's Club in a Woman's Sphere: How Dorothy Whitney Straight Created the *New Republic*," *Journal of Women's History* 11 (Summer 1999): 60–85. On the United War Work campaign, see Breen, *Uncle Sam at Home*, 63, 69. On National League for Women's Service, see Steinson, *American Women's Activism*, 300–349. Despite supporting the war once it was declared, the NCJW opposed the Selective Service Act, the Espionage Act and the Sedition Act. See Rogow, *Gone to Another Meeting*, 242.

29. *Monthly Bulletin of the American Jewish Relief Committee for Sufferers from the War* 1 (April 1915): 1; *Bulletin of the Joint Distribution Committee of the American Funds for Jewish War Sufferers* 1 (February/March 1917): 77–79; *Bulletin of the Joint Distribution Committee of the American Funds for Jewish War Sufferers* 2 (April 1918): 118–19; and *Bulletin of the Joint Distribution Committee of the American Funds for Jewish War Sufferers* 1 (April 1917): 93. On other instances of "feminizing" victims, see Margaret Kelleher, *The Feminization of Famine: Expressions of the Inexpressible?* (Durham, NC: Duke University Press, 1997); and Elizabeth Thompson, *Colonial Citizens: Republican Rights, Paternal Privilege, and Gender in French Syria and Lebanon* (New York: Columbia University Press, 2000), 19–38.

30. Edward Bristow, *Prostitution and Prejudice: The Jewish Fight against White Slavery* (New York: Clarendon, 1982); Marion A. Kaplan, *The Jewish Feminist Movement in Germany: The Campaigns of the Jüdischer Frauenbund, 1904–1938* (Westport, CT: Greenwood, 1979); Linda Gordon Kuzmack, *Women's Cause: The Jewish Woman's Movement in England and the United States, 1881–1933* (Columbus: Ohio State University Press, 1990), 56–58, 65–73. Kuzmack argues that many American Jewish men considered prostitution a female problem and expressed little interest in the issue. Aside from genuine concern for the girls, middle-class Jewish women were certainly subject to the class bias of other American women interested in reforming "wayward girls." See Kuzmack, *Women's Cause*, 70–71. For the broader American context, see Mary E. Odem, *Delinquent Daughters: Protecting and Policing Adolescent Female Sexuality in the United States, 1885–1920* (Chapel Hill: University of North Carolina Press, 1995). Recent work on Great Britain and

France reveals the heightened concern about rising rates of venereal disease and the perceived increase in female sexual autonomy during the war years. See Philippa Levine, "Battle Colors: Race, Sex, and Colonial Soldiery in World War I," *Journal Of Women's History* 9 (Winter 1998): 104–30; and Angela Woollacott, "'Khaki Fever' and Its Control: Gender, Class, Age and Sexual Morality on the British Homefront in the First World War," *Journal of Contemporary History* 29, no. 2 (1994): 325–47.

31. Zipperstein, "The Politics of Relief," 32–33. For similar concerns in Syria and Lebanon, see Thompson, *Colonial Citizens*, 25.

32. *Bulletin of the Joint Distribution Committee of the American Funds for Jewish War Sufferers* 1 (January 1917): 63. For works addressing concerns about women's safety during World War I and the issue of rape specifically, see Susan R. Grayzel, *Women's Identities at War: Gender, Motherhood, and Politics in Britain and France during the First World War* (Chapel Hill: University of North Carolina Press, 1999), 50–85; Nicoletta F. Gullace, "Sexual Violence and Family Honor: British Propaganda and International Law during the First World War," *American Historical Review* 102 (June 1997): 714–47; and Leila J. Rupp, *Worlds of Women: The Making of an International Women's Movement* (Princeton, NJ: Princeton University Press, 1997), 86–87, 226.

33. *Proceedings of the Annual Meeting of the Council of Jewish Women,* Boston, 27 November–2 December 1921, pp. 240–42, Box 2, Folder 4, NCJW collection, LC.

34. Frankel, "Paradoxical Politics of Marginality," 9; Bauer, *My Brother's Keeper,* 6–8.

35. "Workingmen Give $20,000," *Monthly Bulletin of the American Jewish Relief Committee for Sufferers from the War* 1 (November 1915): 15–16; Herts, *50 yohr,* 125.

36. "Der arbayter ring un di milkhome korbones: Der arbayter ring helft oykh di milkhome korbones in palestina" [The Workmen's Circle and the war victims: the Workmen's Circle also helps the war victims in Palestine], *Der fraynd* 7 (January 1916): 50; Herts, *50 yohr,* 129–30.

37. Philip Grosman, "Geshikhtlekhe erinerungen fun lubliner yong mens brentsh 392 arbeter ring" [Historical reminiscences of the Lublin Young Men's Branch 392, Workmen's Circle], in *Lubliner yong men's brentsh yariger yubileyum 1909–1934* [Lubliner Young Men's Branch 392 annual jubilee 1909–1934] (New York: n.p., 1934), pp. 8–9, Box 31, Folder 172, YIVO. On Jewish landsmanshaftn during this period, see Daniel Soyer, *Jewish Immigrant Associations and American Identity in New York, 1880–1939* (Cambridge, MA: Harvard University Press, 1997), 161–89.

38. *Monthly Bulletin of the American Jewish Relief Committee for Sufferers from the War* 2 (April 1916): 15; and *Monthly Bulletin of the American Jewish Relief Committee for Sufferers from the War* 2 (May 1916): 14–15. On Tag Day see Melech Epstein, *Jewish Labor in the U.S.A.: An Industrial, Political, and Cultural History of the Jewish Labor Movement,* vol. 2, *1914–1952* (New York: KTAV, 1969), 60.

39. A. S. Zaks, *Di geshikhte fun arbeter ring, 1892–1925, ershter teyl*

[The history of the Workmen's Circle, 1892–1925, vol. 1] (n.p.: National Executive Committee, Arbeter Ring, 1925), 611, 662, 667.

40. *In dorem-land funfte oysgabe/45 yor arbeter ring brentsh 207/25 yor binush mikhalevitsh arbeter ring froyen brentsh 207-B* [In the southern land fifth edition/Forty-five years of Workmen's Circle Branch 207/25 years Binush Mikhalevitsh Women's Club Branch 207-B] (Atlanta: n.p., 1954), pp. 6–7, Box 19, Folder 119, YIVO; "People's Relief Committee Bazaar," *Monthly Bulletin of American Jewish Relief Committee for Sufferers from the War* 2 (April 1916): 15.

41. "Monat tsu monat: amerikaner 'hori-op' in der milkhome" [Month to month: American 'hurry-up' in the war] and "di 'konskripshon' fun arbayter-ring" [The "conscription" of the Workmen's Circle], *Der fraynd* 8 (October 1917): 3; and "Monat tsu monat: di milkhome oyf'n ferten yohr" [Month to month: the war in the fourth year] and "Der arbayter ring un di milkhome" [The Workmen's Circle and the war], *Der fraynd* 8 (September 1917): 3; "Akhtsehnter yehrlikher barikht tsu der nayntsehnter yehrlikher konvenshon" [Eighteenth yearly report to the nineteenth yearly convention], *Der fraynd: konvenshon numer* [The friend: convention number] (May 1919): 18, located in Box 4, Folder 19, YIVO.

42. Hadassah *Bulletin* no. 12 (July 1915), p. 4, RG 3, Box 1, Folder 2, HA. See also various pamphlets from the war years in RG 4 Box 21, HA. On *Vulcan* shipment see Urofsky, *American Zionism*, 154–55.

43. Carol Kur, "Hadassah, The Women's Zionist Organization of America, Part I," in *Jewish American Voluntary Organizations*, ed. Michael N. Dobkowski (Westport, CT: Greenwood, 1985), 152–53.

44. Hadassah *Bulletin* no. 23 (July–August, 1916): 1, 8–9, 10, located in RG 3, Box 1, Folder 3, HA.

45. "Report of the Proceedings at the Fifth Convention," June 24–26, 1918, pp. 1–4, RG 3, Box 1, Folder 5, HA; Dash, *Summoned to Jerusalem*, 116–17.

46. Dash, *Summoned to Jerusalem*, 125–27.

47. Kur, "Hadassah," 153; L. D. Geller, "Alice L. Seligsberg, 1873–1940: A Zionist Portrait," in *The Alice L. Seligsberg-Rose G. Jacobs Papers in the Hadassah Archives, 1918–1957: A Guide to the Microfilm* (New York: Hadassah, the Women's Zionist Organization of America, 1985), 4–6; Alice Seligsberg, "The Aims and Achievements of the Jewish Woman in the Field of Social Work in Palestine," paper presented to the Women's Guild of the First Congregational Church in Montclair, NJ (handwritten date 1932), p. 2, RG 7, Reel 2, HA.

48. *NCJW The First Fifty Years*, 45.

49. Kohut, *My Portion*, 265.

50. "Proceedings of the Board of Managers of the Council of Jewish Women," 26 April 1916, pp. 176–77, 181–82, Box 2, Folder 1, NCJW collection, LC; Helen Winkler, "Report: Department of Immigrant Aid," *Official Report of the Council of Jewish Women's Eighth Triennial Convention*, November 1917, p. 200, Box 5, Folder 1, Solomon collection, LC.

51. Winkler, "Report: Department of Immigrant Aid," 194–202.

52. Ibid.; Hannah Soloman, "An Expanding Universe" (handwritten on top "Minneapolis—in the 1930s"), p. 4, Box 6, Folder 10, Solomon collection, LC.

53. Kohut, *My Portion*, 265–66; *Report of the Ninth Triennial Convention*, 1920, p. 409, Box 35, NCJW collection, LC. See also Joyce Antler, *The Journey Home: Jewish Women and the American Century* (New York: Free Press, 1997), 54.

54. David A. Brown, "It Happened Years Ago . . . A Story or Two about the National Council of Jewish Women," *American Hebrew and Jewish Tribune* vol. 136, no. 17 (8 March 1935): 345–46, clipping in Box 102, NCJW collection, LC.

55. Ibid. Brown led many fund-raising drives for a variety of organizations, including the first drive ever for the Michigan American Legion. His support for women might have derived from his fund-raising experience in the past and his desire for these drives to be as successful as possible. See entry in *Who's Who in American Jewry* (New York: Jewish Biographical Bureau, 1926), 84.

56. Oscar I. Janowsky, *The Jews and Minority Rights (1898–1919)* (New York: Columbia University Press, 1933), 168–89.

57. "Proceedings of the Board of Managers of the Council of Jewish Women," 27 April 1916, pp. 271–79, Box 2, Folder 1, NCJW Collection, LC.

58. "Proceedings of the Outgoing Board of Managers of the Council of Jewish Women Chicago, ILLS., 5 November 1917," pp. 84–100, Box 2, Folder 2, NCJW Collection, LC. On allotments, see Morris Frommer, "The American Jewish Congress: A History, 1914–1950," vol. 1 (PhD diss., Ohio State University, 1978), 101–2, n. 85. On labor Zionism, see Mark A. Raider, *The Emergence of American Zionism* (New York: New York University Press, 1998).

59. Dr. Askowith's presentation on the congress to Third Convention (1916), reported in Hadassah *Bulletin* no. 23 (July–August, 1916): 13, issue located in RG 3, Box 1, Folder 3, HA. No action was taken on the issue at this convention. See also Hadassah *Bulletin* no. 33 (June 1917): 19; and *Bulletin* 4 (November 1917): 3. This last article reported that eight of the eighteen women serving as delegates to the congress were Hadassah members, including Dora Askowith.

60. "Report of the Fourth Convention," June 1917, p. 19, RG 3, Folder 1, Box 4, HA.

61. Dora Askowith, "The Call of the Jewish Woman to the American Jewish Congress," *Maccabaean* 30 (April 1917): 208.

62. Kutscher, "Early Years," 199–200. Hadassah was not alone in its ambivalence toward the Congress movement. Yonathan Shapiro argues that the German Jewish leadership of the general Zionist movement, including such men as Brandeis, were also reluctant to found an American Jewish Congress. See Y. Shapiro, *Leadership*, 86–98. On the other hand, another

Hadassah founder, Sarah Kussy, did play a major role in founding the American Jewish Congress. See Lauren B. Strauss, "Sarah Kussy," in vol. 1 of *Jewish Women in America: An Historical Encyclopedia*, ed. Paula E. Hyman and Deborah Dash Moore (New York: Routledge, 1997), 769–70.

63. Epstein, *Jewish Labor*, 62; Janowsky, *Jews and Minority Rights*, 246–47.

64. Donald H. Miller, "A History of Hadassah, 1912–1935" (PhD diss., New York University, 1969), 65–72.

65. "Report of the Proceedings at the Fifth Convention," June 1918, pp. 7, 10–11, RG 3, Box 1, Folder 5, HA.

66. Szold to Mrs. Benjamin Davis, 1 August 1918; and Szold to Alice Seligsberg, 28 August 1918; both quoted in Miller, "History of Hadassah," 110–11. See also Kutscher, "Early Years," 208–11.

67. Kutscher, "Early Years," 211. Mrs. A. H. Fromenson headed the Palestine Supplies Division under Jacob DeHaas of the Palestine Bureau, and Ida Danziger served as the executive secretary of the Bureau for Propaganda among Women.

68. On antisemitism in the late-nineteenth-century woman's movement, see Kuzmack, *Women's Cause*, 38–40; and Suzanne M. Marilley, *Woman Suffrage and the Origins of Liberal Feminism in the United States, 1820–1920* (Cambridge, MA: Harvard University Press, 1996), 164–67, 178–80. On Progressive women and changes in Catt's rhetoric, see Marilley, *Woman Suffrage*, 187–216. For Jewish women and suffrage in the war years, see Kuzmack, *Women's Cause*, 146–54, 158.

69. "Report of the Proceedings at the Fifth Convention," June 1918, p. 102, RG 3, Box 1, Folder 5, HA.

70. "Woman Suffrage in Jewish Palestine," *Maccabaean* 31 (June 1918): 160. On women's suffrage in Palestine before 1918, see Ruth Abrams, "Jewish Women in the International Woman's Suffrage Alliance, 1899–1926" (PhD diss., Brandeis University, 1996), 243–47; and Abrams, "'Pioneering Representatives of the Hebrew People': Campaigns of the Palestinian Jewish Women's Equal Rights Association, 1918–1948," in *Women's Suffrage in the British Empire: Citizenship, Nation, and Race*, ed. Ian Christopher Fletcher, Laura E. Nym Mayhall, and Philippa Levine (London: Routledge, 2000), 121–37.

71. Mrs. Desha (Madeline McDowell) Breckinridge, "The Feminist Movement," *Official Report of the Council of Jewish Women's Seventh Triennial*, December 1914, pp. 153–62, Box 4, Folder 5, Solomon collection, LC. Breckinridge was the sister-in-law of Sophonsiba Breckinridge. She served as president of the Kentucky Equal Rights Association from 1912–1915 and from 1919 until her death in 1920. She also served as vice president of the National American Woman Suffrage Association from 1913 to 1915. As the great-grandaughter of Henry Clay, she was very distantly related to Rebecca Gratz, whose younger brother Benjamin married Clay's niece Maria Gist in 1820. See Anne F. Scott, *Notable American Women, 1607–1950: A Biographical Dictionary*, ed. Edward T. James, Janet Wilson James, Paul S. Boyer (Cam-

bridge, MA: Harvard University Press, 1971), 231–33; and Dianne Ashton, *Rebecca Gratz: Women and Judaism in Antebellum America* (Detroit: Wayne State University Press, 1997), 17.

72. Mrs. Carl Wolf, "Paper: The Feminist Movement," *Official Report of the Council of Jewish Women's Eighth Triennial*, November 1917, pp. 160–62, Box 5, Folder 1, Solomon collection, LC.

73. Ibid., 160. On the other hand, Council did support the NAACP over the objections of some of its southern members. *Proceedings of the Executive Board of the Council of Jewish Women November 27–December 1, 1914*, pp. 553–59, Box 1, Folder 1, NCJW collection, LC. On racism in the suffrage movement, see Marilley, *Woman Suffrage*, 159–86; and Aileen S. Kraditor, *The Ideas of the Woman Suffrage Movement, 1890–1920* (1965; reprint, New York: Norton, 1981), 163–218.

74. Rogow, *Gone to Another Meeting*, 78–82; and Charlotte Baum, Paula Hyman, and Sonya Michel, *The Jewish Woman in America* (New York: Dial Press, 1976), 52–53. The group's postwar embrace of women's right to vote reveals the high level of support for women's suffrage within the NCJW. Although concrete statistics on membership attitudes are unavailable, it seems likely that Council's official refusal to come out in support of the suffrage amendment had more to do with its commitment to avoiding "controversy" than the presence of a majority of members in opposition to women's suffrage. The Central Conference of American Rabbis, the organization of Reform rabbis, passed a resolution supporting women's suffrage in 1917, after having twice defeated similar resolutions in previous years. See Michael A. Meyer, *Response to Modernity: A History of the Reform Movement in Judaism* (New York: Oxford University Press, 1988), 285. Jacob Rader Marcus argues that Reform rabbis moved so slowly on the issue because they too wanted to avoid conflict and controversy. Once it appeared that suffragists had gained greater support throughout the nation, they were more willing to take a stand in favor of women's right to vote. See Jacob Rader Marcus, *The American Jewish Woman: A Documentary History* (New York: KTAV, 1981), 389.

75. "Iber der froyen velt" [About the women's world] *Der fraynd* 6 (April 1915): 19. On the Second International, woman's suffrage, and Theresa Malkiel, see Mari Jo Buhle, *Women and American Socialism, 1870–1920* (Urbana: University of Illinois Press, 1981), 222–29, 234–41. Outside New York City, American socialists worked in concert with women's suffrage organizations. See Buhle, *Women and American Socialism*, 229–39; Marilley, *Woman Suffrage*, 205–6. For a discussion of Jewish attitudes about suffrage in this period, see Elinor Lerner, "Jewish Involvement in the New York City Woman Suffrage Movement," *American Jewish History* 70 (June 1981): 442–46. She notes that by the end of 1915 suffrage leaders reported complete support from the New York Yiddish press editorial pages.

76. "Iber der froyen velt," *Der fraynd* 6 (August 1915): 12; and "Iber der froyen velt," *Der fraynd* 8 (March 1917): 7–8. On women's liberation see "Iber der froyen velt," *Der fraynd* 8 (February 1917): 7–8; on suffrage internationally see "Iber der froyen velt," *Der fraynd* 8 (December 1917): 16–17;

on the national and international suffrage movements see *Der fraynd* 7 (December 1916): 22–23; *Der fraynd* 8 (February 1917): 7–8; (March 1917): 7–8; and (December 1917): 16–17; *Der fraynd* 9 (February 1918): 12–14; (December 1918): 8–9; *Der fraynd* 10 (March 1919): 8–10; (June–July 1919): 9–10; for columns regarding women and war work see *Der fraynd* 7 (December 1916): 22–23; *Der fraynd* 8 (March 1917): 7–8; (October 1917): 14–16; *Der fraynd* 9 (December 1918): 8–9; for columns on the influence of women on the legislative and political processes see *Der fraynd* 7 (December 1916): 22–23; *Der fraynd* 8 (July 1917): 6–8; (October 1917): 14–16; *Der fraynd* 9 (February 1918): 12–14.

77. "Di froyen velt" [The women's world], 8 (October 1917): 16–17. This column does not have a byline but the topics are in concert with those pursued by Zametkin.

78. "Iber der froyen velt," *Der fraynd* 6 (June 1915): 8; "Iber der froyen velt," *Der fraynd* 6 (August 1915): 10–12.

79. "Iber der froyen velt," *Der fraynd* 7 (December 1916): 22–23.

80. Socialist Theresa Malkiel similarly refrained from critiquing domestic relations in her political writings. See Sally M. Miller, "From Sweatshop Worker to Labor Leader: Theresa Malkiel, A Case Study," *American Jewish History* 68 (December 1978): 189–203.

81. "Iber der froyen velt," *Der fraynd* 6 (March 1915): 13–16; "Iber der froyen velt," *Der fraynd* 6 (June 1915): 7; on war babies see "Iber der froyen velt," *Der fraynd* 6 (August 1915): 11; on mothers' pensions, especially the inadequacy of charities to help, see "Iber der froyen velt," *Der fraynd* 8 (July 1917): 9.

Chapter 3

1. Nancy F. Cott, *The Grounding of Modern Feminism* (New Haven, CT: Yale University Press, 1987); and Leila J. Rupp, *Worlds of Women: The Making of an International Women's Movement* (Princeton, NJ: Princeton University Press, 1997), 89–92, 102–3. See also Billie Melman, introduction to *Borderlines: Genders and Identities in War and Peace, 1870–1930*, ed. Billie Melman (New York: Routledge, 1998), 5, 18–19.

2. See, for example, Maurine Weiner Greenwald, *Women, War and Work: The Impact of World War I on Women Workers in the United States* (Westport, CT: Greenwood, 1980). For more recent works, see Birgitte Soland, *Becoming Modern: Young Women and the Reconstruction of Womanhood in the 1920s* (Princeton, NJ: Princeton University Press, 2000); and Mary Louise Roberts, *Civilization without Sexes: Reconstructing Gender in Postwar France, 1917–1927* (Chicago: University of Chicago Press, 1994).

3. Judah J. Shapiro, *The Friendly Society: A History of the Workmen's Circle* (New York: Media Judaica, 1970), 78. The Circle's National Executive Committee sued the state and won in State Supreme Court. On Jews and Bolsheviks being used nearly interchangeably, see Leonard Dinnerstein, *Antisemitism in America* (New York: Oxford University Press, 1994), 79–81. See also John Higham, *Strangers in the Land: Patterns of American Nativism,*

1860–1925, 2nd ed. (New Brunswick, NJ: Rutgers University Press, 1988).

    4. Dinnerstein, *Antisemitism*, 80–82.

    5. Henry L. Feingold, *A Time for Searching: Entering the Mainstream, 1920–1945*, vol. 4 of *The Jewish People in America*, ed. Henry L. Feingold (Baltimore: Johns Hopkins University Press, 1992), 26–29; Dinnerstein, *Antisemitism*, 93–96.

    6. Yehuda Bauer, *My Brother's Keeper: A History of the American Jewish Joint Distribution Committee, 1929–1939* (Philadelphia: Jewish Publication Society of America, 1974), 9.

    7. Mark Levene, *War, Jews, and the New Europe: The Diplomacy of Lucien Wolf, 1914–1919* (Oxford: Oxford University Press, 1992), 229; *Bulletin of the Joint Distribution Committee of the American Funds for Jewish War Sufferers* 3 (November/December 1918): 25. Here, cables from Jacobus Kahn, a well-known banker in the Hague, confirm pogroms in Galicia and Poland.

    8. Zosa Szajkowski, "Concord and Discord in American Jewish Overseas Relief, 1914–1924," *YIVO Annual of Jewish Social Science* 14 (1969): 141.

    9. Melvin I. Urofsky, *American Zionism from Herzl to the Holocaust* (New York: Doubleday, 1975), 324–26.

    10. Ibid., 323–39.

    11. Boris D. Bogen, *Born A Jew* (New York: Macmillan, 1930), 125–29.

    12. Bauer, *My Brother's Keeper*, 9.

    13. Ibid., 9–11.

    14. Ibid., 57–61. Tel Hai refers to the famous settlement in Palestine where Josef Trumpeldor died defending it from an Arab attack in 1920.

    15. *Proceedings of the Annual Meeting of the Council of Jewish Women*, November–December 1921, p. 12, Box 2, Folder 4, NCJW collection, LC. In January 1922 *The Jewish Woman* reported that Rose Brenner was asked to serve on the Executive Committee of the AJRC and that she and Estelle Sternberger were chosen to represent Council at American Jewish Committee meetings. "In Woman's World," *Jewish Woman* 2 (January 1922): 15–16.

    16. National Appeal for Jewish Sufferers, *The Victory Conference and Testimonial to David A. Brown at Detroit, MI April 9th, 1922* (New York: Clarence S. Nathan, n.d.), 42.

    17. Henry Hirsch of Toledo, OH, quoted in ibid., 31–32.

    18. Ibid., 87–88.

    19. Joyce Antler, *The Journey Home: Jewish Women and the American Century* (New York: Free Press, 1997), 40–54; and Karla Goldman, "Rebekah Bettelheim Kohut," in vol. 1 of *Jewish Women in America: An Historical Encyclopedia*, ed. Paula E. Hyman and Deborah Dash Moore (New York: Routledge, 1997), 749–51. See also Dora Askowith, *Three Outstanding Women: Mary Fels, Rebekah Kohut, Annie Nathan Meyer* (New York: Bloch, 1941), 11–25.

    20. Rebekah Kohut, *My Portion* (New York: Albert and Charles

Boni, 1927), 267.

21. Rebekah Kohut, *More Yesterdays* (New York: Bloch, 1950), 19.

22. For a general description of the trip and the refugees see Kohut, *My Portion*, 268–69.

23. "Report of the Committee on Reconstruction," *Official Report of the Ninth Triennial Convention*, November 1920, pp. 409–22, Box 5, Folder 1, Solomon collection, LC; Kohut, *My Portion*, 265–73.

24. "Report of the Committee on Reconstruction," *Official Report of the Ninth Triennial Convention*, November 1920, pp. 414–21, Box 5, Folder 1, Solomon collection, LC; Kohut, *More Yesterdays*, 125–26. On Müller-Cohen's work and popularity in Vienna, see Michael Berkowitz, *Western Jewry and the Zionist Project, 1914–1933* (Cambridge: Cambridge University Press, 1997), 180, 181; and Marsha L. Rozenblit, *Reconstructing a National Jewish Identity: The Jews of Habsburg Austria during World War I* (New York: Oxford University Press, 2001), 72–73, 197 n. 130.

25. Kohut, *My Portion*, 269.

26. "Report of the Committee on Reconstruction," *Official Report of the Ninth Triennial Convention*, November 1920, p. 422, Box 5, Folder 1, Solomon collection, LC. On Bertha Pappenheim, see Marion A. Kaplan, *The Jewish Feminist Movement in Germany: The Campaigns of the Jüdischer Frauenbund, 1904–1938* (Westport, CT: Greenwood, 1979).

27. "Report of the Committee on Reconstruction," *Official Report of the Ninth Triennial Convention*, November 1920, p. 422, Box 5, Folder 1, Solomon collection, LC.

28. Ibid., p. 425.

29. Mrs. Mack reports for the Reconstruction Committee, *Proceedings of the Annual Meeting of the Council of Jewish Women*, November–December 1921, pp. 187–93, Box 2, Folder 4, NCJW collection, LC.

30. Eleanor Sachs, "The Council Unit: How It Served Europe," *Jewish Woman* 2 (January 1922): 4.

31. Mrs. Alexander Kohut, "Report, Committee on Reconstruction" (read by Mrs. Sporborg), *Official Report of the Tenth Triennial Convention*, November 1923, pp. 208–9, Box 5, Folder 2, Solomon collection, LC.

32. "Our World Work," report from Annual Board of Managers meeting, *Jewish Woman* 2 (December 1922): 17; and Mrs. A. Salkind (President, Riga CJW), "The Jewish Women of Latvia: Their Progress in Social Work," *Jewish Woman* 3 (February 1923): 2–3. NCJW chapters were in Antwerp, Paris, Amsterdam, Arnhem (Holland), Rotterdam, The Hague, Trieste (Italy), Riga, Lodz, Geneva, and New South Wales. See Winifred Lancashire Rich, "The National Council of Jewish Women," *Woman Citizen* 10 (1925): 13. Evidently they did not move as quickly as some Council leaders would have liked. At the 1921 board meeting Janet Harris reported that on her trip to Europe the previous summer to increase interest in starting up new Council sections, she felt that European women were moving forward very slowly. Janet Harris, "Report, Committee on Foreign Relations," *Proceedings of the Annual Meeting of the Council of Jewish Women*, November–December

1921, pp. 238–39, Box 2, Folder 4, NCJW collection, LC.

33. *Proceedings of the Annual Meeting of the Council of Jewish Women,* November–December 1921, pp. 259–64, Box 2, Folder 4, NCJW collection, LC.

34. Hadassah *Newsletter,* vol. 3, no. 2 (November 1922): 1.

35. Joan Dash, *Summoned to Jerusalem: The Life of Henrietta Szold* (New York: Harper and Row, 1979), 179–82. Dash argues that even after Hadassah's tussle with the ZOA in 1921 funding for the unit remained haphazard. She maintains that the JDC agreed to raise its level of support if Hadassah would relinquish control of their Palestinian projects to the JDC. Henrietta Szold refused what she called a "vile proposition." See also Marlin Levin, *Balm in Gilead: The Story of Hadassah* (New York: Schocken, 1973), 69–73.

36. Levin, *Balm in Gilead,* 73–80. On Brandeis's antimalarial efforts, see Philippa Strum, *Louis D. Brandeis: Justice for the People* (Cambridge, MA: Harvard University Press, 1984), 279.

37. Levin, *Balm in Gilead,* 84.

38. Ibid., 80–88; "Hadassah, the Women's Zionist Organization of America: The Achievements of Twelve Years," copy of speech given by Mrs. Ethel Cohen, p. 2, 1924, Record Group 3, Box 3, Folder 4, HA.

39. See Rafael Medoff, "American Zionist Leaders and the Palestinian Arabs, 1898–1948" (Ph.D. diss., Yeshiva University, 1991), 103–4; Donald H. Miller, "A History of Hadassah, 1912–1935" (PhD diss., New York University, 1969), 307–14.

40. Quoted in Levin, *Balm in Gilead,* 64.

41. *Proceedings of the Tenth Convention,* July 1924, p. 189, Record Group 3, Box 3, Folder 3, HA.

42. Henrietta Szold's speech to convention, *Proceedings of the Tenth Convention,* July 1924, p. 293, Record Group 3, Box 3, Folder 3, HA.

43. Rupp, *Worlds of Women,* 84–86.

44. Henrietta Szold, "Familiar Letter No. 4," Hadassah *Newsletter* 3 (March 1923): 8. On Szold's account of the Jaffa massacre see Marvin Lowenthal, *Henrietta Szold: Life and Letters* (New York, 1942), 175–80.

45. "3,000 Greet Palestine Leader," *New York Times,* 1 May 1923, p. 4, col. 2.

46. *Proceedings of the 12th Convention,* 1926, p. 89, Record Group 3, Box 5, Folder 1, HA.

47. Sheepshanks and 'Sha'rawi quoted in Rupp, *Worlds of Women,* 84; Williams quoted in Boisseau, "White Queens," 47.

48. Michael Berkowitz's work on tourism to Palestine reveals that of all Zionist groups, Hadassah stood out in its insistence that its members familiarize themselves with Arab history and culture. Berkowitz, *Western Jewry,* 141–42. On *Brit Shalom,* see Walter Laqueur, *A History of Zionism* (New York: Holt, Rinehart and Winston, 1972), 251–55.

49. Adlerblum quoted in *Proceedings of the 12th Convention,* 1926, p. 37, Record Group 3, Box 5, Folder 1, HA. On maternalism, see Seth Koven

and Sonya Michel, eds., *Mothers of a New World: Maternalist Politics and the Origins of Welfare States* (New York: Routledge, 1993); Molly Ladd-Taylor, *Mother-Work: Women, Child Welfare, and the State, 1890–1930* (Urbana: University of Illinois Press, 1994); and Lynn Y. Weiner, et al., "Maternalism as a Paradigm," *Journal of Women's History* 5 (Fall 1993): 95–131.

50. "Letter from Henrietta Szold," 1921 Convention Proceedings, p. 5, Record Group 3, Box 2, Folder 4, HA.

51. "The Woman in Zionism," *Maccabaean* 30 (February 1917): 148, located in Record Group 4, Box 2, Folder 20, HA. This issue was edited by the Central Committee of Hadassah.

52. *Proceedings of the Tenth Convention*, 1924, p. 220, Record Group 3, Box 3, Folder 3, HA.

53. Hadassah *Newsletter* 4 (October 1923): 2.

54. Charlotte Weber, "Unveiling Scheherazade: Unveiling Orientalism in the International Alliance of Women, 1911–1950," *Feminist Studies* 27 (Spring 2001): 145–48. In 1926 the IWSA changed its name to the International Alliance of Women.

55. I. Burn, "Hadassah Chapter in Yanishik, Lithuania," Hadassah *Newsletter* 4 (October 1923): 3.

56. Hadassah *Newsletter* 4 (March 1924): 5–6.

57. See Carol Kutscher, "The Early Years of Hadassah, 1912–1921" (PhD diss., Brandeis University, 1976), 208–50; Carol Bosworth Kutscher, "From Merger to Autonomy: Hadassah and the ZOA, 1918–1921," in *The Herzl Yearbook*, vol. 8, *Essays in American Zionism, 1917–1948*, ed. Melvin I. Urofsky (New York, 1978), 64–67; Urofsky, *American Zionism*, 344, 351–57; "Address by Mr. Lipsky at Hadassah Convention," 1921 Convention Proceedings, p. 1, Record Group 3, Box 2, Folder 4, HA. While Hadassah's membership, like that of the FAZ, increased during World War I, reflecting American Jews' concern for the plight of Jews overseas, its greatest growth did not occur until after the war. Although in the 1920s many women might have had more time to devote to organizational life as their children were older and their families financially secure, this cannot entirely account for Hadassah's growth, particularly due to the fact that membership in Zionist organizations did not require active involvement but only payment of membership dues.

58. For an analysis of the conflict between the Brandeis and Lipsky factions, see Ben Halpern, *A Clash of Heroes: Brandeis, Weizmann, and American Zionism* (New York: Oxford University Press, 1987), 205–69. For a rereading of this episode placing the issue of fund-raising at the center of the conflict, see Berkowitz, *Western Jewry*, 56–76.

59. Kutscher, "From Merger to Autonomy," 67–68.

60. Notes for Rose Jacobs's history of Hadassah in Record Group 7, Reel 3; Urofsky, *American Zionism*, 343. On Jacobs's background and career in Hadassah, see Antler, *Journey Home*, 204–14.

61. Kutscher, "From Merger to Autonomy," 69–70.

62. Rose Jacobs Papers, Record Group 7, Reel 3, HA.

63. Irma L. Lindheim, *Parallel Quest: A Search of a Person and a People* (New York: T. Yoseloff, 1962), 215.

64. Rose Jacobs Papers, Record Group 7, Reel 2, HA.

65. Ibid.

66. Rose Jacobs's notes for Hadassah history, Record Group 7, Reel 3, HA.

67. Mrs. Natkin, *Proceedings of the Eighth Annual Convention,* November 1921, p. 22, Record Group 3, Box 2, Folder 1, HA.

68. Mrs. Minkin of Rochester in *Proceedings of the Eighth Annual Convention,* November 1921, p. 14, Record Group 3, Box 2, Folder 1, HA.

69. Phoebe (Mrs. Moses) Ruslander in *Proceedings of the Eighth Convention,* November 1921, p. 23, Record Group 3, Box 2, Folder 2, HA. Ruslander was also prominent in the NCJW.

70. Kutscher, "From Merger to Autonomy," 74.

71. Confidential letter from Alice L. Seligsberg to "like-minded delegates," 23 November 1921, Record Group 3, Box 2, Folder 4, HA.

72. Dash, *Summoned to Jerusalem,* 174.

73. Henrietta Szold to "Dear Family," 4 July 1924, microfilm reel 386B, AJA.

74. Miller, "History of Hadassah," 146–48; Urofsky, *American Zionism,* 345–46. The UPA was founded in October 1925 when American Zionists, angered by what they perceived as a lack of JDC attention to Palestine, broke from the United Jewish Appeal. See also Urofsky, *American Zionism,* 325–26.

75. Emanuel Neumann, *Proceedings of the Twelfth Convention,* pp. 11–13, Record Group 3, Box 5, Folder 1, HA. At the 1927 convention Judge William M. Lewis, chairman of the UPA, stated that women did most of the "house-to-house hard plugging and getting of funds." See Hadassah *Newsletter* 7 (August 1927): 15, located in Record Group 3, Box 6, Folder 1, HA.

76. *Proceedings of the Twelfth Convention,* June–July 1926, pp. 175–207, Record Group 3, Box 5, Folder 1, HA.

77. "Report of the National Board to the 13th Annual Convention of Hadassah, the Women's Zionist Organization of America," p. 12, Record Group 3, Box 6, Folder 1, HA.

78. "Statement of National Board to meeting July 15, 1927," Record Group 3, Box 6, Folder 1, HA; Hadassah *Newsletter* vol. 7, no. 10 (August 1927): 9, located in Record Group 3, Box 6, Folder 1, HA. In 1927 Hadassah's membership was 34,371 while that of the ZOA was only 21,806. See Miller, "History of Hadassah," 154.

79. Lindheim, *Parallel Quest,* 211–13; quote on 213. On Lindheim's life, see Shulamit Reinharz, "Irma 'Rama' Lindheim: An Independent American Zionist Woman," *Nashim: A Journal of Jewish Women's Studies and Gender Issues* 1 (Winter 1998): 106–35.

80. Urofsky, *American Zionism,* 355; "Head of Hadassah Joins Zion-

ist Split," *New York Times*, March 31, 1928. Szold came under her share of fire as well. She and her organization were said to be insufficiently willing to sacrifice for the movement at large. See Berkowitz, *Western Jewry*, 188–89.

81. "Mrs. Lindheim's Greetings," *Proceedings and Speeches at the Fourteenth Annual Convention*, June 1928, p. 3, Record Group 3, Box 6, Folder 2, HA. See also Michael Berkowitz, *Western Jewry*, 70; Urofsky, *American Zionism*, 355–56.

82. Ibid., 260–61.

83. Zip Szold to Henrietta Szold, 19 July 1928, Record Group 7, Box 16, Folder 163, HA.

84. *Proceedings and Speeches at the Fourteenth Annual Convention*, pp. 9–10.

85. Mrs. Kamenetsky in ibid., 12.

86. Ibid., 195.

87. Irma Lindheim to Henrietta Szold, 10 April 1928, Record Group 7, Box 16, Folder 159, HA.

88. Nellie Straus Mochenson to Alice L. Seligsberg, 23 August 1928, Record Group 7, Reel 1, HA.

89. Hadassah *Newsletter* vol. 8, no. 18 (May 11, 1928): 2. See too "Cleaning the Atmosphere," Hadassah *Newsletter* no. 8, no. 20 (May 25, 1928): 2. This article alerted members to the fact that the Yiddish press in particular was making statements about Hadassah's alleged attempts to undermine Chaim Weizmann, the WZO, and the Jewish Agency.

90. Irma Lindheim to Pearl Franklin, 8 April 1928, Record Group 4, Box 1, Folder 7.

91. On the outcome of the battle, see Urofsky, *American Zionism*, 359–60; Kristi Andersen, *After Suffrage: Women in Partisan and Electoral Politics Before the New Deal* (Chicago: University of Chicago Press, 1996).

Chapter 4

1. Kristi Andersen, *After Suffrage: Women in Partisan and Electoral Politics Before the New Deal* (Chicago: University of Chicago Press, 1996); Nancy F. Cott, *The Grounding of Modern Feminism* (New Haven, CT: Yale University Press, 1987), 83–114, 243–67; and Deborah Gray White, *Too Heavy a Load: Black Women in Defense of Themselves, 1894–1994* (New York: Norton, 1999), 134–41.

2. Michael Berkowitz, *Zionist Culture and West European Jewry before the First World War* (London: Cambridge University Press, 1993; Chapel Hill: University of North Carolina Press, 1996), 188–90. Citations are to the 1996 UNC Press edition.

3. Mrs. Moses Sanders of Springfield, Ohio, in "Section Problems," *Jewish Woman* 6 (January 1926): 55.

4. Faith Rogow, *Gone to Another Meeting: The National Council of Jewish Women, 1893–1993* (Tuscaloosa: University of Alabama Press, 1993), 33, 206.

5. "Convention Problems," Hadassah *Newsletter* 7 (May 1927): 6. For similar debates regarding clothing and its meaning, see Birgitte Soland, *Becoming Modern: Young Women and the Reconstruction of Womanhood in the 1920s* (Princeton, NJ: Princeton University Press, 2000), 63–64.

6. Mrs. (Brocha) Reis-Zuckerman(-Reichel) in "Proceedings of the Eleventh Convention," July 1925, pp. 120, 249, RG 3, Box 4, Folder 1, HA. See also description of convention resolution in Hadassah *Newsletter* 5 (August 1925): 11.

7. "Liebe shvester fun Hadassah!" [Dear sisters of Hadassah!], Hadassah *Newsletter* 3 (November 1922): 4.

8. There was a Yiddish-oriented, socialist-Zionist organization, *Poale Zion*. The women's group associated with Poale Zion was Pioneer Women. See Mark A. Raider, *The Emergence of American Zionism* (New York: New York University Press, 1998).

9. Blanche B. Goldman, "Immigrant Aid and Immigrant Education," *Jewish Woman* 9 (April–June 1929): 20.

10. Quoted in Rogow, *Gone to Another Meeting*, 150–51. The works of Anzia Yezierska also show the working-class distrust of benevolent ladies. See in particular, *Salome of the Tenements* (1923; reprint, Urbana: University of Illinois Press, 1995); and *Arrogant Begger* (1927; reprint, Durham, NC: Duke University Press, 1996).

11. "From All Corners," *Jewish Woman* 4 (December 1924): 37.

12. "Proceedings of the Eighth Convention," Fifth Session, 25 November 1921, pp. 15–31, Record Group 3, Box 2, Folder 2, HA.

13. Ezekiel Rabinowitz, "Jubilee Convention of the Council of Jewish Women," *Jewish Tribune and Hebrew Standard*, 23 November 1923, p. 5, [page number missing on second page], clipping in Part II, Box 34, NCJW Collection, LC.

14. "Special Committee: Reconciliation of the NCJW and the Representatives of the Disaffected Sects, Informal Meeting between Committee on Reconciliation of Council of Jewish Women and Representatives of Disaffected Sections," 21 January 1915, pp. 12–13, Part I, Box 103, NCJW collection, LC.

15. "Proceedings of the Executive Board of the Council of Jewish Women," November–December 1914, pp. 553–60, Box 1, Folder 1, NCJW collection, LC. Inez Lopez Cohen was the new wife of soon-to-be writer Octavus Cohen. In 1915 Cohen embarked on a career as a short story and mystery writer. He is best known for his "Negro dialect fiction," which appeared regularly in the *Saturday Evening Post*. Two of the figures he created for his detective stories were quite well known: the black detective Florian Slappey and the white private eye Jim Hanvey, the latter the subject of a 1937 film and the former of a 1920 stage production. Cohen also wrote for the radio program *Amos 'n' Andy* from 1945 to 1946. See *Encyclopedia of Mystery and Detection* (New York: McGraw-Hill, 1976), 92–93; and *Contemporary Authors*, 112 (Detroit: Gale, 1985), 106. During the 1920s the Chicago NCJW cooperated with Ida B. Wells in the wake of race riots occurring in

that city. In 1955 the NCJW board passed a resolution in favor of integration and it supported the major civil rights legislation of the 1950s and 1960s. See Rogow, *Gone to Another Meeting*, 186–87.

16. For example, Jennie Franklin Purvin, known as the "Jewish Jane Addams," was involved in many non-Jewish organizations in Chicago. Hannah G. Solomon considered Jane Addams a friend, while Rebekah Kohut and Sadie American both claimed friendships with Susan B. Anthony. See Joyce Antler, *The Journey Home: How Jewish Women Shaped Modern America* (New York: Schocken, 1997), 62; and Karla Goldman, "Jennie Franklin Purvin (1873–1958)," in *Jewish Women in America: An Historical Encyclopedia*, ed. Paula E. Hyman and Deborah Dash Moore (New York: Routledge, 1997), 1114. Two Council women, Janet Harris and Fanny Brin, held prominent posts in the Women's International League for Peace and Freedom. Brin counted Carrie Chapman Catt and Jane Addams among her friends and served as an alternate consultant to the U.S. delegation at the founding conference of the United Nations in San Francisco. See Linda Mack Schloff, "Building Communities, Building Bridges: Jewish American Women's Organizations in Minneapolis, 1945–1975," (PhD diss., University of Minnesota, 1998), 127–28, 142. On the founding of the WJCC, see Cott, *Grounding*, 97–99.

17. On immigrant aid, see "Bureau of International Service," *Jewish Woman* 8 (January–March 1928): 15; "Immigrant Aid and Immigrant Education: International Service," *Jewish Woman* 9 (October–December 1929): 21.

18. "Council Appeals for Immigration Law Changes," *American Hebrew* 116 (December 12, 1924): 180; see also "International Problems Increase with Immigration Exclusion," *American Hebrew* 116 (March 20, 1925): 584.

19. Florina Lasker, "The Perils of the Emigrant: Who Shall Receive Them?" *Jewish Woman* 2 (January 1922): 9–10, 16. On the Jüdischer Frauenbund in the 1920s, see Marion A. Kaplan, *The Jewish Feminist Movement in Germany: The Campaigns of the Jüdischer Frauenbund, 1904–1938* (Westport, CT: Greenwood, 1979), 86–87.

20. Gertrude Feibleman, "Public Opinion: The Creator of World Peace," *Jewish Woman* 2 (January 1922): 7–8. Individual Jews, such as Lillian Wald, Rabbi Judah Magnes and Rabbi Stephen Wise worked on peace issues, and Wald was instrumental in founding the American Union against Militarism. See Linda Gordon Kuzmack, *Woman's Cause: The Jewish Woman's Movement in England and the United States, 1881–1933* (Columbus: Ohio State University Press, 1990), 102–4; and Barbara J. Steinson, *American Women's Activism in World War I* (New York: Garland, 1982), 9–16, 114–62, 265–68. The Union of American Hebrew Congregations adopted a resolution supporting the outlaw of war in 1925, and many rabbis came to support peace during the 1920s; many, though, still supported Jews' right to self-defense. See Michael A. Meyer, *Response to Modernity: A History of the Reform Movement in Judaism* (New York: Oxford University Press, 1988), 313.

21. Carrie Chapman Catt, "War or Peace," *Official Report of the Tenth Triennial Convention*, 1923, p. 153, Box 5, Folder 2, Solomon Collection, LC; "Momentous Peace Conference," *Jewish Woman* 4 (December 1924): 14. See also "Jewish Women at Momentous Peace Conference," *American Hebrew* 116 (January 2, 1925): 278; and "Council Head Presides at Peace Conference," *American Hebrew* 116 (February 6, 1925): 416. On the Conference on the Cause and Cure of War and later the National Committee on the Cause and Cure of War, see Cott, *Grounding*, 94–95, 257–58; Joan M. Jensen, "All Pink Sisters: The War Department and the Feminist Movement in the 1920s," in *Decades of Discontent: The Women's Movement, 1920–1940*, ed. Lois Scharf and Joan M. Jensen (Westport, CT: Greenwood, 1983), 214–17; and Linda Schott, "'Middle-of-the-Road' Activists: Carrie Chapman Catt and the National Committee on the Cause and Cure of War," *Peace and Change* 21 (January 1996): 1–21.

22. National Council of Jewish Women column in *American Hebrew* 116 (November 14, 1924): 16; Fanny Brin, "Has the Victory of Peace Been Won?" *Jewish Woman* 9 (January–March 1929): 1; "Council to Urge World Court on Congress," *American Hebrew* 117 (August 28, 1925): 468; "Council Officers in Europe," *Jewish Woman* 8 (July–September, 1928): 39; Fanny Brin, "Report on Peace," *Jewish Woman* 8 (October–December 1928): 8; Estelle M. Sternberger, "Has Woman's Vote Improved Politics?" *Jewish Woman* 5 (October 1925): 15–17; *Council Pioneer: A History of Council in the Vanguard of Social Advance*, compiled by Mrs. Mortimer Brenner (published by the NCJW, 1955), 4.

23. Rabinowitz, "Jubilee Convention," pp. 5, [page number missing on second page].

24. See Cott, *Grounding*, 117–42; William H. Chafe, *The Paradox of Change: American Women in the 20th Century* (New York: Oxford University Press, 1991), 45–60. See also Susan D. Becker, *The Origins of the Equal Rights Amendment: American Feminism between the Wars* (Westport, CT: Greenwood, 1981). Faith Rogow notes that Council opposed the ERA, but she fails to place their opposition in sufficient context or to elaborate on other female reformers who also opposed the measure, conveying the impression that Council women valued motherhood over all other concerns and thereby muting their feminism. Like other feminists, the NCJW came to support the ERA by the early 1970s. It also supported *Roe v. Wade*, legalizing abortion. See Rogow, *Gone to Another Meeting*, 83–85, 243.

25. Therese M. Loeb, "The Lucretia Mott Amendment: Pro and Con," *Jewish Woman* 4 (February 1924): 3–4, 27. The version of the resolution adopted by the triennial toned down its essentialist language while more firmly maintaining Council's official position on women's equality. It read, in part, "Whereas, We believe that its enactment would imperil the rights and privileges secured by women in industry and would render insecure the legal and economic basis of marriage and the family, be it Resolved, That the National Council of Jewish Women opposes blanket legislation on these sub-

jects and endorses the method of securing separate, specific legislation to remedy the existing inequalities involving injustices to women in the laws of most of the states of the nation." See, "A Correction," *Jewish Woman* 4 (April 1924): 35.

26. Gray White, *Too Heavy*, 150.

27. Mrs. Alexander Wolf quoted in "Council Declares for Woman's Equality by State Action," *American Hebrew* 116 (March 6, 1925): 542.

28. Winifred Lancashire Rich, "The National Council of Jewish Women," *Woman Citizen* 10 (1925): 13. See also Seth Korelitz, "'A Magnificent Piece of Work': The Americanization Work of the National Council of Jewish Women," *American Jewish History* 83 (June 1995): 192–97. The Workmen's Circle had a similar program, but with different ends in mind. An editorial in February 1918 urged women to take their new suffrage seriously and to engage in "naturalization" work. "Capitalist" women, the editors argued, were already citizens and would use the new vote to advance their class interests. The Workmen's Circle branches needed to ensure that working-class women became citizens and utilized their vote to further the workers' interests. "Undzere naye birger" [Our new citizens], *Der fraynd* 9 (February 1918): 4.

29. Rose Brenner, "The Organized Expression of Woman's Conscience," *Jewish Woman* 1 (October 1921): 14–15.

30. Rose Brenner, "The Great Interpreter," *Jewish Woman* 2 (April 1922), 3–4. See also Jennie Franklin Purvin, "The Jewish Woman in Civic Life," *Jewish Woman* 2 (April 1922): 10, 16. Montague Glass was a Jewish writer of British origin who popularized the Jewish immigrant figures Morris ("Mawruss") Perlmutter and Abraham Potash, partners in the garment business. Some Jews at the time took offense at the characterizations, which one literary critic describes as "lovable but one-dimensional ethnic stereotypes." Nevertheless the stories, and later stage productions, had a wide appeal particularly in Great Britain. See entry on Glass by Gregory S. Sojka, in *Dictionary of Literary Biography*, vol. 11, *American Humorists, 1800–1950* (Detroit: Gale, 1982). On Hurst, see Antler, *Journey Home*, 151–54, 158–75. Interestingly, Antler points out that Hurst was born in a small town in Ohio to German-Jewish parents who were very class-conscious. She looked down on Eastern European Jews to such a degree that for awhile she kept her own marriage to an immigrant musician a secret. This disdain was reflected in her fictional works.

31. "Jewish Woman Is 'Thankful' There Is Ku Klux Klan: Tells National Council Work of Organization Has Helped to Solidify Judaism in America," *Cleveland Plain Dealer*, n.d., ["11/15" handwritten on clipping], located in the Cleveland NCJW Scrapbook for August 1923 through September 1926, Ms. 3629, Box 27, Folder 2, WRHS. See also Rabinowitz, "Jubilee Convention." He notes that the leadership tried to stem discussion of Ford's antisemitism and "even criticism of the Ku Klux Klan" by Long and others.

32. Article fragment located in NCJW Scrapbook in Pittsburgh

Section files. Possibly *Jewish Criterion*. Series C, Box 59, Folder 1, Archives of Industrial Society, Pittsburgh.

33. See exhortation for members to contact congressmen in opposition to the proposed changes, in Hadassah *Newsletter* 4 (January 1924): 1; Henrietta Szold, "Women's Work in Palestine," Ninth Convention Proceedings, 1923, pp. 1–9, Record Group 3, Box 3, Folder 1, HA. Her Polish counterpart, Puah Rakovsky, echoed her thoughts regarding rabbinical opposition to women's equality. Writing about her own experiences organizing Jewish women in Poland, Rakovsky insisted that "the Jewish clerics, the Agude, were terrified by the awakening of Jewish women. They saw the Jewish women's movement as an attack on their allegedly exclusive right to obscure and dull the minds of the women, so that women would never, God forbid, grasp how much undeserved grief and suffering they experienced, or what old-fashioned laws—like levirate marriage, the *agune* [the "chained" wife, whose husband will not grant her a divorce] question, the prohibition of the marriage of a Cohen and a divorcee, etc.—those men had created." See Puah Rakovsky, *My Life as a Radical Jewish Woman: Memoirs of a Zionist Feminist in Poland*, ed. Paula E. Hyman, trans. Barbara Harshav and Paula E. Hyman (Bloomington: Indiana University Press, 2002), 83–84.

34. Sylvie Fogiel-Bijaoui, "On the Way to Equality? The Struggle for Women's Suffrage in the Jewish *Yishuv*, 1917–1926," in *Pioneers and Homemakers: Jewish Women in Pre-State Israel*, ed. Deborah S. Bernstein (Albany: State University of New York Press, 1992), 262–68; and Ruth Abrams, "Jewish Women in the International Woman Suffrage Alliance, 1899–1926" (PhD diss., Brandeis University, 1996), 232–68. The creation of the Jewish government in Palestine was complex, with numerous changes occurring in a very short period of time. Throughout this process the ultra-Orthodox [*Haredi*] factions threatened to boycott elections and participation in governments even they had helped to create. In the spring 1920 election, Haredi women did not vote, and the votes of men in that community counted twice.

"The Jewish community in Palestine was organized in a legal body known as *Knesset Israel* (Community of Israel), with which every Jew was automatically affiliated unless he elected not to be. The members of the *Knesset Israel* elected a parliamentary body known as the *Assefat ha-Nivharim* (Elected Assembly), from which in turn, the *Va'ad Leumi* (National Council) was elected." Defined in Anita Shapira, *Land and Power: The Zionist Resort to Force, 1881–1948* (New York, Oxford University Press, 1992), 421.

35. Rakovsky, *My Life*, 148.

36. Abrams, "Jewish Women," 232–68; Fogiel-Bijaoui, "On the Way," 268–72.

37. "Proceedings of the Eleventh Convention," July 1925, pp. 229–30, Record Group 3, Box 4, Folder 1, HA; and Hadassah *Newsletter* 5 (August 1925): 14.

38. Rakovsky, *My Life*, 148.

39. Hadassah *Newsletter* 4 (December 1925): 7.

40. Rakovsky, *My Life*, 148.

41. Hadassah *Newsletter* 6 (April 1926): 3; Fogiel-Bijaoui, "On the Way," 270–72. Fogiel-Bijaoui presents a much more detailed version of the events than the one provided in the *Newsletter*. Unlike the Hadassah account, which discusses only "Orthodox" opposition, Fogiel-Bijaoui maintains that the ultra-Orthodox were seeking to end women's suffrage while the Mizrachi tried to work out compromises on the issue. Abrams concurs with this interpretation, arguing that Mizrachi eventually concluded that it would be impossible to bring the far-right, non-Zionist Orthodox elements into agreement with secular Jews on the matter of women's suffrage. See Abrams, "Jewish Women," 232–68. The PJWERA continued to exist but never formally affiliated with any Zionist party. After the establishment of the state of Israel, the association became part of WIZO. See Hanna Herzog, "The Fringes of the Margin: Women's Organizations in the Civic Sector of the *Yishuv*," in Bernstein, *Pioneers and Homemakers*, 289.

42. On the Jewish Women's Organization and its work, see the unsigned report from Haifa, 26 June 1925; "First Report of the Jerusalem Baby Home of the JWO," 1924–1925; Henrietta Szold's "Report to the Hadassah National Board" on relations with the JWO, 26 February 26 1926; and "Report of JWO Executive on Activities of the Organization during the Period November 1927 through May 1928"; all located in Record Group 2, Box 62, Folder 1, HA. See also Fay Grove-Pollak, ed., *The Saga of a Movement: WIZO, 1920–1970* (n.p.: Women's International Zionist Organization, n.d.), 11–14. Hadassah routinely referred to Histadrut Nashim Ivriot as the Jewish Women's Organization. Hanna Herzog translates the Histadrut Nashim Ivriot as the Federation of Hebrew Women.

43. In 1925 Henrietta Szold wrote Nellie Straus Mochenson that she had seen the JWO claim responsibility for founding the infant welfare centers in Jerusalem. This was a false presentation, Szold complained, because the Hadassah Medical Organization had already started such a program; Henrietta Szold to Nellie Straus Mochenson, 23 March 1925, Record Group 2, Box 62, Folder 1, HA. Herzog credits the JWO with devising the infant and mother welfare services. Sources produced by or about Hadassah attribute it with helping create the JWO, while sources relying on WIZO documents or perspectives downplay Hadassah's interest in that group. Compare, for instance, Herzog, "Fringes of the Margin," 290–91 with Joan Dash, *Summoned to Jerusalem: The Life of Henrietta Szold* (New York: Harper and Row, 1979), 181.

44. "Report of the National Board" in Seventeenth Convention Proceedings, 1931, pp. 12–13, Record Group 3, Box 6, Folder 5, HA.

45. Puah Rakovsky, living in Palestine and working for WIZO in 1920, persuaded women involved in other social welfare projects to join her in creating "a broad WIZO chapter in the country." She recalled that "I tried to persuade them that that activity would be neither competition nor contradiction to their previous work, but could in time contribute to the development and reinforcement of their already existing institutions." Her proposal

was accepted by, among others, Henrietta Szold. Rakovsky, *My Life*, 139. "Proceedings and Resolutions of the Ninth Convention," 1923, pp. 11–12, Record Group 3, Box 3, Folder 2, HA. Szold commented at this convention that when WIZO was founded the ZOA did not think it advisable for Hadassah to affiliate with it. She added that she could not remember why the ZOA took that position. See also Grove-Pollak, *Saga of a Movement*, 11–14, 76–77. On WIZO connections to the WZO, see Michael Berkowitz, *Western Jewry and the Zionist Project, 1914–1933* (Cambridge: Cambridge University Press, 1997), 182. Rose Jacobs felt that WIZO was composed of women who were the wives of men supporting the Keren Hayesod. See Antler, *Journey Home*, 368, n.14. On Hadassah as too controlling, see Abrams, "Jewish Women," 242; Berkowitz, *Western Jewry*, 188–89.

46. Herzog, "Fringes of the Margin," 296–97. See also Margalit Shilo, "The Double or Multiple Image of the New Hebrew Woman," *Nashim: A Journal of Jewish Women's Studies and Gender Issues* 1 (Winter 1998): 73–94. Puah Rakovsky, however, criticized the first formal Polish WIZO section, which replaced the organization she had created, as bourgeois and a group that "carried out its activity exclusively among rich Jewish women." Rakovsky, *My Life*, 184.

47. Nellie Straus Mochenson to Alice L. Seligsberg, 2 June 1924, Record Group 7, Reel 1, HA.

48. Ibid.

49. Nellie Straus Mochenson to Alice L. Seligsberg, November 1923, Record Group 7, Reel 1, HA

50. "Proceedings and Resolutions of the Ninth Convention," typed proceedings, 1923, p. 14–15, Record Group 3, Box 3, Folder 2, HA; "Proceedings of the Eleventh Convention," typed proceedings, 1925, pp. 181–93, Record Group 3, Box 4, Folder 1, HA. When the issue arose in 1925 Szold reminded members that the interactions between the two women's groups had always been tense, ever since WIZO's founding. As early as January 1921, Szold recalled, WIZO had expressed interest in opening an infant welfare station. Hadassah, seeing itself as the major organization providing medical services in Palestine, offered to help with this project but never heard back from WIZO. Eventually Hadassah forged ahead by itself and opened its own infant station in June of that year. Early in 1922 WIZO opened a service center in Jaffa, funded by money received from Australia, and this led to conflict with Hadassah and the Hadassah Medical Organization (HMO). Both groups disapproved of the administration in the WIZO center, where a nurse was authorized to make decisions independently of a physician. While the medical aspect may have been a major issue for HMO doctors, Hadassah's chief concern centered on its belief that all social welfare should fall under the auspices of the HMO. The HMO, Szold believed, should have control over its own affairs, and if women disagreed with the way the HMO was run, they could opt to withdraw their support. Although Szold personally supported cooperation between the two women's groups, she concluded from this incident that the most important relationship to foster was that

between the HMO and WIZO. See "Proceedings of the Eleventh Convention," pp. 181–93.

51. Rose Jacobs to "Hal," n.d., Record Group 7, Reel 2, HA. The Canadian situation was unique. In 1917 Szold oversaw the founding of the Hadassah Organization of Canada, which held its first national convention in 1921. Chaim Weizmann, head of the World Zionist Organization, and his wife Vera, head of WIZO, attended this convention, after which the group became a part of WIZO. In later years the group was known as the Hadassah-WIZO Organization of Canada. See Grove-Pollack, *Saga of a Movement*, 115–16.

52. Nellie Straus Mochenson to Alice L. Seligsberg, 27 May 1923, Record Group 7, Reel 1, HA. Mochenson wrote that those who complained the most lived in Amsterdam, Zurich, and Vienna.

53. Henrietta Szold to Ruth Cohen, 2 June 1926, Record Group 2, Box 62, Folder 1, HA; Henrietta Szold to Hadassah National Board, 27 April 1926, Record Group 2, Box 62, Folder 1, HA.

54. "President" of Hadassah to Tamar Buchstab, 15 January 1926, Record Group 2, Box 62, Folder 1, HA.

55. Henrietta Szold to Ruth Cohen, 2 June 1926, RG 2, Box 62, Folder 1, HA. On WIZO and Hadassah not allowing JWO to raise funds, see Herzog, "Fringes of the Margin," 290.

56. Mrs. E. (Rose) Jacobs to Histadrut Nashim Ivriot, 20 December 1929, Record Group 2, Box 62, Folder 1, HA.

57. Rose Jacobs to "Hal," n.d., Record Group 7, Reel 2, HA; Zip Szold to Irma Lindheim, 30 July 1929, Record Group 7, Box 16, Folder 163, HA; "The Israel Federation of WIZO in Grove-Pollack, *Saga of a Movement*, 11; Herzog, "Fringes of the Margin," 290. Grove-Pollack states the groups affiliated in 1933, Herzog in 1931.

58. Mrs. William Loeb, chair of the Extension Committee, *Jewish Woman* 1 (October 1921): 11. See too Mrs. William Loeb, chair of the Extension Committee, "Vigorous Extension Campaign," *Jewish Woman* 2 (April 1922): 2 . The NCJW goal was to reach 300 sections and 100,000 members in 1923. In the same issue Rose Brenner stated that the organization currently had 45,000 members. Rose Brenner, "The Great Interpreter," 4.

59. *Jewish Woman* 4 (April 1924): 21. See also "A Challenge to Our Women," *Jewish Woman* 3 (February 1923): 18–19; *Jewish Woman* 4 (April 1924): 36; *Jewish Woman* 5 (March 1925): 28–29; and *Jewish Woman* 9 (January–March 1929): 33–34.

60. Henrietta Szold to Nellie Straus Mochenson, 23 March 1925, Record Group 2, Box 62, Folder 1, HA.

61. "Hadassah Sabbath," Hadassah *Newsletter* 7 (November 1926): 2.

62. "Report of Proceedings of the Fifth Convention," June 1918, pp. 35, 111, Record Group 3, Box 1, Folder 5, HA .

63. "Proceedings and Resolutions of the Ninth Convention," 1923, pp. 19–23, Record Group 3, Box 3, Folder 2, HA.

64. Hadassah *Bulletin* no. 26 (November 1916): 2–3.

65. Ruth Cohen, "Report of Miss Ruth Cohen, Executive Secretary of Hadassah," 1926 Convention, p. 2, Record Group 3, Box 5, Folder 2, HA; This report notes on p. 17 that "naturally the Council has not yet taken action regarding Palestinian work." For sewing circle figures see "Palestine Supplies Bureau Report," 1924 Convention Proceedings, p. 1, Record Group 3, Box 3, Folder 4, HA; Ruth B. Fromenson, "A Decade of Sewing," Hadassah *Newsletter* 7 (March 1927): 9.

66. Hadassah *Newsletter* 7 (January 1927): 3.

67. "Proceedings and Resolutions of the Ninth Convention," 1923, p. 28, Record Group 3, Box 3, Folder 2, HA. A similar resolution passed the following year directing each chapter to "form a committee to enlist the interest and cooperation of other organized groups of Jewish women in their respective communities." "Proceedings of the Tenth Convention," 1924, p. 189, Record Group 3, Box 3, Folder 3, HA.

68. "Proceedings of the Tenth Convention," 1924, pp. 232–37, Record Group 3, Box 3, Folder 3, HA.

69. Ibid., 241–43.

70. "Report of the National Board of Hadassah, the Women's Zionist Organization of America," 1924–1925, p. 8, Record Group 3, Box 4, Folder 2, HA. The resolution reads as follows: "Whereas Palestine is assuming importance in the solution of the world problems of the Jewish people, particularly in relation to the tasks which the National Council of Jewish Women has adopted as its province, viz: immigration, women on farms, and the welfare of unprotected girls, therefore, Be it resolved that the Pennsylvania State Conference recommend that the Board of the NCJW invite to its meeting an accredited representative of Hadassah, the Women's Zionist Organization of America." Ibid., 8; Hadassah *Newsletter* 5 (August 1925): 3.

71. Typescript report to Board of Managers by Rose Brenner, November 1925, pp. 2–3, 9, Box 100, Klau Library, Hebrew Union College. The handwritten words "most unwisely" were added to the typed speech but were also crossed out.

72. Ibid., 3–4. See also "Membership and Extension Campaign," *Jewish Woman* 5 (March 1925): 28–29. Membership campaign information indicates that the organization comprised 229 sections, forty-three of which were in Pennsylvania. The next largest were New York with twenty-two and New Jersey with twenty-one.

73. *Official Report of the Eleventh Triennial*, November 1926 (New York: National Council of Jewish Women, 1927), 9–10.

74. Ida W. Friend, "Point of View of the National Council of Jewish Women," *Jewish Woman* 8 (April–June 1928): 4–6.

75. "Proceedings of the Meeting of the Board of Managers of the National Council of Jewish Women," January 1927, pp. A29–30, Box 3, Folder 2, NCJW collection, LC.

76. Hadassah *Newsletter* 10 (December 1929): 5, located in Record Group 3, Box 6, Folder 3, HA; Rose Jacobs's handwritten notes, Record

Group 7, Reel 4, HA.

77. "Proceedings of the 12th Triennial Convention of the NCJW," January 1930, pp. 397–402, Part I, Box 37, NCJW collection, LC; and Rebekah Kohut, "Address on the World Organization of Jewish Women," *Jewish Woman* 10 (January–March 1930): 5–6. On the riots, see Melvin I. Urofsky, *American Zionism from Herzl to the Holocaust* (New York: Doubleday, 1975), 361; and Naomi W. Cohen, *The Year After the Riots: American Responses to the Palestinian Crisis of 1929–1930* (Detroit: Wayne State University Press, 1988).

78. Rebekah Kohut, "Report: Committee on Reconstruction," *Official Report of the Tenth Triennial Convention*, 1923, pp. 210–11, Box 5, Folder 2, Solomon collection, LC. For the precursor organization, the ICJW, see Nelly Las, *Jewish Women in a Changing World: A History of the International Council of Jewish Women (ICJW), 1899–1995* (Jerusalem: A. Harman Institute of Contemporary Jewry, 1996). 29–31. See also Janet Harris in *Official Report of the Ninth Triennial Convention*, 1920, pp. 30, 46, 427, Box 5, Folder 1, Solomon collection, LC. After attending the 1920 quinquennial of the International Council of Women in Norway, Janet Harris reported that she had used the meeting to begin arranging an international congress of Jewish women. While European women favored the idea, they could not initially agree on where to hold the congress. Great Britain's Union of Jewish Women insisted it play host to the international gathering but, according to Harris, German and Austrian women rejected that idea, stating that their delegates would be unable to obtain the necessary travel documents. Although no permanent decisions were made at the quinquennial, the NCJW committed itself to pursuing the organizational effort.

79. Estelle M. Sternberger, "Jewry's World Crisis," *Jewish Woman* 3 (April 1923): 12.

80. Janet Harris, "Report: Committee on Foreign Relations," *Official Report of the Tenth Triennial Convention*, 1923, p. 233, Box 5, Folder 2, Solomon collection, LC; "Council of Jewish Women" column in *American Hebrew* 113 (May 18, 1923): 16; Rebekah Kohut, *My Portion* (New York: Albert and Charles Boni, 1927), 281–82.

81. Kohut quoted in *World Congress of Jewish Women. Proceedings* (Vienna: Druckerei-U. Verlags—A.G. Ignaz Steinmann, 1923), 12; Anitta Müller-Cohen, "What the Conference will Achieve," *Jewish Woman* 3 (April 1923): 7. See also Rebekah Kohut, "The Vienna Conference: Its World Significance," *Jewish Woman* 3 (April 1923): 22; and Kohut, *My Portion*, 279–80. For similar rhetoric in other organizations, see Leila J. Rupp, *Worlds of Women: The Making of an International Women's Movement.* (Princeton, NJ: Princeton University Press, 1997); and Cott, *Grounding*, 244.

82. See *World Congress of Jewish Women. Proceedings*, 63–65, 92–96.

83. Nellie Straus Mochenson to Alice L. Seligsberg, 27 May 1923, Record Group 7, Reel 1, HA. Van Geldern, in *World Congress of Jewish Women. Proceedings*, 125.

84. Harris, "Report: Committee on Foreign Relations," p. 233. Also

Henrietta Szold, "Women's Work in Palestine," Ninth Convention Proceedings, pp. 14–16, Record Group 3, Box 3, Folder 1, Hadassah Archives.

85. *World Congress of Jewish Women*, 129. Mochenson as reported by Henrietta Szold in "Women's Work in Palestine," Ninth Convention Proceedings, pp. 14–16, Record Group 3, Box 3, Folder 1, HA. The unanimously adopted resolution declared that: "Whereas with the Balfour Declaration, and its incorporation into the Public Law of Europe by the San Remo Decision and the acceptance by Great Britain of the Mandate for Palestine, Palestine has been made available as a home for the Jews. Be it resolved that the Conference deems it to be the duty of all Jews to contribute to the physical reconstruction of Palestine, to aid in its social and economic rehabilitation and to promote the settlement in that country of such Jews as wish to go there."

86. Henrietta Szold, "Women's Work in Palestine," Ninth Convention Proceedings, pp. 14–16, Record Group 3, Box 3, Folder 1, HA.

87. The Jüdischer Frauenbund went through changes regarding Zionism similar to those of the NCJW in the 1920s. Shortly after the war, pro-Zionist members attempted to win a resolution supporting the movement despite leader Bertha Pappenheim's desire to avoid the issue. While the organization never embraced Zionism officially it did support Palestine's "importance and great interest as a Jewish women's and a cultural question." Quoted in Kaplan, *Jewish Feminist Movement*, 87.

88. Rosa Welt-Strauss, *Protokoll der Gründungsversammlung des 'Weltbundes jüdischer Frauen' vom 4.–6. Juni 1929* [Record of the founding meeting of the 'World Congress of Jewish Women' from 4–6 June 1929] (Berlin: B. Levy, 1929), 96. For Anitta Müller-Cohen and others, see same program, 127–41.

89. *Protokoll der Gründungsversammlung*, 143–44.

90. Meeting of the Board of Managers, National Council of Jewish Women, October 1929, pp. 292–93, Part 1, Box 6, Folder 2, NCJW collection, LC. The Palestine resolution reads: "In recognition of the fact that upbuilding efforts in Palestine are of fundamental importance for all Jews of the world, the World Conference demands that the yet-to-be-founded World Federation [Weltbund] strongly urge its member organizations to take part in these efforts."

91. Rebekah Kohut, "Proceedings of the Twelfth Triennial Convention of the National Council of Jewish Women," January 1930, p. 400, Part 1, Box 37, NCJW collection, LC. This statement also reflects Kohut's concerns about the violence against Jews in Palestine that occurred in August 1929.

92. *Protokoll der Gründungsversammlung*, 147–48, 152, 160. For similar dynamics in other international women's organizations, see Rupp, *Worlds of Women*, 51–81.

93. *Protokoll der Gründungsversammlung*, 96–97; see also Rupp, *Worlds of Women*, 58.

94. "A Brief History of Hadassah's Activities," pamphlet published

in June 1932, RG 4, Box 21, HA.

95. "Baricht fun ershten tsuzamenfahr fun di froyen kluben fun a.r." [Report from the first convention of the women's clubs of the Workmen's Circle], *Der fraynd* 20 (March–April 1929): 19.

Chapter 5

1. Estelle B. Freedman, "Separatism Revisted: Women's Institutions, Social Reform, and the Career of Miriam Van Waters," in *U.S. History as Women's History: New Feminist Essays*, ed. Linda K. Kerber, Alice Kessler-Harris, and Kathryn Kish Sklar (Chapel Hill: University of North Carolina Press, 1995), 170–88; and Freedman, "Separatism as Strategy: Female Institution Building and American Feminism, 1870–1930," *Feminist Studies* 5 (Fall 1979): 512–29. For separatism in a different context, see Temma Kaplan, "Women and Spanish Anarchism," in *Becoming Visible: Women in European History*, ed. Renate Bridenthal and Claudia Koonz (Boston: Houghton Mifflin, 1977), 401–21.

2. On the importance of nonpolitical work in sustaining radical organizations, see Paul Buhle, "Jews and American Communism: The Cultural Question," *Radical History Review* 23 (Spring 1980): 12–17.

3. See the National Executive Committee meetings notes from the 1920s, unprocessed materials, YIVO; Yehuda Bauer, *My Brother's Keeper: A History of the American Jewish Joint Distribution Committee, 1929–1939* (Philadelphia: Jewish Publication Society of America, 1974), 35. For an in-depth look at overseas relief during these years, see three essays by Zosa Szajkowski, "Private and Organized American Jewish Overseas Relief (1919–1938)," *American Jewish Historical Quarterly* 57 (September 1967): 52–106; "Private and Organized American Jewish Overseas Relief and Immigration (1914–1938)," *American Jewish Historical Quarterly* 57 (December 1967): 191–253; and "Private and Organized American Jewish Overseas Relief (1919–1938): Problems and Attempted Solutions," *American Jewish Historical Quarterly* 57 (March 1968): 285–352.

4. M. Ivenski, "Tsvey kongressen" [Two congresses], *Der fraynd* 17 (October 1927): 7–9; Yakov Pat, "Di geshehenishen in palestina un der 'bund' in poylen" [The events in Palestine and the 'Bund' in Poland], *Der fraynd* 20 (November–December 1929): 10–12; and Pat, "Palestine," *Der fraynd* 21 (November–December 1930): 2–3. See also M. Ivenski, "'Ahad Ha'am' un zeyn literarishe badaytung" ["Ahad Ha'am" and his literary meaning], *Der fraynd* 16 (September 1926): 17–19; Gina Medem, "Di naye froy" [The new woman], *Der fraynd* 17 (November–December 1927): 7–9; and Harold Berman, "The Youth Movement in Palestine," *Friend* 21 (November–December 1930): 5–6.

5. Judah J. Shapiro, *The Friendly Society: A History of the Workmen's Circle* (New York: Media Judaica, 1970), 79–85; and Maximilian Hurwitz, *The Workmen's Circle: Its History, Ideals, Organizations and Institutions* (New York: Workmen's Circle, 1936), 55–78. For more general context, see Melech Epstein, *Jewish Labor in the U.S.A.: An Industrial, Political, and Cultural His-*

tory of the Jewish Labor Movement, vol. 2, *1914–1952* (New York: KTAV, 1969), 124–56.

6. J. Shapiro, *Friendly Society,* 79–85; Hurwitz, *Workmen's Circle,* 55–78; and Epstein, *Jewish Labor,* 124–56. On the IWO, see Joyce Antler, "Between Culture and Politics: The Emma Lazarus Federation of Jewish Women's Clubs and the Promulgation of Women's History, 1944–1989," in *U.S. History as Women's History: New Feminist Essays,* 267–95; Thomas J. E. Walker, *Pluralistic Fraternity: The History of the International Worker's Order* (New York: Garland, 1991); and Arthur J. Sabin, *Red Scare in Court: New York versus the International Workers Order* (Philadelphia: University of Pennsylvania Press, 1993).

7. "Di grindung fun froyen klub in brentsh 392" [The founding of the women's club in Branch 392], in *50th Anniversay Jubilee Lubliner Ehrlich Branch 392 W.C., 1909–1959* (New York: n.p., 1956), pp. 22–23, Box 31, Folder 172, YIVO; "Anshtot a bagrisung" [Instead of a greeting], in *In doremland* [In the southern land] (Atlanta: n.p., 1928), p. 43, Box 19, Folder 119, YIVO.

8. I. Sh. Herts, *50 yohr arbeter ring in yidishn lebn* [Fifty years of Workmen's Circle in Jewish life] (New York: National Executive Committee, Arbeter Ring, 1950), 184. In 1926 the National Executive Committee (NEC) reported that the number of new members inducted that year amounted to 2,000 less than the year before. General Secretary Joseph Baskin also reported that in 1926 the Circle lost 3,070 members. National Executive Committee meeting minutes, in English, 9 January 1927, unprocessed material at YIVO.

9. Herts, *50 yohr,* 170–71, 184–85. He maintains that by 1922, 11 percent of Arbeter Ring members were businessmen, generally running small operations, who had retained their ideals.

10. J. Shapiro, *Friendly Society,* 78; A. S. Zaks, *Di geshichte fun arbeter ring, 1892–1925, tsveyter teyl* [The history of the Workmen's Circle, vol. 2] (n.p.: National Executive Committee, Arbeter Ring, 1925), 705–6.

11. *Der fraynd. Konvenshon numer* [The friend. Convention number] May 1919, pp. 17–18. Box 4, Folder 19, YIVO. On youth groups see Herts, *50 yohr,* 187–88.

12. "Wives of Wo[r]kmen's Circle Members," *Friend* 16 (February 1926): 1–2.

13. Hurwitz, *Workmen's Circle,* 212–14. As he was writing the book in 1936, six ladies' branches still existed: two in Newark and one each in New York City, Syracuse, Pittsburgh, and Richmond, VA.

14. Ibid.; *Konvenshon buletin* [Convention bulletin] 9 (5 May 1927), p. 28, Box 4, Folder 22, YIVO. In December 1924 plans were laid for a joint conference between members of the 3rd class (members' wives) and the Organizing Committee. This conference established a campaign to enroll more wives into the 3rd class. See Report of the Office Committee, NEC minutes, 7 December 1924, p. 206, in English, unprocessed material located at YIVO.

15. *Konvenshon buletin* [Convention bulletin] 7 (5 May 1925), p. 6, Box 4, Folder 21, YIVO.

16. *Konvenshon buletin* [Convention bulletin] 10 (7 May 1929), p. 5, Box 4, Folder 23, YIVO.

17. "Leydies okzileri fun brentsh 27 a.r." [Ladies' auxiliary of Branch 27 A.R.], in *Branch 27 Workmen's Circle, 25th Jubiliee, 1903–1928/Ladies Auxiliary of Branch 27, 20th Jubilee, 1908–1928* (Rochester, NY: n.p., 1928), pp. 14–16, Box 16, Folder 94 YIVO.

18. Sara Eybishoz, "Mayn troym farvirklikht" [My dream realized], *Boro park froyen brentsh 315–B acht-yoriker yubiley suvenir zhurnal* [Borough Park Women's Branch 315-B eight year anniversary journal] (Borough Park, NY: n.p.,1937), n.p., Box 22, Folder 137, YIVO; and Rokhl Vol, "Di froy—frier un yitst" [The woman—earlier and now], *Tsen-yoriger yubiley zhurnal pinsker froyen brentsh 210–B arbeter ring, 1929–1939* [Ten-year anniversary journal of Pinsker Women's Branch 210-B Workmen's Circle, 1929–1939] (New York: n.p., 1939), n.p., Box 20, Folder 121, YIVO.

19. Laura Z. Hobson, *Laura Z.: A Life* (New York: Arbor House, 1983), 23. Hobson writes: "To think that I might have been a linguist! But the whole purpose of their moving away from New York in my earliest childhood, first to Brooklyn, and then to a small town on Long Island, away from their colleagues and friends, away from their co-workers on newspapers and in labor unions—the whole point was to bring up their children as total Americans, with no trace of foreign accent, no smallest inflection or gesture that was not native to this their beloved country."

20. Ibid., 27–28, 63–64.

21. Ibid., 64, 100. Socialist Theresa Malkiel similarly refrained from critiquing domestic relations in her political writings; see Sally M. Miller, "From Sweatshop Worker to Labor Leader: Theresa Malkiel, A Case Study," *American Jewish History* 68 (December 1978): 189–203.

22. See Steven Cassedy, *To the Other Shore: The Russian Jewish Intellectuals Who Came to America* (Princeton, NJ: Princeton University Press, 1997), 101–2. Adela Kean Zametkin, *Der froy's handbukh* [The wife's handbook] (Jamaica, NY: privately published, 1930).

23. Other socialist and mutual aid groups also saw a rise in female organizing in the 1920s. See Mari Jo Buhle, *Women and American Socialism, 1870–1920* (Urbana: University of Indiana Press, 1981) 300–304; Daniel Soyer, *Jewish Immigrant Associations and American Identity in New York, 1880–1939* (Cambridge, MA: Harvard University Press, 1997), 192.

24. Hannah Klein, "Yorn loyfn" [Years run], in *Tsen yoriger yubiley zhurnal pinsker froyen brentsh 210-B arbeter ring*, n.p.

25. Rokhl Vol, "Di froy—frier un yitst," n.p.

26. "Froyen" [Women], in *Di geshikhte fun 60 yor arbeter ring brentsh 207/40 yor arbeter ring brentsh 207-b yubiley feyering* [The history of 60 years,Workmen's Circle Branch 207/40 years Workmen's Circle Branch 207-b jubilee celebration] (Atlanta: n.p., 1968), pp. 6–7, Box 19, Folder 119, YIVO; Beki Kohen, "Ikh dermon zikh" [I reminisce], in *Tsen yoriger yubiley*

zshurnal pinsker froyen brentsh 210-B arbeter ring, n.p. In this article Kohen describes how busy women were in the home, unable to attend Arbeter Ring meetings more than once or twice a week. See also Philip Grosman, "Geshikhlakhe erinerungen fun lubliner yong mans brentsh 392 arbeter ring" [Historical reminiscences of the Lublin Young Men's Branch 392 Workmen's Circle], *Lubliner yong manis brentsh 392 yoriger yubileyum, 1909–1934* [Lubliner Young Men's Branch 392 annual jubilee 1909–1934] (New York: n.p., 1934), pp. 12–13, Box 31, Folder 172, YIVO.

27. Jeni Goldberg, "Tsvelf zeynen mir geven" [We were twelve], in *Tsen yoriger yubiley zshurnal pinsker froyen brentsh 210-B arbeter ring*, n.p.

28. "Di grindung fun froyen klub in brentsh 392," pp. 22–23.

29. Esther Lurie, "Der 'Fraynd' un di froy" ["The friend" and the woman], *Der Fraynd* 11 (November–December 1920): 21. Maxine Seller points out that in similar articles for *Forverts* in 1919 Esther Lurie fails to mention the Workmen's Circle Yiddish school movement. This could indicate a change in Lurie's interest or position on the movement. It is also a reminder of the importance of newspaper editors in determining the content of articles printed in this and other papers. While much can be gleaned of the women's positions from their printed articles, editorial influence and input cannot be ignored. Maxine S. Seller, "Defining Socialist Womanhood: The Women's Page of the *Jewish Daily Forward* in 1919," *American Jewish History* 76 (June 1987): 432. On Lurie see Norma Fain Pratt, "Culture and Radical Politics: Yiddish Women Writers in America, 1890–1940," in *Decades of Discontent: The Women's Movement, 1920–1940*, ed. Lois Scharf and Joan M. Jensen (Westport, CT: Greenwood, 1983), 137–38.

30. Rokhl Holtman, "Di oyftuungen fun der amerikaner froy in 1922" [The achievements of the American woman in 1922], *Der fraynd* 14 (January 1923): 20–22. See also Rokhl Holtman, *Mayn lebns-veg* [My lifepath] (New York: Rokhl Holtman book committee, 1948); and Fain Pratt, "Culture and Radical Politics," 142–43. Like Zametkin and Lurie, Holtman led an extraordinary life. Born in Memel, near the Baltic Sea, in 1882, Holtman struggled for years to achieve an education. As a youth she opened a night school for working girls and read widely in Russian. At a young age she expressed an interest in women's rights and read such authors as George Eliot, Emma Lazarus, Harriet Beecher Stowe, Lucretia Mott, Frances Wright, and Mother Jones. She later studied in Vilna, Warsaw, and Berlin before emigrating to the United States with her husband in 1913. After living in Minneapolis and Pittsburgh, they eventually landed in New York City, where her husband became the editor of *Der kampf.* He was also an editor of the Communist *Frayhayt*, whose Sunday women's page Holtman edited. Holtman was a member of the Workmen's Circle and wrote for *Der fraynd* as well as other Yiddish papers. After divorcing Holtman, she traveled to Moscow, where she met Nadezhda Krupskaya, and to South Africa where all her brothers had emigrated. See Holtman, *Mayn lebns-veg;* and Fain Pratt, "Culture and Radical Politics," 142–43.

31. Rokhl Holtman, "Di froy un der industrie" [The woman and

industry], *Der fraynd* 14 (March 1923): 17–18.

32. Rokhl Holtman, "Di antshteyung fun der moderner froyen-bavegung" [The rise of the modern women's movement], *Der fraynd* 14 (August 1923): 20–21.

33. Rokhl Holtman, "Froyen-kluben in Amerike" [Women's clubs in America], *Der fraynd* 13 (November 1922): 21–23.

34. Rose Asch-Simpson, "Vorum members froyen darfen zikh onshlisen in dem arbeyter ring" [Why members' wives should join the Workmen's Circle], in *Grodner brentsh 74 20 yeriger yubileyum* [Grodner branch 74 twentieth anniversary] (New York: n.p., 1926), n.p., Box 17, Folder 100, YIVO.

35. Anna Kronshtadt, "Vos ikh gedenk fun undzer froyen brentsh: erinerungen" [What I think of our women's branch: memoirs], in *40 yehriger yubiley zshurnal fun pruzhener brentsh 244 arbeter ring*, [Forty-year anniversary journal of Purzhene Branch 244 Workmen's Circle] (New York: n.p., 1948) Box 21, Folder 127, YIVO; See also Roze Selnik, "Tsen yor" [Ten years], in *Tsen yoriger yubiley zhurnal pinsker froyen brentsh 210-b arbeter ring*, n.p.; and Grosman, "Geshikhlakhe erinerungen," pp. 12–13.

36. "Leydies okzileri"; J. Flekser, "Froyen organizatsies beym arbeter ring in montreal" [Women's organizations in Workmen's Circle in Montreal], *Suvenir bukh aroysgegeben fun mayer london brentsh 151* [Souvenir book published by Meyer London Branch 151] (Montreal: Branch 151, 1932), pp. 23–25, Box 18, Folder 111, YIVO; Anna H. Yifah, "Tsen yor froyen klub geshikhte" [Ten year women's club history], in *Arbeter Ring yubileyum shtime: 25 yoriker yubileyum fun brentsh 208, a.r.* [Workmen's Circle jubilee voice: 25 year anniversary of Branch 208, W.C.] (New Brunswick, NJ: n.p., 1933), pp. 11–13, Box 19, Folder 120, YIVO; Roze Selnik, "Tsen yor" [Ten years].

37. Mini Shneyder, "Di role fun der froy in dem arbeter ring" [The role of the woman in the Workmen's Circle], in *30 yoriker yubiley khotiner beserabier brentsh 200, 1909–1939* [30 year jubilee of Khotin Besarabia Branch 200, 1909–1939] (New York: n.p., 1939), n.p., Box 19, Folder 117, YIVO.

38. Hurwitz, *Workmen's Circle*, 213. For a description of the schools, see Israel Kugler, "A Life in the Workmen's Circle: Reminiscence and Reflection," *Labor's Heritage* 3 (October 1991): 42–44. The Workmen's Circle schools began as "socialist Sunday schools" in 1906. Many of the early teachers were women. The Sunday schools were not ultimately successful and ceased to exist in 1914. The following year proponents of Yiddish education began to work in the Circle to open Yiddish school programs. The proponents met opposition from more orthodox socialists. These opponents were won over by a promise that the schools would stress both radical politics and Yiddish education. In 1918 the first part-time elementary schools opened in the New York area, followed in later years by programs for older children, summer camps, and teacher education classes. By 1928 there were 105 schools with 6,500 total students. See Epstein, *Jewish Labor*, 275–79. See also Zaks, *Geshichte*, 508–27.

39. N. Chanin, "Di froyen arum der arbeter ring shul bavegung"

[The women in the Workmen's Circle school movement], *Shul Almanakh: di yidishe moderne shul oyf der velt* [School almanac: the Jewish modern school in the world] (April 1935): 196–98. Hurwitz, *Workmen's Circle*, 213–14.

40. "Leydies okzileri," pp. 14–16; Flekser, "Froyen organizatsies," pp. 23–5; Yifah, "Tsen yor froyen klub," pp. 11–13.

41. "A Historic Conference," *Der fraynd* 20 (March–April 1929): 1–2 [in the English section].

42. "Di konvenshon fun di leydis okzileris" [The convention of the ladies' auxiliaries], *Der fraynd* 20 (February 1929): 5; and in the same issue's English section, "The Ladies Auxiliaries Conference."

43. "Barikht fun ershten tsuzamenfohr fun di froyen kluben fun a.r." [Report of the first convention of the women's clubs of W.C.], *Der fraynd* 20 (March–April 1929): 17–20. The NEC continued to take full credit for devising the women's clubs. See "Barikht fun natsionaler ekzekutiv komite" [Report of the National Executive Committee], *Der fraynd* 20 (May 1929): 20. "Klas 3 froyen members in leydis ukzileris" [Class 3 female members in ladies' auxiliaries], *Der fraynd* 20 (March–April 1929): 2–3.

44. "Der ershter tsuzamenfohr fun unzere froyen kluben" [The first convention of our women's clubs], *Der fraynd* 20 (March–April 1929): 4.

45. Mrs. Levin in *Konvenshon buletin* [Convention bulletin] 10 (7 May 1929): 13, 26; Herts, *50 yohr*, 189; Hurwitz, *Workmen's Circle*, 212–13. For explanation of class 3 status see "Vikhtige informatsiyes vegen klas 3 members" [Important information about class 3 members], *Der fraynd* 19 (September 1928): 3. Class 3 membership was for wives of Circle members who belonged to the same branch as their husbands. If a member whose wife was in Class 3 died, resigned, was expelled, or disappeared, the wife was able to remain in class 3 by paying her own fees. The same situation held if the members divorced. Explication of class 5 rights and duties can be found in "Membership kampeyn notitsehn" [Membership campaign notes], *Der fraynd* 20 (September 1929): 2. All classes of women could join a women's club, but those outside classes 3 and 5 could only do so on the local level.

46. Herts, *50 yohr*, 190; for 1936 figures, see Hurwitz, *Workmen's Circle*, 214.

47. Yifah, "Tsen yor froyen klub," pp. 11–13.

48. Joseph Baskin, *In dinst fun der yidisher gezelshaft* [In service of Jewish society] (New York: National Executive Committee of the Workmen's Circle, 1945), 20–21. In this passage, Baskin discusses the formation of the Social Service Department, using Asch's arguments but without once mentioning her centrality to its creation.

49. Zaks, *Geshikhte* (vol. 2), 841, 856–57; Hurwitz, *Workmen's Circle*, 137–38. See also information on Asch in *Arbeter Ring: Boyer un Tuer* [Workmen's Circle: builders and active members] (New York: Marstin Press, 1962), 31.

50. Rose Asch-Simpson, "The Origins of Social Service in the Workmen's Circle," *Social Service Review of Workmen's Circle*, pp. 2–3, Box 9, Folder 56, YIVO; and Rose Asch-Simpson, "Di 'soshel soyrvis byuro' in

arbeter ring" [The "social service bureau" in Workmen's Circle), in *Yubileum oyfgabe tsu dem 25 yorigen fest fun dem minsker progresiv brentsh 99 arbeter ring* [Anniversary task of the 25 year festival of the Minsk Progressive Branch 99 of the Workmen's Circle], pp. 28–30, Box 16, Folder 105, YIVO;

51. Rose Asch, "A New Plan for the Workmen's Circle," quoted in Hurwitz, *Workmen's Circle*, 197.

52. Rose Asch-Simpson, *Der soshel soyrvis department fun arbeter ring* [The social service department of the Workmen's Circle], 1943–1944, n.p., Box 9, Folder 56, YIVO. (One half in Yiddish, one half in English.)

53. Hurwitz, *Workmen's Circle*, 199–200; Herts, *50 yohr*, 193. The Committee of Six included Rose Asch, Nathan Chanin of the NEC, Boris Fingerhut, Henry Fruchter, Philip Geliebter, and Samuel Koner. The other NEC representative attending the conference was Louis Zinderman. See also National Executive Committee meeting minutes, in English, 7 November 1926, p. 95, unprocessed material located at YIVO.

54. NEC minutes, 1 February 1927, pp. 15–16, in English; NEC minutes, 21 March 1927, p. 36, in English, unprocessed material, YIVO.

55. "Joint Meeting with Committee of Social Service Conference," 11 April 1927, pp. 46–47, in English, and continuation of meeting on 18 April 1927, p. 50, in English. The joint committee included Dinerstein, J. Rothman (recording secretary of NEC), Bruskin, Haskell, and Padnick. In June the committee was composed of Davidoff, Padnick, Fischman, Berman, and Cohen. NEC mintues, 5 June 1927, p. 60, in English. All in unprocessed materials, YIVO.

56. NEC minutes from 5 June 1927, in English, pp. 60–61, unprocessed material, YIVO.

57. See Hurwitz, *Workmen's Circle*, 196–201. The Jewish Women's Organization of Palestine faced similar opposition to its activities. Some Zionists felt that its social services undermined the strength and independence of the "new Jews." See Hanna Herzog, "The Fringes of the Margin: Women's Organizations in the Civic Sector of the *Yishuv*," in *Pioneers and Homemakers: Jewish Women in Pre-State Israel*, ed. Deborah Bernstein (Albany: State University of New York Press, 1992), 292.

58. Nathan Rothman, "Is a Social Service Department Necessary?" *Der fraynd* 16 (February 1926): 3–4.

59. NEC minutes, 7 September 1927, pp. 175–76, in Yiddish. At the August 2, 1927, meeting, a Social Service supporter recommended that the department begin to function in September. NEC minutes, 2 August 1927, pp. 168–69, in Yiddish. Both in unprocessed material, YIVO.

60. NEC minutes, 1 April 1928, pp. 264–65, in Yiddish, unprocessed material, YIVO.

61. *Konvenshon buletin* [Convention bulletin] 9 (5 May 1927), p. 8, Box 4, Folder 22, YIVO.

62. Hurwitz, *Workmen's Circle*, 201–6; For the services offered by the Social Service Department, see Y. Kaminski, *Fertsik yor arbeter-ring: a geshikhte in bilder* [Forty years of the Workmen's Circle: A history in pictures]

(New York: National Executive Committee of Workmen's Circle, 1940), 50–51. At the center of the two-page spread on the department is a large heart, from which the services are listed as if emanating from the heart.

63. Greetings [in English] sent from The Matrix Young Circle Branch 1022 Workmen's Circle, in *Suvenir zshurnal lozsher froyen brentsh 342-b arbeter ring* [Souvenir journal of the Lodzer Women's Branch 342-B Workmen's Circle], 1935, Box 22, Folder 144, YIVO. Such language is not unique for this period; in discussing women in the order, Kaminski states that "when she finally freed herself from the greyness of kitchen walls, when she sought recreation and social intercourse, she came to the Workmen's Circle." See Kaminski, *Fertsik yor arbeter-ring*, 42.

Conclusion

1. Quoted in Kristi Andersen, *After Suffrage: Women in Partisan and Electoral Politics before the New Deal* (Chicago: University of Chicago, 1996), 166.

2. Quoted in Judah J. Shapiro, *The Friendly Society: A History of the Workmen's Circle* (New York: Media Judaica, 1970), 180; also 177–89. See Faith Rogow, *Gone to Another Meeting: The National Council of Jewish Women, 1893–1993* (Tuscaloosa: University of Alabama Press, 1993), 173–76; and Joyce Antler, *The Journey Home: Jewish Women and the American Century* (New York: Free Press, 1997), 125–26, 209–11, 218–23.

3. Rogow, *Gone to Another Meeting*, 176–78; J. Shapiro, *Friendly Society*, 195–207.

4. Hadassah, the Women's Zionist Organization of America, "Hadassah Associates," and "Membership: Every Action Counts, Every Member Counts," http://www.hadassah.org (26 July 2002); and Zionist Organization of America, "What Is the ZOA?" http://www.zoa.org (26 July 2002). The Hadassah Associates were formed in 1966 to give men a way to support the Hadassah Medical Organization directly. More recently, these groups have developed their own national structure and leadership.

5. See National Council of Jewish Women, "Programs and Projects," http://www.ncjw.org (26 July 2002).

6. See Workmen's Circle, "Contact Us: National Executive Board and Officers," http://www.circle.org (26 July 2002).

BIBLIOGRAPHY

PRIMARY SOURCES

ARCHIVAL

American Jewish Relief Committee. Miscellaneous Publications. Klau Library. Hebrew Union College. Cincinnati.

Brenner, Rose. "Report to the Board of Managers by Rose Brenner, November 1925." National Council of Jewish Women—Miscellaneous Publications. Klau Library. Hebrew Union College. Cincinnati.

Brickner, Rebecca Aronson. Papers. Western Reserve Historical Society. Cleveland.

Brown, Ronald, and Isabelle Brown. Papers. Western Reserve Historical Society. Cleveland.

Hadassah, Pittsburgh Chapter. Records. Archives of Industrial Society, University of Pittsburgh.

Hadassah, the Women's Zionist Organization of America, Cleveland Chapter. Records. Western Reserve Historical Society. Cleveland.

Hadassah, the Women's Zionist Organization of America. Miscellaneous Publications. Klau Library. Hebrew Union College. Cincinnati.

Hadassah, the Women's Zionist Organization of America. Records. Hadassah Archives. New York City.

International Council of Jewish Women. Miscellaneous Publications. Klau Library. Hebrew Union College. Cincinnati.

Kohut, Rebekah. Correspondence, 1896–1951. American Jewish Archives. Cincinnati.

———. Nearprint. American Jewish Archives. Cincinnati.

Landy, Rachel Diane. Papers. Western Reserve Historical Society. Cleveland.

National Council of Jewish Women. Miscellaneous Publications. Klau Library. Hebrew Union College. Cincinnati.

National Council of Jewish Women. Records. Library of Congress. Washington, D.C.

National Council of Jewish Women, Cleveland Section. Records. Western Reserve Historical Society. Cleveland.

National Council of Jewish Women, Pittsburgh Section. Records. Archives of Industrial Society, University of Pittsburgh.

Pittsburgh Conference of Jewish Women's Organizations. Records. Archives of Industrial Society, University of Pittsburgh.

Solomon, Hannah G. Nearprint. American Jewish Archives. Cincinnati.

———. Papers. Library of Congress. Washington, D.C.

———. Scrapbook, 1894–1953. American Jewish Archives. Cincinnati.

Szold, Henrietta. Letters to and from Henrietta Szold, 1866–1944, and Diaries kept by Miss Szold, 1881–1920. American Jewish Archives. Cincinnati.

Workmen's Circle. Records in the Bund Archival collection. YIVO Institute for Jewish Research. New York City.

NEWSPAPERS AND NEWSLETTERS

American Hebrew

Bulletin of the Joint Distribution Committee of the American Funds for Jewish War Sufferers

Council of Jewish Women, New York Section, *The Bulletin*

Der fraynd

Hadassah *Bulletin*

Hadassah *Newsletter*

Jewish Woman

Maccabaean

Monthly Bulletin of the American Jewish Relief Committee for Sufferers from the War

BOOKS AND ARTICLES

American Jewish Relief Committee. *Proceedings of the Chicago Conference of the American Jewish Relief Committee*. n.p., 1921.

American Relief Administration in Austria. *A Review of the Work of the American Relief Administration in Austria*. Vienna: n.p., 1923.

Askowith, Dora. *Three Outstanding Women: Mary Fels, Rebekah Kohut, Annie Nathan Meyer*. New York: Bloch, 1941.

Baskin, Joseph. *In dinst fun der yidisher gezelshaft* [In service of Jewish society]. New York: National Executive Committee of the Workmen's Circle, 1945.

Bogen, Boris D. *Born A Jew*. New York: Macmillan, 1930.

———. *Jewish Philanthropy: An Exposition of Principles and Methods of Jewish Social Science in the United States*. New York: Macmillan, 1917.

Council of Jewish Women. *Department of Immigrant Aid*. New York: Office of the Department of Immigrant Aid, 1922.

———. *Official Report of the Eleventh Triennial*. New York: n.p., 1927.

———. *Official Report of the Ninth Triennial Convention*. n.p., 1920.

———. *Official Report of the Tenth Triennial Convention*, ed. Estelle M. Sternberger. n.p., 1923.

Enlow, H. G. *The Allied Countries and the Jews*. New York: Bloch, 1918.

Engelman, Morris. *Four Years of Relief and War Work by the Jews of America, 1914–1918: A Chronological Review*. New York: Schoen, 1918.

Gorenstein, Lillian. "A Memoir of the Great War, 1914–1924." *YIVO Annual*

20 (1991): 125–83.

Herts, I. Sh. *50 Yohr arbeter ring in yidishn lebn* [Fifty Years of Workmen's Circle in Jewish Life]. New York: National Executive Committee, Arbeter Ring, 1950.

Hirsh, Joseph, ed. *The Hadassah Medical Organization: An American Contribution to Medical Pioneering and Progress in Israel.* New York: Hadassah, 1956.

Hobson, Laura Z. *Laura Z.: A Life.* New York: Arbor House, 1983.

Holtman, Rokhl. *Mayn lebns-veg* [My life-path]. New York: Rokhl Holtman bukh-komitet, 1948.

International Council of Women. *Sixth Quinquennial Convention.* n.p., 1925.

Jacobs, Rose G. "Beginnings of Hadassah." In *Early History of Zionism in America*, ed. Isidore S. Meyer, 233–36. New York: Arno, 1977.

Kaminski, Y. *Fertsik yor arbeter-ring: a geshikhte in bilder* [Forty years of the Workmen's Circle: A history in pictures]. New York: National Executive Committee of the Workmen's Circle, 1940.

Kohut, Rebekah. *As I Know Them: Some Jews and a Few Gentiles.* Garden City, NY: Doubleday, Doran, 1929.

———. "Jewish Women's Organizations." *American Jewish Yearbook* 33 (1931–1932): 165–202.

———. *More Yesterdays.* New York: Bloch, 1950.

———. *My Portion.* New York: Albert and Charles Boni, 1927.

Lindheim, Irma L. *Parallel Quest: A Search of a Person and a People.* New York: T. Yoseloff, 1962.

National Appeal for Jewish War Sufferers. *The Victory Conference and Testimonial to David A. Brown.* New York: Clarence S. Nathan, n.d.

National Council of Jewish Women. *Council Pioneer: A History of Council in the Vanguard of Social Advance.* n.p.: National Council of Jewish Women, 1955.

———. *The First Fifty Years: A History of the National Council of Jewish Women, 1893–1943.* n.p.: National Council of Jewish Women, 1943.

Protokoll der Gründungsversammlung des 'Weltbundes jüdischer Frauen' vom 4.–6. Juni 1929 [Record of the founding meeting of the 'World Congress of Jewish Women' from 4–6 June, 1929]. Berlin: B. Levy, 1929.

Rakovsky, Puah. *My Life as a Radical Jewish Woman: Memoirs of a Zionist Feminist in Poland.* Ed. and intro. Paula E. Hyman. Trans. from the Yiddish by Barbara Harshav and Paula E. Hyman. Bloomington: Indiana University Press, 2002.

Razovsky, Cecilia. *Making Americans.* New York: National Council of Jewish Women, 1938.

Rich, Winifred Lancashire. "The National Council of Jewish Women." *Woman Citizen* 10 (1925): 13, 29.

Rosenfelt, Henry H. *The First Six Months of 1919.* n.p.: n.p., n.d.

Sampter, Jessie E. *The Coming of Peace.* New York: Publishers Printing, 1919.

———. "Cure the Causes." In *How to Combat Anti-Semitism in America: The*

BIBLIOGRAPHY

Six Prize Winning Essays in the Contest Conducted by Opinion—A Journal of Life and Letters, 71–9. New York: Jewish Opinion, 1937.

Solomon, Hannah G. *Fabric of My Life*. New York: Bloch, 1946.

Sternberger, Estelle M. *Daily Readings in Human Service: A Handbook of Information on Council Ideas and Activities*. n.p.: National Council of Jewish Women, 1925.

———. *Triennial Report of the Office of the Executive Secretary. Twelfth Triennial Convention*. n.p., 1930.

Veintroyb, Y. "Der arbayter ring (a kurtser historisher iberblik)" [The Workmen's Circle: A short overview]. In *Der arbayter ring zamel bukh* [The Workmen's Circle collection book]. New York: Arbayter Ring, 1910.

Wolfson, Miriam. *The Spirit of Hadassah: A One-Act Play*. New York: Bloch, 1927.

World Congress of Jewish Women. *Proceedings*. Vienna: Druckerei-U. Verlags—A. G. Ignaz Steinmann, 1923.

Yezierska, Anzia. *Arrogant Begger*. 1927. Reprint, Durham, NC: Duke University Press, 1996.

———. *Salome of the Tenements*. 1923. Reprint, Urbana: University of Illinois Press, 1995.

SECONDARY SOURCES

Abrams, Ruth. "Jewish Women in the International Woman's Suffrage Alliance, 1899–1926." PhD diss., Brandeis University, 1996.

———. "'Pioneering Representatives of the Hebrew People': Campaigns of the Palestinian Jewish Women's Equal Rights Association, 1918–1948." In *Women's Suffrage in the British Empire: Citizenship, Nation, and Race*, ed. Ian Christopher Fletcher, Laura E. Nym Mayhall, and Philippa Levine, 121–37. London: Routledge, 2000.

Almog, Shmuel. "Antisemitism as a Dynamic Phenomenon: The 'Jewish Question' in England at the Time of the First World War." *Patterns of Prejudice* 21 (winter 1987): 3–18.

Alonso, Harriet Hyman. *Peace as a Women's Issue: A History of the U.S. Movement for World Peace and Women's Rights*. Syracuse: Syracuse University Press, 1993.

Andersen, Kristi. *After Suffrage: Women in Partisan and Electoral Politics before the New Deal*. Chicago: University of Chicago Press, 1996.

Anderson, Benedict. *Imagined Communities: Reflections on the Origin and Spread of Nationalism*. London: Verso, 1983.

Anderson, Bonnie S. *Joyous Greetings: The First International Women's Movement, 1830–1860*. New York: Oxford University Press, 2000.

Antler, Joyce. "Between Culture and Politics: The Emma Lazarus Federation of Jewish Women's Clubs and the Promulgation of Women's History, 1944–1989." In *U.S. History as Women's History: New Feminist Essays*, ed. Linda K. Kerber, Alice Kessler-Harris, and Kathryn Kish Sklar, 267–95. Chapel Hill: University of North Carolina Press, 1995.

———. *The Journey Home: Jewish Women and the American Century*. New

York: Free Press, 1997.

———. "Zion in Our Hearts: Henrietta Szold and the American Jewish Women's Movement." In *Daughter of Zion: Henrietta Szold and American Jewish Womanhood*, ed. Barry Kessler, 35–55. Baltimore: Jewish Historical Society of Maryland, 1995.

Aronson, Judith. "The National Council of Jewish Women: A Study of the Los Angeles Section in Transition." In *Speaking of Faith: Global Perspectives on Women, Religion and Social Change*, ed. Diana L. Eck and Devaki Jain, 196–202. Philadelphia: New Society, 1987.

Aschheim, Steven. *Brothers and Strangers: The East European Jew in German and German Jewish Consciousness, 1800–1923.* Madison: University of Wisconsin Press, 1982.

———. "The East European Jew and German Jewish Identity." In *Studies in Contemporary Jewry*. Vol. 1, *Ostjuden in Central and West Europe*, ed. Ezra Mendelsohn, 3–25. New York: Oxford University Press, 1984.

Ashton, Dianne. *Rebecca Gratz: Women and Judaism in Antebellum America.* Detroit: Wayne State University Press, 1997.

Bair, Barbara. "True Women, Real Men: Gender, Ideology, and Social Roles in the Garvey Movement." In *Gendered Domains: Rethinking Public and Private in Women's History*, ed. Dorothy O. Helly and Susan M. Reverby, 154–66. Ithaca, NY: Cornell University Press, 1992.

Banner, Lois W. *Elizabeth Cady Stanton: A Radical for Women's Rights.* Boston: Little, Brown, 1980.

Baron, Salo W. *The Russian Jew under Tsars and Soviets.* 2nd ed. New York: Schocken, 1987.

Basch, Francoise. "The Socialist Party of America, the Woman Question, and Theresa Serber Malkiel." Translated by Nancy Festinger. In *Women in Culture and Politics: A Century of Change*, ed. Judith Friedlander, Blanche Wiesen Cook, Alice Kessler-Harris, Carroll Smith-Rosenberg, 344–57. Bloomington: Indiana University Press, 1986.

Baskin, Judith R., ed. *Jewish Women in Historical Perspective.* Detroit: Wayne State University Press, 1991.

Bauer, Yehuda. *My Brother's Keeper: A History of the American Jewish Joint Distribution Committee, 1929–1939.* Philadelphia: Jewish Publication Society of America, 1974.

Baum, Charlotte. "What Made Yetta Work? The Economic Role of Eastern European Jewish Women in the Family." *Response: A Contemporary Jewish Review* 18 (1973): 32–38.

Baum, Charlotte, Paula Hyman, and Sonya Michel. *The Jewish Woman in America.* New York: Dial, 1976.

Becker, Susan D. *The Origins of the Equal Rights Amendment: American Feminism between the Wars.* Westport, CT: Greenwood, 1981.

Beito, David T. "Mutual Aid, State Welfare, and Organized Charity: Fraternal Societies and the 'Deserving' and 'Undeserving' Poor, 1900–1930." *Journal of Policy History* 5, no. 4 (1993): 419–34.

Bellah, Robert N. "Civil Religion in America." *Daedalus* (Winter 1967):

1–21.

Bender, Daniel E. "From Sweatshop to Model Shop: Anti-Sweatshop Campaigns and Languages of Labor and Organizing, 1880–1934." PhD diss., New York University, 2001.

Berkowitz, Michael. "Transcending 'Tzimmes and Sweetness': Recovering the History of Zionist Women in Central and Western Europe, 1897–1933." In *Active Voices: Women in Jewish Culture*, ed. Maurie Sacks, 41–62. Urbana: University of Illinois Press, 1995.

———. *Western Jewry and the Zionist Project, 1914–1933.* Cambridge: Cambridge University Press, 1997.

———. *Zionist Culture and West European Jewry before the First World War.* London: Cambridge University Press, 1993.

Berman, Myron. *The Attitude of American Jewry towards East European Jewish Immigration, 1881–1914.* New York: Arno, 1980.

Bernstein, Deborah. *Struggle for Equality: Urban Women Workers in Pre-State Israeli Society.* New York, Praeger, 1987.

———. "The Women Workers' Movement in Pre-State Israel, 1919–1939." *Signs: The Journal of Women in Culture and Society* 12 (spring 1987): 454–70.

Bernstein, Deborah, ed. *Pioneers and Homemakers: Jewish Women in Pre-State Israel.* Albany: State University of New York Press, 1992.

Berrol, Selma. "Class or Ethnicity: The Americanized German Jewish Woman and Her Middle Class Sisters in 1895." *Jewish Social Studies* 47 (winter 1985): 21–32.

———. "When Uptown Met Downtown: Julia Richman's Work in the Jewish Community of New York, 1880–1912." *American Jewish History* 70 (September 1980): 35–51.

Biale, David. "Zionism as an Erotic Revolution." In *People of the Body: Jews and Judaism from an Embodied Perspective*, ed. Howard Eilberg-Schwartz, 283–307. Albany: State University of New York Press, 1992.

Blair, Karen J. *The Clubwoman as Feminist: True Womanhood Redefined, 1868–1914.* New York: Holmes and Meier, 1980.

Blatman, Daniel. "Women in the Jewish Labor Bund in Interwar Poland." In *Women in the Holocaust*, ed. Dalia Ofer and Lenore J. Weitzman, 68–84. New Haven: Yale University Press, 1998.

Bodek, Evelyn. "'Making Do': Jewish Women and Philanthropy." In *Jewish Life in Philadelphia, 1830–1940*, ed. Murray Friedman, 143–62, 327–30. Philadelphia: ISHI, 1983.

Boisseau, T. J. "White Queens at the Chicago World's Fair, 1893: New Womanhood in the Service of Class, Race, and Nation." *Gender and History* 12 (April 2000): 33–81.

Bordin, Ruth. *Frances Willard: A Biography.* Chapel Hill: University of North Carolina Press, 1986.

Boyarin, Daniel, and Jonathan Boyarin. "Diaspora: Generation and the Ground of Jewish Identity." *Critical Inquiry* 19 (summer 1993): 693–725.

BIBLIOGRAPHY

Brandes, Joseph. "From Sweatshop to Stability: Jewish Labor between Two World Wars." *YIVO Annual of Jewish Social Science* 16 (1976): 1–149.

Braude, Anne. "Jewish Women's Encounter with American Culture." In *Women and Religion in America*. Vol. 1, *The Nineteenth Century*, ed. Rosemary Radford Ruether and Rosemary Skinner Keller, 150–92. San Francisco: Harper and Row, 1981.

Breen, William J. *Uncle Sam at Home: Civilian Mobilization, Wartime Federalism, and the Council of National Defense, 1917–1919*. Westport, CT: Greenwood, 1984.

Bremner, Robert H. *American Philanthropy*. 2d ed. Chicago: University of Chicago Press, 1988.

Brinner, William M., and Moses Rischin, eds. *Like All the Nations? The Life of Judah L. Magnes*. Albany: State University of New York Press, 1987.

Bristow, Edward. *Prostitution and Prejudice: The Jewish Fight against White Slavery*. New York: Clarendon Press, 1982.

Brown, Michael. "The American Element in the Rise of Golda Meir, 1906–1929." *Jewish History* 6, nos. 1–2 (1992): 35–50.

———. "Henrietta Szold's Progressive American Vision of the Yishuv." In *Envisioning Israel: The Changing Ideals and Images of North American Jews*, ed. Allon Gal, 60–80. Detroit: Wayne State University Press, 1996.

Buhle, Mari Jo. *Women and American Socialism, 1870–1920*. Urbana: University of Illinois Press, 1981.

Buhle, Paul. "Jews and American Communism: The Cultural Question." *Radical History Review* 23 (spring 1980):

———. "Themes in American Jewish Radicalism." In *The Immigrant Left in the United States*, ed. Paul Buhle and Dan Georgakas, 77–118. Albany: State University of New York Press, 1996.

Cassedy, Steven. *To the Other Shore: The Russian Jewish Intellectuals Who Came to America*. Princeton: Princeton University Press, 1997.

Cesarani, David. "Anti-Alienism in England after the First World War." *Immigrants and Minorities* 6 (March 1987): 5–29.

Chafe, William H. *The Paradox of Change: American Women in the 20th Century*. New York: Oxford University Press, 1991.

Chateauvert, Melinda. *Marching Together: Women of the Brotherhood of Sleeping Car Porters*. Urbana: University of Illinois Press, 1998

Clawson, Mary Ann. *Constructing Brotherhood: Class, Gender, and Fraternalism*. Princeton: Princeton University Press, 1989.

Cohen, Naomi. *American Jews and the Zionist Idea*. New York: KTAV, 1975.

———. *Not Free to Desist: The American Jewish Committee, 1906–1966*. Philadelphia: Jewish Publication Society of America, 1972.

———. *The Year after the Riots: American Responses to the Palestinian Crisis of 1929–1930*. Detroit: Wayne State University Press, 1988.

Cohen, Stuart A. "Ideological Components in Anglo-Jewish Opposition to Zionism before and during the First World War: A Restatement." *Jewish Historical Studies* 30 (1987–88): 149–62.

Cohn, Norman. *Warrant for Genocide: The Myth of the Jewish World-Conspiracy and the Protocols of the Elders of Zion.* New York: Harper and Row, 1966.

Cott, Nancy F. *The Grounding of Modern Feminism.* New Haven: Yale University Press, 1987.

———. "What's in a Name? The Limits of 'Social Feminism,' or, Expanding the Vocabulary of Women's History." *Journal of American History* 6 (December 1989): 809–28.

Curti, Merle. *American Philanthropy Abroad: A History.* New Brunswick, NJ: Rutgers University Press, 1963.

Dancis, Bruce. "Socialism and Women in the United States, 1900–1917." *Socialism Revolution* 6 (January–March 1976): 81–144.

Daniels, Doris Groshen. *Always a Sister: The Feminism of Lillian D. Wald.* New York: Feminist Press, 1989.

Dash, Joan. *Summoned to Jerusalem: The Life of Henrietta Szold.* New York: Harper and Row, 1979.

Davis-Kram, Harriet. "No More a Stranger Alone: Trade Union, Socialist and Feminist Activism: A Route to Becoming American (Rose Schneiderman, Pauline Newman)." PhD diss., City University of New York, 1997.

———. "Story of the Sisters of the Bund." *Contemporary Jewry* 5 (winter 1980): 27–43.

Diner, Hasia R. "Before the Promised City: Eastern European Jews in America before 1880." In *An Inventory of Promises: Essays on American Jewish History in Honor of Moses Rischin,* ed. Jeffrey S. Gurock and Marc Lee Raphael, 43–62. Brooklyn: Carlson, 1995.

———. *A Time for Gathering: The Second Migration, 1820–1880.* Vol. 2, *The Jewish People in America,* ed. Henry L. Feingold. Baltimore: Johns Hopkins University Press, 1992.

Dinnerstein, Leonard. *Antisemitism in America.* New York: Oxford University Press, 1994.

Dobkowski, Michael N., ed. *Jewish American Voluntary Organizations.* Westport, CT: Greenwood, 1985.

DuBois, Ellen Carol. "Woman Suffrage and the Left: An International Socialist-Feminist Perspective." *New Left Review* no. 186 (March/April 1991): 20–45.

———. "Woman Suffrage and the World: Three Phases of Suffragist Internationalism." In *Suffrage and Beyond: International Feminist Perspectives,* ed. Caroline Daley and Melanie Nolan, 252–74. New York: New York University Press, 1994.

DuBois, Ellen Carol, Mari Jo Buhle, Temma Kaplan, Gerda Lerner, and Carroll Smith-Rosenberg. "Politics and Culture in Women's History: A Symposium," *Feminist Studies* 6 (spring 1980): 26–63.

Elwell, Ellen Sue Levi. "The Founding and Early Programs of the National Council of Jewish Women: Study and Practice as Jewish Women's Religious Expression." PhD diss., Indiana University, 1982.

Endelman, Todd. "Making Jews Modern: Some Jewish and Gentile Misunderstandings in the Age of Emancipation." In *What Is Modern about the Modern Jewish Experience?*, ed. Marc Lee Raphael, 18–32. Williamsburg, VA: College of William and Mary, 1997.

———. *Radical Assimilation in English Jewish History, 1656–1945.* Bloomington: Indiana University Press, 1990.

Epstein, Melech. *Jewish Labor in the U.S.A.: An Industrial, Political, and Cultural History of the Jewish Labor Movement, 1882–1914.* New York: KTAV, 1969.

Faber, Eli. *A Time for Planting: The First Migration, 1654–1820.* Vol. 1, *The Jewish People in America*, ed. Henry L. Feingold. Baltimore: Johns Hopkins University Press, 1992.

Feingold, Henry L. *A Time for Searching: Entering the Mainstream, 1920–1945.* Vol. 4, *The Jewish People in America*, ed. Henry L. Feingold. Baltimore: Johns Hopkins University Press, 1992.

Fink, Carole. "The League of Nations and the Minorities Question." *World Affairs* 157 (spring 1995): 197–205.

Flanagan, Maureen A. *Seeing With Their Hearts: Chicago Women and the Vision of the Good City, 1871–1933.* Princeton: Princeton University Press, 2002.

Fogiel-Bijaoui, Sylvie. "On the Way to Equality? The Struggle for Women's Suffrage in the Jewish *Yishuv*, 1917–1926." In *Pioneers and Homemakers: Jewish Women in Pre-State Israel*, ed. Deborah S. Bernstein, 261–72. Albany: State University of New York Press, 1992.

Frager, Ruth A. "Politicized Housewives in the Jewish Communist Movement of Toronto, 1923–1933." In *Beyond the Vote: Canadian Women and Politics*, ed. Linda Kealey and Joan Sangster, 258–75. Toronto: University of Toronto Press, 1989.

———. *Sweatshop Strife: Class, Ethnicity, and Gender in the Jewish Labour Movement of Toronto, 1900–1939.* Toronto: University of Toronto Press, 1992.

Frank, Dana. "Housewives, Socialists, and the Politics of Food: The 1917 New York Cost-of-Living Protests." *Feminist Studies* 11 (summer 1985): 255–85.

Frankel, Jonathan. *Prophecy and Politics: Socialism, Nationalism and the Russian Jews, 1882–1917.* London: Cambridge University Press, 1981.

———, ed. *Studies in Contemporary Jewry: An Annual.* Vol. 4, *The Jews and the European Crisis, 1914–1921.* New York: Oxford University Press, 1988.

Freedman, Estelle B. "Separatism Revisited: Women's Institutions, Social Reform, and the Career of Miriam Van Waters." In *U.S. History as Women's History: New Feminist Essays*, ed. Linda K. Kerber, Alice Kessler-Harris, and Kathryn Kish Sklar, 170–88. Chapel Hill: University of North Carolina Press, 1995.

———. "Separatism as Strategy: Female Institution Building and American Feminism, 1870–1930," *Feminist Studies* 5 (fall 1979): 512–29.

Friesel, Evyatar. "The Influence of American Zionism on the American Jewish Community, 1900–1950." *American Jewish History* 75 (December 1985): 130–48.

Frommer, Morris. "The American Jewish Congress: A History, 1914–1950." PhD diss., Ohio State University, 1978.

Gal, Allon. *Brandeis of Boston*. Cambridge, MA: Harvard University Press, 1980.

———. "Hadassah and the American Jewish Political Tradition." In *An Inventory of Promises: Essays on American Jewish History in Honor of Moses Rischin*, ed. Jeffrey S. Gurock and Marc Lee Raphael, 89–114. Brooklyn: Carlson, 1995.

———. "The Mission Motif in American Zionism, 1898–1948." *American Jewish History* 75 (June 1986): 363–85.

———. "The Motif of Historical Continuity in American Zionist Ideology, 1900–1950." *Studies in Zionism* 13 (spring 1992): 1–20.

Gere, Anne Ruggles, *Intimate Practices: Literacy and Cultural Works in U.S. Women's Clubs, 1880–1920*. Urbana: University of Illinois Press, 1997.

Gilbert, Martin. *The First World War: A Complete History*. New York: Henry Holt, 1994.

Ginzburg, Lori D. "'Moral Suasion is Moral Balderdash': Women, Politics, and Social Activism in the 1850s." *Journal of American History* 73 (December 1986): 601–22.

———. *Women and the Work of Benevolence: Morality, Politics, and Class in the 19th-Century United States*. New Haven: Yale University Press, 1990.

Gitelman, Zvi. "A Centenary of Jewish Politics in Eastern Europe: The Legacy of the Bund and Zionist Movements." *East European Politics and Societies* 11 (fall 1997): 555–56.

———, ed. *The Quest for Utopia: Jewish Political Ideas and Institutions through the Ages*. Armonk, NY: M. E. Sharpe, 1992.

Glanz, Rudolf. *The Jewish Woman in America: Two Female Immigrant Generations, 1820–1929*. Vol. 1, *The Eastern European Jewish Woman*. New York: KTAV, 1976.

———. *The Jewish Woman in America: Two Female Immigrant Generations, 1820–1929*. Vol. 2, *The German Jewish Woman*. New York: KTAV, 1976.

Glenn, Susan. *Daughters of the Shtetl: Life and Labor in the Immigrant Generation*. Ithaca, NY: Cornell University Press, 1990.

Gluck, Sherna Berger. "Socialist Feminism between the Two World Wars: Insights from Oral History." In *Decades of Discontent: The Women's Movement, 1920–1940*, ed. Lois Scharf and Joan M. Mitchell, 279–97. Westport, CT: Greenwood, 1983.

Goldin, Milton. *Why They Give: American Jews and Their Philanthropies*. New York: Macmillan, 1976.

Goldman, Karla. *Beyond the Synagogue Gallery: Finding a Place for Women in American Judaism*. Cambridge, MA: Harvard University Press, 2001.

Goldscheider, Calvin and Alan S. Zuckerman. *The Transformation of the Jews*. Chicago: University of Chicago Press, 1984.

Goldstein, Eric L. "The Practical as Spiritual: Henrietta Szold's American Zionist Ideology, 1878–1820." In *Daughter of Zion: Henrietta Szold and American Jewish Womanhood*, ed. Barry Kessler, 17–33. Baltimore: Jewish Historical Society of Maryland, 1995.

Golomb, Deborah Grand. "The 1893 Congress of Jewish Women: Evolution or Revolution in American Jewish History." *American Jewish History* 70 (September 1980): 52–67.

Gordon, Linda. "Putting Children First: Women, Maternalism, and Welfare in the Early Twentieth Century." In *U.S. History as Women's History: New Feminist Essays*, ed. Linda K. Kerber, Alice Kessler-Harris, and Kathryn Kish Sklar, 63–86, 364–69. Chapel Hill: University of North Carolina Press, 1995.

———, ed. *Women, the State, and Welfare*. Madison: University of Wisconsin Press, 1990.

Grayzel, Susan R. *Women's Identities at War: Gender, Motherhood, and Politics in Britain and France during the First World War*. Chapel Hill: University of North Carolina Press, 1999.

Graziani, Bernice. *Where There's a Woman: Seventy-Five Years of History as Lived by the National Council of Jewish Women*. New York: McCall, 1967.

Greenwald, Maurine Weiner. *Women, War and Work: The Impact of World War I on Women Workers in the United States*. Westport, CT: Greenwood, 1980.

Grose, Peter. *Israel in the Mind of America*. New York: Alfred A. Knopf, 1983.

Grove-Pollack, Fay. *Saga of a Movement: WIZO 1920–1970*. n.p.: Department of Organisation and Education of Wizo, The Women's International Zionist Organisation, n.d.

Grubbs, Frank L., Jr. *The Struggle for Labor Loyalty: the A. F. of L., and the Pacifists, 1917–1920*. Durham, NC: Duke University Press, 1968.

Gullace, Nicoletta F. "Sexual Violence and Family Honor: British Propaganda and International Law during the First World War." *American Historical Review* 102 (June 1997): 714–47.

Halperin, Samuel. *The Political World of American Zionism*. Detroit: Wayne State University Press, 1961.

Halpern, Ben. *The American Jew: A Zionist Analysis*. New York: Theodore Herzl Foundation, 1956.

———. *A Clash of Heroes: Brandeis, Weizmann, and American Zionism*. New York: Oxford University Press, 1987.

Handlin, Oscar. *A Continuing Task: The American Jewish Joint Distribution Committee, 1914–1964*. New York: Random House, 1964.

Hertzberg, Arthur. *The Jews in America: Four Centuries of an Uneasy Encounter*. New York: Simon and Schuster, 1989.

Herzog, Hanna. "The Fringes of the Margin: Women's Organizations in the Civic Sector of the *Yishuv*." In *Pioneers and Homemakers: Jewish Women in Pre-State Israel*, ed. Deborah Bernstein, 283–304. Albany: State University of New York Press, 1992.

Hewitt, Nancy A. "Re-Rooting American Women's Activism: Global Perspectives on 1848." In *Women's Rights and Human Rights: International Historical Perspectives*, ed. Patricia Grimshaw, Katie Holmes, and Marilyn Lake, 123–37. New York: Palgrave, 2001.

———. *Southern Discomfort: Women's Activism in Tampa, Florida, 1880s–1920s.* Urbana: University of Illinois Press, 2001.

———. *Women's Activism and Social Change: Rochester, New York, 1822–1872.* Ithaca, NY: Cornell University Press, 1984.

Higham, John. *Strangers in the Land: Patterns of American Nativism, 1860–1925.* 2d ed. New Brunswick, NJ: Rutgers University Press, 1988.

Higonnet, Margaret Randolph, et al., eds. *Behind the Lines: Gender and the Two World Wars.* New Haven: Yale University Press, 1987.

Honeycutt, Karen. "Clara Zetkin: A Socialist Approach to the Problem of Women's Oppression." In *European Women on the Left: Socialism, Feminism, and the Problems Faced by Political Women, 1880 to the Present*, ed. Jane Slaughter and Robert Kern, 29–49. Westport, CT: Greenwood, 1981.

Hopkins, C. Howard, and John W. Long. "American Jews and the Root Mission to Russia in 1917: Some New Evidence." *American Jewish History* 69 (March 1980): 342–354.

Howe, Irving, with Kenneth Libo. *World of Our Fathers.* New York: Harcourt Brace Jovanovich, 1976.

Hunt, Karen. *Equivocal Feminists: The Social Democratic Federation and the Woman Question, 1884–1911.* Cambridge: Cambridge University Press, 1996.

Hurwitz, Maximilian. *The Workmen's Circle: Its History, Ideals, Organizations and Institutions.* New York: Workmen's Circle, 1936.

Hyman, Paula. *Gender and Assimilation in Modern Jewish History: The Roles and Representation of Women.* Seattle: University of Washington Press, 1995.

———. "Immigrant Women and Consumer Protest: The New York City Kosher Meat Boycott of 1902." *American Jewish History* 70 (September 1980): 91–105.

———. "The Jewish Body Politic: Gendered Politics in the Early Twentieth Century." *Nashim: A Journal of Jewish Women's Studies and Gender Issues* 1 (spring 1999): 37–51.

———. "The Voluntary Organizations: Vanguard or Rearguard?" *Lilith* 5 (1978): 17, 22.

Izraeli, Dafna N. "The Women Workers' Movement: First-Wave Feminism in Pre-State Israel." In *Women and Social Protest*, ed. Guida West and Rhoda Lois Blumenberg, 134–55. New York: Oxford University Press, 1990.

———. "The Zionist Women's Movement in Palestine, 1911–1927: A Sociological Analysis." *Signs: Journal of Women's Culture and Society* 7 (autumn 1981): 87–114.

Jacobson, Matthew Frye. *Special Sorrows: The Diasporic Imagination of Irish, Polish, and Jewish Immigrants in the United States.* Cambridge, MA: Harvard University Press, 1995.

Janowsky, Oscar I. *The Jews and Minority Rights (1898–1919)*. New York: Columbia University Press, 1933.

Jensen, Joan M. "All Pink Sisters: The War Department and the Feminist Movement in the 1920s." In *Decades of Discontent: The Women's Movement, 1920–1940*, ed. Lois Scharf and Joan M. Jensen, 199–222. Westport, CT: Greenwood, 1983.

Joselit, Jenna Weissman. "The Special Sphere of the Middle-Class American Jewish Woman: The Synagogue Sisterhood, 1890–1940." In *The American Synagogue: A Sanctuary Transformed*, ed. Jack Wertheimer, 206–30. New York: Cambridge University Press, 1987.

Joseph, Judith Lee Vaupen. "The Nafkeh and the Lady: Jews, Prostitution and Progressives in New York City, 1900–1930." PhD diss., State University of New York at Stony Brook, 1986.

Kadish, Sharman. *Bolsheviks and British Jews: The Anglo-Jewish Community, Britain, and the Russian Revolution*. London: Frank Cass, 1992.

———. "Jewish Bolshevism and the 'Red Scare' in Britain." *Jewish Quarterly* 34, no. 4 (1987): 13–19.

Kaganoff, Nathan M. "The Jewish Landsmanshaftn in New York City in the Period Preceding World War I." *American Jewish History* 76 (September 1986): 56–66.

Kahn, Ava. "Pragmatists in the Promised Land: American Immigrant Voluntary Associations in Israel, 1948–1978." PhD diss., University of California, Santa Barbara, 1989.

Kaplan, Marion A. *The Jewish Feminist Movement in Germany: The Campaigns of the Jüdischer Frauenbund, 1904–1938*. Westport, CT: Greenwood, 1979.

———. *The Making of the German Jewish Middle Class: Women, Family and Identity in Imperial Germany*. New York: Oxford University Press, 1991.

Kaplan, Temma. "Women and Spanish Anarchism." In *Becoming Visible: Women in European History*, ed. Renate Bridenthal and Claudia Koonz, 401–21. Boston: Houghton Mifflin, 1977.

Katz, Sherry J. "A Politics of Coalition: Socialist Women and the California Suffrage Movement, 1900–1911." In *One Woman, One Vote: Rediscovering the Woman Suffrage Movement*, ed. Marjorie Spruill Wheeler, 245–62. Troutdale, OR: New Sage, 1995.

Katz, Sherry Jeanne. "Dual Commitments: Feminism, Socialism, and Women's Political Activism in California, 1890–1920." PhD diss., University of California, Los Angeles, 1991.

Katznelson-Rubashow, Rachel, ed. *The Plough Woman: Records of the Pioneer Women of Palestine*. Trans. Maurice Samuel. New York: Nicholas L. Brown, 1932.

Kelleher, Margaret. *The Feminization of Famine: Expressions of the Inexpressible?* Durham, NC: Duke University Press, 1997.

Kerber, Linda K. "Separate Spheres, Female Worlds, Woman's Place: The Rhetoric of Women's History." *Journal of American History* 75 (June

1988): 9–39.

Kessler-Harris, Alice. "Designing Women and Old Fools: The Construction of the Social Security Amendments of 1939." In *U.S. History as Women's History: New Feminist Essays*, ed. Linda K. Kerber, Alice Kessler-Harris, and Kathryn Kish Sklar, 87–106. Chapel Hill: University of North Carolina Press, 1995.

———. "Organizing the Unorganizable: Three Jewish Women and Their Union." *Labor History* 17 (winter 1976): 5–23.

———. "Rose Schneiderman and the Limits of Women's Trade Unionism." In *Labor Leaders in America*, ed. Melvyn Dubofsky and Warren Van Tine, 160–84. Urbana: University of Illinois Press, 1987.

Klepfisz, Irena. "*Die Mames, Dos Loshn*/The Mothers, The Language: Feminism, Yidishkayt, and the Politics of Memory." *Bridges* 4 (winter/spring 1994): 12–40.

Knee, Stuart E. *The Concept of Zionist Dissent in the American Mind, 1917–1941.* New York: Robert Speller, 1979.

Korelitz, Seth. "'A Magnificent Piece of Work': The Americanization Work of the National Council of Jewish Women." *American Jewish History* 83 (June 1995): 177–203.

Kosmin, Barry A., and Paul Ritterbad, eds. *Contemporary Jewish Philanthropy in America.* Savage, MD: Rowman and Littlefield, 1991.

Koven, Seth, and Sonya Michel, eds. *Mothers of a New World: Maternalist Politics and the Origins of Welfare States.* New York: Routledge, 1993.

Kraditor, Aileen S. *The Ideas of the Woman Suffrage Movement, 1890–1920.* 1965. Reprint, New York: Norton, 1981.

Kugler, Israel. "A Life in the Workmen's Circle: Reminiscence and Reflection." *Labor's Heritage* 3 (October 1991): 36–49.

Kur, Carol. "Hadassah, The Women's Zionist Organization of America, Part I." In *Jewish American Voluntary Organizations*, ed. Michael N. Dobkowski, 151–54. Westport, CT: Greenwood, 1985.

Kutscher, Carol. "The Early Years of Hadassah, 1912–1921." PhD diss., Brandeis University, 1976.

Kutscher, Carol Bosworth. "From Merger to Autonomy: Hadassah and the ZOA, 1918–1921." In *The Herzl Yearbook.* Vol. 8, *Essays in American Zionism, 1917–1948*, ed. Melvin I. Urofsky, 61–76. New York: Herzl, 1978.

Kutzik, Alfred Jacob. "The Social Basis of American Jewish Philanthropy." PhD diss., Brandeis University, 1962.

Kuzmack, Linda Gordon. "The Emergence of the Jewish Women's Movement in England and the United States, 1881–1933: A Comparative Study." PhD diss., George Washington University, 1986.

———. *Woman's Cause: The Jewish Woman's Movement in England and the United States, 1881–1933.* Columbus: Ohio State University Press, 1990.

Ladd-Taylor, Molly. *Mother-Work: Women, Child Welfare, and the State, 1890–1930.* Urbana: University of Illinois Press, 1994.

Lash, Joseph P. *Eleanor and Franklin*. New York: Smithmark, 1995.

Laqueur, Walter. *A History of Zionism*. New York: Holt, Rinehart and Winston, 1972.

Las, Nelly. *Jewish Women in a Changing World: A History of the International Council of Jewish Women (ICJW), 1899–1995*. Jerusalem: A. Harman Institute of Contemporary Jewry, 1996.

Lemons, J. Stanley. *The Woman Citizen: Social Feminism in the 1920s*. Urbana: University of Illinois Press, 1973.

Leonoff, Cyril E. "Letters from the Front during the Great War." *Western States Jewish History* 23 (July 1991): 344–57.

Lerner, Elinor. "American Feminism and the Jewish Question, 1890–1940." In *Anti-Semitism in American History*, ed. David A. Gerber, 305–28. Urbana: University of Illinois Press, 1986.

———. "Jewish Involvement in the New York City Woman Suffrage Movement." *American Jewish History* 70 (June 1981): 442–61.

Levene, Mark. "Anglo-Jewish Foreign Policy in Crisis: Lucien Wolf, The Conjoint Committee and the War, 1914–1918." *Jewish Historical Studies* 30 (1987–88): 179–197.

———. "The Balfour Declaration: A Case Study of Mistaken Identity." *English Historical Review* 107 (January 1992): 54–77.

———. *War, Jews, and the New Europe: The Diplomacy of Lucien Wolf, 1914–1919*. Oxford: Oxford University Press, 1992.

Levin, Marlin. *Balm in Gilead: the Story of Hadassah*. New York: Schocken, 1973.

Levin, Nora. *While the Messiah Tarried: Jewish Socialist Movements, 1871–1917*. New York: Schocken, 1977.

Levine, Philippa. "Battle Colors: Race, Sex, and Colonial Soldiery in World War I." *Journal Of Women's History* 9 (winter 1998): 104–30.

Lewis, Jane. "Women, Social Work and Social Welfare in Twentieth-Century Britain: From (Unpaid) Influence to (Paid) Oblivion?" In *Charity, Self-Interest and Welfare in the English Past*, ed. Martin Daunton, 203–23. New York: St. Martin's Press, 1996.

Lichtenstein, Diane. *Writing Their Nations: The Tradition of Nineteenth-Century American Jewish Women Writers*. Bloomington: Indiana University Press, 1992.

Liebman, Arthur. *Jews and the Left*. New York: John Wiley, 1979.

Lindley, Susan Hill. *"You Have Stept Out of Your Place": A History of Women and Religion in America*. Louisville, KY: Westminster John Knox Press, 1996.

Lowenthal, Marvin. *Henrietta Szold: Life and Letters*. New York: Viking, 1942.

Lurie, Harry L. *A Heritage Affirmed: The Jewish Federation Movement in America*. Philadelphia: Jewish Publication Society of America, 1961.

Maclean, Pam. "Control and Cleanliness: German-Jewish Relations in Occupied Eastern Europe during the First World War." *War and Society* 6 (September 1988): 47–69.

Marcus, Jacob Rader. *The American Jewish Woman, 1654–1980*. New York:

KTAV, 1981.

———. *The American Jewish Woman: A Documentary History.* New York: KTAV, 1981.

Marilley, Suzanne M. *Woman Suffrage and the Origins of Liberal Feminism in the United States, 1820–1920.* Cambridge, MA: Harvard University Press, 1996.

Marks, Lara. "'Dear Old Mother Levy's': The Jewish Maternity Home and Sick Room Helps Society 1895–1939." *Social History of Medicine* 3 (April 1990): 61–87.

McCarthy, Kathleen D., ed. *Lady Bountiful Revisited: Women, Philanthropy, and Power.* New Brunswick, NJ: Rutgers University Press, 1990.

Medoff, Rafael. "American Zionist Leaders and the Palestinian Arabs, 1898–1948." PhD diss., Yeshiva University, 1991.

Melman, Billie, ed. *Borderlines: Genders and Identities in War and Peace, 1870–1930.* New York: Routledge, 1998.

Mendelsohn, Ezra. *Class Struggle in the Pale: The Formative Years of the Jewish Workers' Movement in Tsarist Russia.* Cambridge: Cambridge University Press, 1970.

———. *The Jews of East Central Europe between the World Wars.* Bloomington: Indiana University Press, 1983.

———. *On Modern Jewish Politics.* New York: Oxford University Press, 1993.

Meyer, Isidore, ed. *Early History of Zionism in America.* New York: Theodore Herzl Foundation, 1958.

Meyer, Michael A. *The Origins of the Modern Jew: Jewish Identity and European Culture in Germany, 1749–1824.* Detroit: Wayne State University Press, 1967.

———. *Response to Modernity: A History of the Reform Movement in Judaism.* New York: Oxford University Press, 1988.

Michels, Tony E. "Socialist Politics and the Making of Yiddish Culture in New York City, 1890–1923." PhD diss.: Stanford University, 1998.

Miller, Donald H. "A History of Hadassah, 1912–1935." PhD diss., New York University, 1969.

Miller, Sally M. "From Sweatshop Worker to Labor Leader: Theresa Malkiel, A Case Study." *American Jewish History* 68 (December 1978): 189–205.

———. "In the Shadow of Giants: American Socialists and Policies of the Second International on Race, Ethnicity, and Gender." In *Race, Ethnicity, and Gender in Early Twentieth-Century American Socialism*, ed. Sally M. Miller, 3–29. New York: Garland, 1996.

———. "Women in the Party Bureaucracy: Subservient Functionaries." In *Flawed Liberalism: Socialism and Feminism*, ed. Sally M. Miller, 13–35. Westport, CT: Greenwood, 1981.

Mink, Gwendowlyn. *The Wages of Motherhood: Inequality in the Welfare State, 1917–1942.* Ithaca, NY: Cornell University Press, 1995.

Muncy, Robyn. *Creating a Female Dominion in American Reform, 1890–1930.* New York: Oxford University Press, 1991.

BIBLIOGRAPHY

Nadell, Pamela S. "From Shtetl to Border: East European Jewish Emigrants and the 'Agents' System, 1868–1914." In *Studies in the American Jewish Experience II*, ed. Jacob R. Marcus and Abraham J. Peck, 49–78. Lanham, MD: University Press of America, 1984.

———. *Women Who Would Be Rabbis: A History of Women's Ordination, 1889–1985.* Boston: Beacon, 1998.

Nadell, Pamela S., and Rita J. Simon. "Ladies of the Sisterhood: Women in the American Reform Synagogue, 1900–1930." In *Active Voices: Women in Jewish Culture*, ed. Maurie Sacks, 63–75. Urbana: University of Illinois Press, 1995.

Odem, Mary E. *Delinquent Daughters: Protecting and Policing Adolescent Female Sexuality in the United States, 1885–1920.* Chapel Hill: University of North Carolina Press, 1995.

Olsen, Tillie. "Tell Me a Riddle." In *Tell Me a Riddle*, 72–125. New York: Dell, 1976.

Orleck, Annelise. *Common Sense and a Little Fire: Women and Working-Class Politics in the United States, 1900–1965.* Chapel Hill: University of North Carolina Press, 1995.

Palmer, Phyllis. *Domesticity and Dirt: Housewives and Domestic Servants in the United States, 1920–1945.* Philadelphia: Temple University Press, 1989.

Peled, Yoav. *Class and Ethnicity in the Pale: The Political Economy of Jewish Workers' Nationalism in Late Imperial Russia.* London: Macmillan, 1989.

Phillips, Anne. "Images of Fraternity: Socialist Slogans, Feminist Values." *Dissent* 32 (winter 1985): 69–76.

Pittenger, Mark. "Evolution, 'Woman's Nature' and American Feminist Socialism, 1900–1915." *Radical History Review* 36 (September 1986): 47–61.

Pratt, Norma Fain. "Culture and Radical Politics: Yiddish Women Writers, 1890–1940." *Decades of Discontent: The Women's Movement, 1920–1940*, ed. Lois Scharf and Joan M. Jensen, 131–52. Westport, CT: Greenwood, 1983.

———. "Transitions in Judaism: Jewish American Women through the 1930s." *American Quarterly* 30 (winter 1978): 681–702.

Prestel, Claudia T. "Zionist Rhetoric and Women's Equality (1897–1933): Myth and Reality." *San Jose Studies* 20 (fall 1994): 4–28.

Raider, Mark A. *The Emergence of American Zionism.* New York: New York University Press, 1998.

———. "Toward a Re-examination of American Zionist Leadership: The Case of Hayim Greenberg." *Journal of Israeli History* 15 (summer 1994): 133–60.

Raphael, Marc Lee. "The Origins of Organized National Jewish Philanthropy in the United States, 1914–1939." In *The Jews of North America*, ed. Moses Rischin, 213–23. Detroit: Wayne State University Press, 1987.

Raphael, Marc Lee, ed. *Understanding American Jewish Philanthropy.* New York: KTAV, 1979.

————. *What Is American about the American Jewish Experience?* Williamsburg, VA: College of William and Mary, 1993.

Rauchway, Eric. "A Gentleman's Club in a Woman's Sphere: How Dorothy Whitney Straight Created the *New Republic*." *Journal of Women's History* 11 (summer 1999): 60–85.

Reagin, Nancy R. *A German Women's Movement: Class and Gender in Hanover, 1880–1933.* Chapel Hill: University of North Carolina Press, 1995.

Reinharz, Shulamit, "Irma 'Rama' Lindheim: An Independent American Zionist Woman." *Nashim: A Journal of Jewish Women's Studies and Gender Issues* 1 (winter 1998): 106–35.

Rich, J. C. *The Jewish Daily Forward: An Achievement of Dedicated Idealists.* New York: Forward, 1967.

Rischin, Moses. "Germans versus Russians." In *The American Jewish Experience*, ed. Jonathan D. Sarna, 120–32. New York: Holmes and Meier, 1986.

————. *An Inventory of American Jewish History.* Cambridge: Harvard University Press, 1954.

————. *The Promised City: New York's Jews, 1870–1914.* 1962. Reprint, Cambridge, MA: Harvard University Press, 1977.

Roberts, Mary Louise. *Civilization without Sexes: Reconstructing Gender in Postwar France, 1917–1927.* Chicago: University of Chicago Press, 1994.

Rogow, Faith. *Gone to Another Meeting: The National Council of Jewish Women, 1893–1993.* Tuscaloosa: University of Alabama Press, 1993.

Rosenstock, Morton. *Louis Marshall, Defender of Jewish Rights.* Detroit: Wayne State University Press, 1965.

Roskies, David G., ed. *The Literature of Destruction: Jewish Responses to Catastrophe.* Philadelphia: Jewish Publication Society, 1988.

Rozenblit, Marsha L. *Reconstructing a National Jewish Identity: The Jews of Habsburg Austria during World War I.* New York: Oxford University Press, 2001.

Rupp, Leila J. *Worlds of Women: The Making of an International Women's Movement.* Princeton: Princeton University Press, 1997.

Sabin, Arthur J. *Red Scare in Court: New York versus the International Workers Order.* Philadelphia: University of Pennsylvania Press, 1993.

Sarna, Jonathan D. *JPS: The Americanization of Jewish Culture, 1888–1988.* Philadelphia: Jewish Publication Society, 1989.

Sarvasy, Wendy. "Beyond the Difference versus Equality Policy Debate: Postsuffrage Feminism, Citizenship, and the Quest for a Feminist Welfare State." *Signs* 17 (winter 1992): 329–62.

Schlesinger, Yaffa. "Hadassah: The National Women's Zionist Organization of America." *Contemporary Jewry* 15 (1994): 121–39.

Schloff, Linda Mack. "Building Communities, Building Bridges: Jewish American Women's Organizations in Minneapolis, 1945–1975." PhD diss., University of Minnesota, 1998.

Schott, Linda. "'Middle-of-the-Road' Activists: Carrie Chapman Catt and the National Committee on the Cause and Cure of War." *Peace and*

Change 21 (January 1996): 1–21.

Scott, Anne Firor. *Natural Allies: Women's Associations in American History*. Chicago: University of Illinois Press, 1991.

Seller, Maxine S. "Defining Socialist Womanhood: The Women's Page of the *Jewish Daily Forward* in 1919." *American Jewish History* 76 (June 1987): 416–38.

———. "World of Our Mothers: The Women's Page of the Jewish Daily Forward." *Journal of Ethnic Studies* 16, no. 2 (1988): 95–118.

Seltzer, Robert M., and Norman J. Cohen, eds. *Americanization of the Jews*. New York: New York University Press, 1995.

Shapira, Anita. *Land and Power: The Zionist Resort to Force, 1881–1948*. New York: Oxford University Press, 1992.

Shapiro, Judah J. *The Friendly Society: A History of the Workmen's Circle*. New York: Media Judaica, 1970.

Shapiro, Yonathan. *Leadership of the American Zionist Organization, 1897–1930*. Urbana: University of Illinois Press, 1971.

Shargel, Baila Round. *Lost Love: The Untold Story of Henrietta Szold*. Philadelphia: Jewish Publication Society, 1997.

Shepard, Naomi. *A Price below Rubies: Jewish Women as Rebels and Radicals*. Cambridge, MA: Harvard University Press, 1993.

Shilo, Margalit. "The Double or Multiple Image of the New Hebrew Woman." *Nashim: A Journal of Jewish Women's Studies and Gender Issues* 1 (winter 1998): 73–94.

Shpiro, David H. *From Philanthropy to Activism: The Political Transformation of American Zionism in the Holocaust Years, 1933–1945*. Oxford: Pergamon Press, 1994.

Silberstein, Laurence J. "Others Within and Others Without: Rethinking Jewish Identity and Culture." In *The Other in Jewish Thought and History: Constructions of Jewish Culture and Identity*, ed. Laurence J. Silberstein and Robert L. Cohn, 1–34. New York: New York University Press, 1994.

Sinkoff, Nancy B. "Educating for 'Proper' Jewish Womanhood: A Case Study in Domesticity and Vocational Training, 1897–1926." *American Jewish History* 77 (June 1988): 572–98.

Sklar, Kathryn Kish. "'Women Who Speak for an Entire Nation': American British Women Compared at the World Anti-Slavery Convention, London, 1840." In *The Abolitionist Sisterhood: Women's Political Culture in Antebellum America*, ed. Jean Fagan Yellin and John C. Van Horne, 301–34. Ithaca, NY: Cornell University Press, 1994.

Sochen, June. *Consecrate Every Day: The Public Lives of Jewish American Women, 1880–1980*. Albany: State University of New York Press, 1981.

———. "Jewish Women as Volunteer Activists." *American Jewish History* 70 (September 1980): 23–34.

Soland, Birgitte. *Becoming Modern: Young Women and the Reconstruction of Womanhood in the 1920s*. Princeton: Princeton University Press, 2000.

Soltes, Mordecai. *The Yiddish Press: An Americanizing Agency*. New York:

Teachers' College, Columbia University, 1925.

Sorin, Gerald. *A Time For Building: The Third Migration, 1880–1920*. Vol. 3, *The Jewish People in America*, ed. Henry L. Feingold. Baltimore: Johns Hopkins University Press, 1992.

———. *Tradition Transformed: The Jewish American Experience in America*. Baltimore: Johns Hopkins University Press, 1997.

Sorkin, David. *The Transformation of German Jewry, 1780–1840*. New York: Oxford University Press, 1987.

Soyer, Daniel. "Between Two Worlds: The Jewish Landsmanshaftn and the Questions of Immigrant Identity." *American Jewish History* 76 (September 1986): 5–24.

———. *Jewish Immigrant Associations and American Identity in New York, 1880–1939*. Cambridge, MA: Harvard University Press, 1997.

Stein, Herman D. "Jewish Social Work in the United States, 1654–1954." *American Jewish Yearbook* 57 (1956): 3–98.

Steinson, Barbara J. *American Women's Activism in World War I*. New York: Garland, 1982.

———. "'The Mother Half of Humanity': American Women in the Peace and Preparedness Movements in World War I." In *Women, War, and Revolution*, ed. Carol R. Berkin and Clara M. Lovett, 259–84. New York: Holmes and Meier, 1980.

Stovall, Tylar. "The Color Line behind the Lines: Racial Violence in France during the Great War." *American Historical Review* 103 (June 1998): 737–69.

Strange, Carolyn. "Mothers on the March: Maternalism in Women's Protest for Peace in North America and Western Europe, 1900–1985." In *Women and Social Protest*, ed. Guida West and Rhoda Lois Blumenberg, 209–24. New York: Oxford University Press, 1990.

Strum, Philippa. *Louis D. Brandeis: Justice for the People*. Cambridge, MA: Harvard University Press, 1984.

Szajkowski, Zosa. "Concord and Discord in American Jewish Overseas Relief, 1914–1924." *YIVO Annual of Jewish Social Science* 14 (1969): 99–158.

———. *Jews, Wars, and Communism*. Vol. 1, *The Attitudes of American Jews to World War I, the Russian Revolution of 1917, and Communism (1914–1945)*. New York: KTAV, 1972.

———. *Jews, Wars, and Communism*. Vol. 2, *The Impact of the 1919–1920 Red Scare on American Jewish Life*. New York: KTAV, 1974.

———. *Jews, Wars, and Communism*. Vol. 4, *The Mirage of American Jewish Aid in Soviet Russia, 1917–1939*. New York: privately published, 1977.

———. "Private and Organized American Jewish Overseas Relief (1914–1938)." *American Jewish Historical Quarterly* 57 (September 1967): 52–106.

———. "Private and Organized American Jewish Overseas Relief and Immigration (1914–1938)." *American Jewish Historical Quarterly* 57 (December 1967): 191–253.

——. "Private American Jewish Overseas Relief (1919–1938): Problems and Attempted Solutions." *American Jewish Historical Quarterly* 57 (March 1968): 285–352.

Tenenbaum, Shelly. *A Credit to Their Community: Jewish Loan Societies in the United States, 1880–1945.* Detroit: Wayne State University Press, 1993.

——. "Immigrants and Capital: Jewish Loan Societies in the United States, 1880–1945." *American Jewish History* 76 (September 1986): 67–77.

Thompson, Elizabeth. *Colonial Citizens: Republican Rights, Paternal Privilege, and Gender in French Syria and Lebanon.* New York: Columbia University Press, 2000.

Toll, William. "A Quiet Revolution: Jewish Women's Clubs and the Widening Female Sphere, 1870–1920." *American Jewish Archives* 41 (spring/summer 1989): 7–26.

Tobias, Henry J. *The Jewish Bund in Russia: From its Origins to 1905.* Stanford: Stanford University Press, 1972.

Trunk, Isaiah. "The Cultural Dimension of the American Jewish Labor Movement." *YIVO Annual of Jewish Social Science* 16 (1976): 342–93.

Tyrrell, Ian R. *Woman's World/Woman's Empire: The Woman's Christian Temperance Union in International Perspective, 1800–1930.* Chapel Hill: University of North Carolina Press, 1991.

Umansky, Ellen M. "Piety, Persuasion, and Friendship: Female Jewish Leadership in Modern Times." In *Embodied Love: Sensuality and Relationship as Feminist Values,* ed. Paula M. Cooey, Sharon A. Farmer, and Mary Ellen Ross, 189–206. San Francisco: Harper and Row, 1987.

Urofsky, Melvin I. *American Zionism from Herzl to the Holocaust.* New York: Doubleday, 1975.

——., ed. *The Herzl Yearbook.* Vol 8., *Essays in American Zionism, 1917–1948.* New York: Herzl, 1978.

Vital, David. *The Origins of Zionism.* Oxford: Clarendon, 1975.

——. *Zionism: The Crucial Phase.* Oxford: Clarendon, 1987.

Walker, Thomas J. E. *Pluralistic Fraternity: The History of the International Worker's Order.* New York: Garland, 1991.

Walkowitz, Daniel J. "The Making of a Feminine Professional Identity: Social Workers in the 1920s." *American Historical Review* 95 (October 1990): 1051–75.

Weber, Charlotte. "Unveiling Scheherazade: Unveiling Orientalism in the International Alliance of Women, 1911–1950," *Feminist Studies* 27 (Spring 2001): 125–57.

Weinberg, Sydney Stahl. *World of Our Mothers: The Lives of Jewish Immigrant Women.* Chapel Hill: University of North Carolina Press, 1988.

Weiner, Lynn Y., et al. "Maternalism as a Paradigm." *Journal of Women's History* 5 (fall 1993): 95–131.

Weissberger, S. J. "The Rise of the Yiddish-American Press." PhD diss., Syracuse University, 1972.

Weisser, Michael R. *A Brotherhood of Memory: Jewish Landsmanshaftn in the*

New World. New York: Basic Books, 1985.

Welt, Mildred G. "The National Council of Jewish Women." *American Jewish Yearbook* 46 (1944–45): 55–72.

Wenger, Beth S. "Jewish Women and Voluntarism: Beyond the Myth of Enablers." *American Jewish History* 79 (autumn 1989): 16–36.

———. "Jewish Women of the Club: The Changing Public Role of Atlanta's Jewish Women, 1870–1930." *American Jewish History* 76 (March 1987): 311–33.

———. *New York Jews and the Great Depression: Uncertain Promise.* New Haven: Yale University Press, 1996.

———. "Radical Politics in a Reactionary Age: The Unmaking of Rosika Schwimmer, 1914–1930." *Journal of Women's History* 2 (fall 1990): 66–99.

White, Deborah Gray. *Too Heavy a Load: Black Women in Defense of Themselves, 1894–1994.* New York: Norton, 1999.

Woocher, Jonathan S. *Sacred Survival: The Civil Religion of American Jews.* Bloomington: Indiana University Press, 1986.

Woollacott, Angela. "From Moral to Professional Authority: Secularism, Social Work, and Middle-Class Women's Self-Construction in World War I Britain." *Journal of Women's History* 10 (summer 1998): 85–111.

———. "'Khaki Fever' and Its Control: Gender, Class, Age and Sexual Morality on the British Homefront in the First World War," *Journal of Contemporary History* 29, no. 2 (1994): 325–47.

———. *On Her Their Lives Depend: Munitions Workers in the Great War.* Berkeley: University of California Press, 1994.

Zaborowska, Magdalena J. *How We Found America: Reading Gender through East European Immigrant Narratives.* Chapel Hill: University of North Carolina Press, 1995.

Zaks, A. S. *Di geshikhte fun arbeter ring, 1892–1925, ershter teyl* [The history of the Workmen's Circle, 1892–1925, vol. 1]. n.p.: National Executive Committee, Arbeter Ring, 1925.

Zeitlin, Rose. *Henrietta Szold: Record of a Life.* New York, Dial Press, 1952.

INDEX